Only Pictures?

Therapeutic Work with Internet Sex Offenders

by

**Ethel Quayle, Marcus Erooga,
Louise Wright, Max Taylor
and Dawn Harbinson**

Russell House Publishing

First published in 2006 by:
Russell House Publishing Ltd.
4 St George's House
Uplyme Road
Lyme Regis
Dorset DT7 3LS

Tel: 01297-443948
Fax: 01297-442722
e-mail: help@russellhouse.co.uk
www.russellhouse.co.uk

British Library Cataloguing-in-publication Data:
A catalogue record for this book is available from the British Library.

ISBN: 1-903855-68-3; 978-1-903855-68-3

Typeset by TW Typesetting, Plymouth, Devon
Printed by Cromwell Press, Trowbridge

Russell House Publishing
is a group of social work, probation, education and
youth and community work practitioners and
academics working in collaboration with a professional
publishing team.
Our aim is to work closely with the field to produce
innovative and valuable materials to help managers,
trainers, practitioners and students.
We are keen to receive feedback on publications and
new ideas for future projects.
For details of our other publications please visit our
website or ask us for a catalogue. Contact details are
on this page.

Contents

Introduction

Even if there are noticeable differences among people in their ability to change, they are deserving of respect for the very possibility of changing. Even the worst criminals are worthy of basic human respect for the possibility that they may radically re-evaluate their past lives and, if they are given the opportunity, may live the rest of their lives in a worthy manner.

Margalit, 1996: 70

On 20th May 2002 the BBC reported mass arrests over 'online child porn'. 'Thirty-six people suspected of downloading paedophile pornography from the web have been arrested in raids across the UK. Police claim this is the tip of the iceberg and they have 2,000 names of offenders they are unable to arrest due to a lack of resources. Officers from 31 forces searched 44 homes and seized about 30 computers, plus discs and videos. Operation Ore targeted computer users suspected of accessing US-based websites which sell images of children aged as young as five being sexually abused. US authorities gave the National Criminal Intelligence Service (NCIS) the names of 2,000 British subscribers between May 1999 and the summer of 2001. They were traced by their credit card details which they gave in order to buy the images' (BBC online news[1]). In the UK, Operation Ore marked a turning point in relation to attitudes about the potential seriousness of the victimisation of children through Internet images. There had been a growing awareness among practitioners that the Internet was being used by some people in a problematic way, but in general this had been seen as yet another vehicle for the abuse of children by a small number of people. Operation Ore forced us both to reconsider this and challenged some of our conceptions of adult sexual interest in children.

The purpose of this book

The research, which underpins this book, was initiated prior to the above events and was part of a larger project that had been monitoring the use of the Internet to trade abusive images of children. Our work was supported by the European Union through the 'Stop' and 'Daphne' Programmes, which was an acknowledgement by those funding bodies of how important it was to understand the ways in which children could be sexually exploited through the new technologies. The material in this book was part of one such initiative and was developed in response to the numerous requests by practitioners for guidance in this area (partners included Greater Manchester Probation Area, NSPCC, COPINE, University College Cork and the Lucy Faithful Foundation). Calder (2004) has suggested that '. . . practice cannot wait until the necessary research has been undertaken and a body of theory and knowledge develops' and it was in this spirit that we decided to try to use the initial

---

[1] (http://news.bbc.co.uk/1/hi/uk/1998515.stm)

findings from our own research and that of others to develop some guidelines for working with offenders. In this context, the work was driven by research, but the area was and remains, too new for us to examine the long-term impact of any intervention on future offending activity. What we offer instead, are potential areas of concern in relation to offending through abuse images, and guidelines as to how these might be approached therapeutically. Throughout this book, we emphasise the heterogeneity of this client group and the need for assessment and intervention strategies to reflect this. Ward et al. (2004: 143) had stressed that, ' . . . unless we understand the processes involved for an individual offender, how can we credibly identify areas for clinical intervention . . .' and this is something that we hope will influence how this book is used. While we offer guidelines, these are not prescriptive, and it is hoped that the practitioner will use the material given by the client to guide the direction and course of therapy.

The structure of this book

The book is organised to provide a review of the current literature, (Chapters 1 and 2), which sets the scene for an understanding of both offences related to the Internet and cognitive behaviour therapy (CBT) for sex offenders. Subsequent chapters are written around a specific therapeutic theme, providing a brief review of the literature before moving on to ways of working with a client and offering exercises and materials that can either be used as they are, or adapted to particular cases. Readers may find that there is some repetition of the material within the chapters and this is due to a realisation that practitioners may use the book in parts, rather than as a whole. Chapter 3 focuses on a model of offending; Chapter 4 on identifying the children in the images as children; Chapter 5 on fantasy and its escalation, Chapter 6 on emotional avoidance; Chapter 7 on social activity and Internet images; Chapter 8 on collecting behaviour and Chapter 9 on maintaining change. Throughout these chapters we have acknowledged new research findings and have tried to incorporate these into the guidelines. Central to this has been the importance of values and about helping clients to learn to live a more valued life.

Therapeutic relationships with Internet sex offenders

Ward and Brown (2004: 252) have stressed that, '. . . motivating offenders and creating a sound therapeutic alliance are pivotal components of effective treatment and should not be viewed as of lesser importance than the administration of strategies and techniques'. The importance of the therapeutic alliance has rarely been explicitly stated in the context of sexual offenders, yet these people are amongst those whose offending actions promote such strong emotional reactions in others. The practitioner is not immune to this, and it has been suggested that, 'The attitude they adopt toward the offender arguably reflects their implicit (rarely explicit) forgiveness (or lack of forgiveness) of the individual in question and the belief that he or she is entitled to be treated with respect because of their value as a person' (Ward and Brown, 2004: 253). In a similar fashion, Wilson and Luciano (2002) have also emphasised the importance of establishing the therapeutic relationship, and have suggested that therapists need to both know their values and be able to state them explicitly. In the context of Acceptance and Commitment Therapy (ACT) they have argued that this assumes that, 'at some level, people hope, aspire, dream, wish for a life that is broader, richer and more meaningful . . . that under any and all conditions it is possible to live a life in the direction of one's core values . . . [and that the] therapist is committed to helping clients achieve the richest life (in terms of the client's own values) that is possible'.

The aspiration of this book

Nowhere more than in the context of the Internet are we forced to confront the fact that in an unregulated and anarchic world, people have the capacity to behave in ways that are ultimately harmful to others. Much of what we struggle with exists on a continuum, and this is clearly the case in terms of adult sexual interest in children. We hope that this book will provide information and resources that practitioners can use when working with clients that will foster respect, understanding and help promote change.

Acknowledgement

We would like to acknowledge the support that we received in the compilation of this book from the Faculty of Arts, University College, Cork.

About the Authors

Ethel Quayle is a lecturer in the Department of Applied Psychology, University College Cork, and researcher with the COPINE project. She is a clinical psychologist and course coordinator for an MA in Behavioural and Cognitive Psychotherapy. Her research has as its focus the use of Internet images by people with a sexual interest in children. She has written widely in this area and is co-author of *Child Pornography: An Internet Crime* which was published in 2003. She is the co-editor, with Max Taylor, of *Viewing Child Pornography on the Internet: Understanding the Offence, Managing the Offender, Helping the Victim.*

Marcus Erooga is an NSPCC Area Children's Services Manager. He has been involved for some 15 years in the development of services for those who sexually offend against children and has written widely both on this and on child protection more generally.

Louise Wright currently works for the Greater Manchester Probation Service – a partner of the COPINE project. She has ten years experience working therapeutically with men who sexually abuse. She is currently a Tutor and Treatment Manager for the Northumbria Sex Offender Group Work Programme.

Max Taylor is Professor of Applied Psychology, University College Cork, and director of the COPINE project. He is a chartered forensic psychologist and has published widely in the areas of terrorism and criminal activity. He is co-author of the book *Child Pornography: An Internet Crime* and co-editor of *Viewing Child Pornography on the Internet.*

Dawn Harbinson is a research forensic psychologist with the COPINE project. She is currently engaged in the CROGA project that seeks to provide Internet support to people engaging in problematic Internet use.

Chapter One

Abuse Images and the Internet

Current usage is tending towards replacing the term 'child pornography' with 'child abuse image', or 'abuse image'. In this book we generally use the term abuse image, but there are occasions when 'child pornography' has been chosen where its use seems appropriate, or when making reference to others who use that term.

Within the last ten years there has been democratisation in the availability and use of the Internet from being a medium used primarily by academic and research staff to one available in many domestic settings. Such availability has brought with it many advantages, but inevitably it has also brought problems. One of these problems, which forms the focus of this book, is the production, distribution and downloading of images of children that have been described as both child pornography and child abuse images (Taylor and Quayle, 2003). These images relate to the victimisation of children and adult sexual interest in children, although not all such images necessarily depict sexual assault.

At present there is very little published literature that relates to these activities that helps inform practitioners dealing with offenders in this area. This book is an effort to partially remedy this, it attempts to draw attention to some of the issues that may be relevant to offence behaviours associated with the use of Internet images, and is based on a number of years of collaborative work between the authors. It is not our intention to detract from current treatment programmes but to further explore issues that may be relevant for treatment that are not exclusively related to the Internet but may be changed or magnified by its use.

The first chapter of this book examines some of the issues that pertain to images and the Internet, while the second provides an overview of offending activity and cognitive behaviour therapy as an approach to treatment. The following chapters bring together relevant current literature that relates to such offending behaviour, and includes materials and exercises for working with offenders. The book concludes with a chapter on the relevance of relapse prevention for this population.

Prevalence

An important starting point relates to an often-asked question as to the extent of the problem. The estimation of any form of deviance in the general population is always a very difficult task, and it is impossible to assess the extent of sexual offending, either in general or that with children as targets. We know that most estimates of the distribution of sexual offenders in the general population are derived from forensic sources, that is, samples of those who are arrested or convicted for sex offences. All researchers acknowledge that those who are arrested represent only a fraction of all sexual offenders, and that sexual crimes have the lowest rates of reporting for all crimes (Terry and Tallon, 2004). Studies of both the incidence and the prevalence of sexual abuse of children in the United States began in the 1960s and suggested that the scope of the problem was extensive, with females more likely to have been sexually abused during childhood than males. Furthermore, it was found that females were more likely than the males to disclose such information; however, disclosure rates were quite low regardless of the victim's gender.

Recent research by Finkelhor and Jones (2004) used data from NCANDS (National Child Abuse and Neglect Data System of the Federal Department of Health and Human Services, US) to make a national estimate of the number of sexual abuse cases substantiated by the Child Protective Service (CPS) for the period from 1992 to 2000. Using data from more than 40 US states they reported that the number of substantiated sexual abuse cases peaked at approximately 149,800 in 1992, followed by annual declines of 2 to 11 per cent per year through 2000, when the number of cases reached a low of approximately 89,355. Inevitably, this research reporting a decline in child sexual abuse has resulted in controversy, with suggestions that the figures relate, for example, to changes in reporting practices. However, when Finkelhor and Jones (2004) examined other indices of sex abuse rates they concluded that, taken together, they suggested that at least part of the drop in cases had resulted from a decline in sexual abuse of children, and that these changes are mirrored by a drop in teenage pregnancies and births. One reason suggested for such changes is the increased incarceration of sexual offenders (Finkelhor and Ormrod, 2000).

The situation in relation to Internet abuse images is even more difficult to assess, both in terms of offending behaviour and the number of children victimised. We have no clear understanding of the number of people who access abuse images. Not only are we reliant on data derived from convictions, it is also the case that many people operate within private Internet networks that are by definition inaccessible to monitoring. However, the problems related to child abuse images on the Internet appear to be growing. As part of its ongoing activities, in the six-week period from August to mid September 2002, the COPINE Project downloaded a total of 140,917 child image files from the Usenet newsgroups monitored by the Project (COPINE is an acronym for a research group based in University College Cork). Over 35,000 of these images were *new* images not already contained within the COPINE Archive of over 500,000 images. Almost 30,000 of the new images were from identifiable web sites (containing reference to a web site in the image). In the remaining images, 20 new children (9 girls, 11 boys) in pictures categorised at level 7 or above (COPINE categorising scale: Taylor et al., 2001) were identified. This represents a considerable rise over the amount of material available in previous years and an increase in the number of children involved in highly abusive images. This level of activity was largely sustained in 2003 (Taylor and Quayle, 2005).

From the limited evidence we have it would appear that people with a sexual interest in children who access Internet abuse images are a heterogeneous group. They include people of all ages and from all social backgrounds, displaying various degrees of technical sophistication. They may include those who have a known history of sexual offending and convictions, and others for whom there has been no previously acknowledged sexual interest in children. To date, other than in media reports, there have been no published accounts of female offending on the Internet (although there are anecdotal accounts) and it appears that at present this is a largely male activity. Although research in this area is limited, the available evidence suggests that in a general sense, the problems associated with Internet abuse images are:

- Production (as distinct from viewing) involves the sexual abuse of a child.
- A photograph preserves visual evidence of that abuse.
- Sexual fantasy may become reality, through imitation or permission giving.
- Images can act as instruments in the grooming process of potential victims.
- It may sexualise other aspects of child and family life.

This latter point is perhaps the most pervasive and worrying effect of this material, although it is difficult to separate this from other forms of abusive practices toward children, and of course it is a most diffuse and difficult effect to quantify (for a discussion of some of the broader issues relevant to this see Kincaid (1998) and Adler, (2001)). However, it must be emphasised that the function of abuse images and their relationship to the commission of contact offences remain for the moment unclear. Seto et al. (2001) in their review of the relationship between pornography and sexual violence, provided an excellent overview of the various psychological models proposed to examine this issue. However, research in this area is often conflicting and in the main predates the advent of the Internet. Goldstein (1999) had suggested that child-pornography could be understood as a by-product of contact offences – one consequence of the commission of an offence against a child. On the other hand authors such as Itzin have described such images as central to child abuse. 'Pornography, in the form of adult and/or child pornography used to season/groom/initiate/coerce children into agreeing to be abused, or the production of child pornography (the records of children being sexually abused) is implicated in every form of child abuse, however it is organised' (Itzin, 1997). In many ways this is difficult to substantiate, as children who are victimised through the production of images remain largely silent (e.g., Svedin and Back, 1994). Furthermore, until recently, many offenders seem never to have been questioned about their use of pornography in the commission of a contact offence. It may well be that many aspects of the sexual victimisation of children, whether through the production or viewing of images, or through Internet child seduction, have at its heart the use of abuse images (Taylor and Quayle, 2005).

Definitions and functions

It is important to address the question as to what are abuse images, although this may prove to be complex. Earlier research by Goldstein (1999) had differentiated between 'pornography' and 'erotica'. Any material that stimulates sexual arousal may be described as erotic, regardless of its content, and in the context of the Internet may include images that are in themselves legal. Both Lanning (1992) and Goldstein (1999) have emphasised that abuse images not only function as an aid to fantasy and masturbation but can also serve to:

- Symbolically keep the child close.
- Remind the offender of what the child looked like at a particular age.
- Make the child feel important, or special.
- Lower the child's inhibitions about being photographed.
- Act as a memento that might give the offender status from other people he associates with.
- Demonstrate propriety by convincing children that what the offender wants them to do is acceptable because he has engaged in a similar way with other children.
- Provide a vehicle for coercion.
- Act as an aid to seduce children, by misrepresenting moral standards and by depicting activities that the offender wishes the child to engage in.

A problem with this analysis is that these functions seem to relate to the planned commission of a contact offence against a child, and collections of images and memorabilia that are primarily obtained for that purpose, may in some ways be qualitatively different from those obtained from the Internet. Given this, a significant point to note is that a person's collection of Internet abuse images in its entirety is less likely to relate to individual children known to the offender (with the exception of an offender who also produces images). It may be useful for us to question, therefore, in what ways the availability of Internet pornography and erotica create additional factors to consider, rather than to see them as identical to the memorabilia collected by offenders prior to the Internet. It has long been argued that pornography and its use leads to the objectification of the people within the pictures. This is seen most clearly in the context of abuse images where offenders literally make objects of

the children photographed, describing them as artefacts to be collected. Evidence of this is seen in 'chat' about the images, where they are referred to as being part of a collection, with little or no reference to the fact that the images are of children. Offenders talk about them as if they were other collectibles, and in some instances edit the images themselves to remove features (for example the child's face) that are of no interest to them, or that do not fit with a particular sexual fantasy or script.

Internet abuse images may also lead to the fragmentation of the viewer's own sexuality – the Internet allows for the expression of sexual behaviour with others that otherwise is unlikely to find expression in the off-line word (Quayle et al., 2001). It is important to note that this extends beyond the use of abuse images to other forms of sexual activities and pornographies. Most people have sexual fantasies, many of which remain publicly unacknowledged, but some of which may be shared with a consenting adult partner and acted upon. What becomes apparent in the on-line world is the ability to relate sexually, either through solitary masturbatory behaviour, or through 'cybersex', in a variety of sexual fantasies and practices that would have been difficult to find either stimulus (as in fantasy material) or audience (another person or persons) in 'real' life. All sexual preferences are catered for in the anarchy that is the Internet, and this is evidenced not only in the amount of email spam that we all receive, but the number of 'hits' that are returned with the use of a search engine when any sexual term is used. It is also the case that sexual behaviour in general is more disinhibited on-line (Cooper et al., 1999), and while this may be seen in a positive light in the new-found ability of adults to explore their sexual feelings and behaviours, where the object of the sexual exploration is the abuse of children, this clearly becomes problematic.

The problem of defining what is child pornography is also complicated by the fact that different jurisdictions have different legal definitions. The COPINE categorisation scale (Taylor et al., 2001) identified some ten types (levels) of images that are attractive to adults with a sexual interest in children. The scale described an ascending series of categories that attempted an objective measure of degrees of apparent victimisation. Of course, the basis for this was inevitably a subjective one on the part of the researchers. There is insufficient evidence to say that from the perspective of the victim, bestiality, for example, is a more abusive practice than oral sexual activity with an adult, or even less invasive acts. However, using this scale, in most jurisdictions levels 5 or 6 upwards are illegal. But, between jurisdictions, critical judgements about what constitute illegal material may differ in terms of an emphasis on obscenity or an emphasis on sexual qualities. As a result of this, countries may take different positions on the illegality of some images, particularly for example those involving naked children, (which might be categorised as level 5 or 6). In the context of the UK, the Sentencing Advisory Panel (2002) believed that for sentencing purposes a five level structure should be created, focusing on levels 5–10 of the COPINE scale. The UK Court of Appeal, with some compression of categories 4 and 5 adopted this, but levels COPINE 1–3 inclusive were dropped, suggesting that such categories of images should not be classed in the view of UK judges as illegal.

Pseudo images

In the context of the United States a recent court ruling (Ashcroft v. Free speech Coalition, 2002) required that evidence be produced that the child in the image is an actual child before an image can be judged to be in a legal sense child pornography (and therefore evidence of the sexual abuse of a child). The distinction drawn here is between a real child and one depicted by a computer-generated image (which of course may or may not be evidence of a crime against a real child). One unintended consequence of this ruling may well be a potential increase in the amount of computer generated images created and circulated. It also raises serious conceptual issues about the significance of, and what constitutes, an image of a real child as opposed to a pseudo or computer generated image. For many practitioners, an assumption is that a pseudo image is similar to a cartoon and bears no relation to an existing child, being created, as it were, without reference to an image of an actual person. However, Akdeniz (2001) has noted that the typical pseudo photograph is when a photograph, or a collage of photographs, of a real person is in some way altered, perhaps by a graphics manipulation package. But in objective terms, the definition of pseudo or computer generated images remains very vague. Gillespie (2003) has given an interesting example of how

problematic this might be: 'Let us take an example of a sexually explicit photograph of a six-year-old girl. This image is scanned and stored in the computer. No difficulty arises with this: it is quite clearly an indecent photograph. Let us assume that the girl has a large birthmark on her face. Using a graphics program, this birthmark is airbrushed out. Is this now a photograph or a pseudo-photograph?' Such a photograph is clearly 'not original', and in this sense has been changed through computer manipulation. This is of considerable importance, because as can be seen from the above, such images may not be restricted to those where there was never a real child being abused or exploited. Equally, the exploitation may not relate to the child portrayed in the image (if, for example the child's head was pasted onto the body of an adult female), but would we really wish to argue that such a representation does not victimise the child in question?

This raises an important issue. A distinction can be made between what constitutes in legal terms child pornography, and in psychological terms images that are attractive to an adult with a sexual interest in children. A wide range of images can enable high levels of sexual arousal for an individual by fuelling fantasy, but those images need not necessarily be explicitly sexual and therefore illegal. The problem is that sexual arousal is highly subjective (and is closely related to and dependent on fantasy), rather than necessarily lying in the objective sexual (in legal terms) qualities of an image. This can clearly be seen in the wide variety of material that is legally available and which is used as an aid to arousal. It might be argued that these issues change if a relationship can be demonstrated between images (of any kind), fantasy and contact offending, because presumably the fantasy activities may then move from the world of fantasy to real life, and contribute to contact offending. However, relatively little is known about the relationship between possession of abuse images of children and contact offending. Sullivan and Beech (2004) have suggested that, 'Evidence obtained from our semi-structured interviews with Internet sex offenders appears not to support the assertion that the offender will eventually do whatever he fantasises and masturbates about' (p 81). However, what does seem to be becoming clearer is that it may be necessary to make distinctions between individuals in terms of their *probability* of committing contact offences (sometimes referred to as 'dangerousness' or level of risk). Individuals who produce abuse images are necessarily involved in the commission of a contact offence, but individuals in possession of abuse images are less clearly 'dangerous' in this sense. For some in this category, engagement with abuse images does seem to act as a catalyst prompting, when opportunity allows, contact offending; for others however, this may not be the case.

Producer, trader and collector

It is important to stress that the complex relationship between sexual offending against children and possession of abuse images, when focusing on the individual, does not invalidate in any way the sense in which the process of trading and collecting abuse images constitutes one of the principal factors driving the production and distribution of new images. Thought of in market terms, collecting abuse images generates the demand that is met by photography of sexual abuse. This is perhaps one of the principal reasons why the trade in abusive images of children, and their possession, is rightly regarded as an aspect of the sexual abuse of children and should attract heavy penalties (Taylor and Quayle, 2005). It is also apparent however that many people access images that may be indicative of sexual interest in children, but which are still legal (Taylor et al., 2001). Given this, it may be more useful to think of such images as lying along a continuum of victimisation. This is an important issue, and has been reflected in sentencing guidelines in the UK (Court of Appeal Criminal Division, 2002). It is important because the offenders' collections of images reflects both their level of engagement with the material, and also provides visible evidence of at least some elements of their sexual fantasy. Until recently, the term 'child pornography' has been used to describe these images, allowing comparison with the depictions of consensual sexual activity between adults that are so widely available from newsagents and video retailers. Many professionals working in this area have expressed the belief that such terminology is problematic and allows us to distance ourselves from the true nature of the material (Quayle, 2004). It is equally true that other professionals feel concerned about moving away from a terminology that is grounded in the common discourse of the legal system (Lanning, 2004).

While it is important that we do not think of the Internet as simply another vehicle for the commission of sexual offences, Calder (2004) has suggested a number of reasons why the Internet may be a very attractive place for both consumers and producers of abuse images. These include:

- Advanced technology which makes for rapid updating of materials.
- Easy access to a global audience and the distribution of materials through different formats, such as pictures, cartoons, video, sound files and text.
- The quality of the material is maintained no matter how frequently it is downloaded. Along with this, live video conferencing has created the capacity for participant interaction.
- Cost effectiveness of production along with a high quality product. New technology also allows for taking secret pictures of children, both as static and moving images.
- Perceived security and anonymity which may be increased through the use of software such as anonymisers.
- The ability to download movies in a way that avoids issues of censorship.
- The ability to create pseudo images or to modify existing images of children, the latter being circulated on the Internet without the victim's knowledge.

Few practitioners have a clear idea as to how people engage with child pornographic images on the Internet, as accessing such material is of itself illegal. Taylor and Quayle (2005) have provided a description of what they termed 'The natural history of trading abusive images on the Internet', which helped give a context to the complex array of behaviours associated with the circulation of images. It is in the nature of the Internet that anyone engaged with it has to identify themselves in some way, by specifying a user name. This may be a real name, but more usually it is an assumed nickname, which may play a part in the self-representation of the individual on the Internet. This nickname may indicate something about the individual (e.g., kidlover) or may simply be a fictitious real name (e.g., malcom3). The names used may change between different Internet activities, or over time. People can be very possessive about nicknames, and in fact they tend to be constant, although individuals may possess multiple names. There is some evidence that the selection of nicknames is purposive and reflects some sense of how the individual sees himself (Bechar-Israeli, 1995).

Trading of images on the Internet takes place in a variety of settings, employing different Internet protocols that involve different degrees of interaction or communication with other people. Some protocols facilitate secret communication between people, others are more open. One of the more potentially secret forms of communication on the Internet relates to what are termed 'e-groups'. These are essentially proprietary chat rooms, which users can establish. The founder or owner of the e-group can specify level of access to other people, forbidding access unless permission is given. A number of e-groups exist for trading abusive images of children; these are secret, and often only allow access to individuals who can themselves prove that they are taking abusive images. (Evidence of this having taken place can often be seen in images where the child is holding up a paper with a message, often in the form of a name and date.) An example of the global nature of such e-groups can be seen in Operation Candyman. In 2001 the FBI initiated this investigation after an undercover agent identified three e-groups that were involved in the posting, exchanging and transmitting of child abuse images. This operation identified 7,000 unique email addresses, with 2,400 from outside of the United States. Other forms of Internet protocols involved in the exchange of abuse images include Internet Relay Chat, which can have similar qualities, proprietary e-groups, and Usenet newsgroups, which are forms of publicly available bulletin boards.

Three broad groups of individuals can be identified in the process of trading abusive images: the producer, the trader and the collector. These are not necessarily mutually exclusive categories, and indeed it is quite likely that producers are also in many cases traders and collectors; the reverse however does not necessarily apply. Collectors may be active (in that they directly communicate with other people through, for example, Internet Relay Chat) or passive (in that they access images through protocols that do not require direct access to other people, e.g., through the Usenet newsgroups, or through web sites). Collectors seem to be much more numerous than producers, but many (if not all) producers are also probably both traders and collectors. However, it also seems likely that not all producers of abuse images necessarily trade their own images with other people, retaining them for personal use, or for trading within a discrete group of 'friends'. The various relationships are probably best seen as a reflection of a process, whereby individuals move between different roles as inclination and opportunity allows (Quayle and Taylor, 2003). It is important to stress that in general no money changes hands in the type of trading activities described here. This trade is essentially not driven by money, but rather it is often a form of barter. However, access to pay web sites represents a different means of obtaining images, where money is absolutely central to the process at least on the part of the web site owner. One example of such commercial trading was Landslide Productions Inc., operated and owned by Thomas and Janice Reedy, who sold access to child abuse image web sites. Customers from around the world paid monthly subscription fees, via a post office box address or the Internet, to access hundreds of web sites, some of which contained extremely graphic abuse images of children (US Postal Inspection Service, 2003). Landslide Productions originally dealt with the sale of adult web sites, but as the business grew, most of the profits came from child abuse image web sites; a measure of the scale of this is that in just one month the business grossed as much as $1.4 million.

That there is a considerable interest in such images is surely evidenced by the size of the market place and the emergence of such commercial web sites selling pictures of children. It would also seem reasonable to assume that the reason people access such images is for sexual purposes – to aid sexual fantasy, masturbation and other sexual activities. What little evidence we have would appear to support this, yet it cannot account for why many convicted offenders are found to have extensive collections of pictures, containing many thousands of images. Consideration needs to be given to the possibility that the functions of a picture collection are various and that these may change over time. Howells et al. (2004) draws our attention to this in the context of other sexual offences, '. . . offending behaviours that are topographically identical may be functionally dissimilar. Thus, for example, individual A and individual B both commit a rape offence of a very similar nature, but the functions of the rape (the antecedent and consequence factors that control it) may be entirely different for the two perpetrators'.

Function of abuse images

In an attempt to look at the function of abuse images, Quayle and Taylor (2002) used a qualitative analysis of the accounts of offenders about their use of abuse images. From this they identified six principle discourses that distinguished offender's engagement with Internet abuse images. These included abuse images as:

- An aid to sexual arousal.
- Collectibles.
- A way of facilitating social relationships.
- A way of avoiding 'real life'.
- A form of therapy.
- Abuse images and the Internet.

Within the COPINE sample of interviewed offenders, all of these appeared common across offenders, with the exception of where abuse images facilitated social relationships. This latter was largely confined to offenders who had gone on to 'chat' on-line with others through protocols such as IRC (Internet Relay Chat). Abuse images functioned for the offender in a number of ways, depending on the nature of the involvement with the Internet. This involvement seems to be best characterised as a process, within which offenders moved between different aspects, depending upon circumstances at the time and opportunity.

The primary function of abuse images was as an aid to sexual arousal, where many of the images accessed (but not all) were used for masturbatory purposes. Offenders may be selective in the images used and this may be related to specific age groups, physical types, gender of the child, or to a particular sexual activity. Images may also be selected to reflect earlier contact offences or to new offending fantasies. For many people involved in accessing abuse images, levels of masturbatory behaviour appeared to increase with access to the Internet.

Abuse images, as previously noted, also function as collectibles, and a medium for exchange and trading. Offenders often called themselves 'collectors', and used this term to differentiate themselves from 'paedophiles'. In this sense collecting abuse images in many ways is no different to the collection of any other artefacts, except that their content is illegal, and functioned (as is also the case for collectors of adult pornographies) as an aid to sexual arousal. Offenders could rapidly build up large collections of images and such rapid acquisition was often accompanied by the ability to trade or exchange images, while maintaining relative anonymity. For some offenders this undoubtedly facilitated the building of community networks, and as a general point, the importance of the 'collection' for some offenders cannot be underestimated. The collected images are often given a sense of structure and unity by being created (by either the originator or by another collector) as a part of a numbered or named series. Inevitably, as with other 'collections', status was gained from having a 'complete' collection, and referral back to 'old images' often took second place to seeking out new material, which was an important aspect of collecting per se. To supply the demand by collectors for new material, more photographs have to be taken that depict the ongoing abuse of children. In some cases this may directly lead to the production of new material through the abuse of children in the offender's immediate social network. In this process we therefore see a combination of sexual and social forces at work.

Indeed, for many people with a sexual interest in children, abuse images can be used to facilitate social relationships with like-minded individuals. Child abuse images and social relationships are almost exclusively seen in the context of offenders who trade images and who use synchronous or asynchronous forms of communication to link up with others. The exchange of images and the discourse surrounding this practice (which may or may not be sexually related) enables social cohesion and allows for the rapid acquisition of images through trading networks. Such networks appear to have their own social hierarchies, associated with the number of images, the ability to complete picture series and access to new or unusual material. Knowledge of Internet systems, especially related to security, may also be associated with social status.

It also seems to be the case that for some people, the Internet and accessing abuse images can be used as a way of avoiding real life relationship and social problems. For many offenders, establishing on-line relationships provides important social support that often replaces unsatisfactory relationships in the off-line world. This is similar to the findings of Morahan-Martin and Schumacher (2000) who described the Internet as providing an attractive alternative to a mundane or unhappy life. It has been suggested that what is often achieved through prolonged engagement with the Internet is a change of mood (Kennedy-Souza, 1998). At its most benign, this may be construed as a form of displacement activity, 'Therefore for whatever reason the Internet is initially accessed, there is every inducement to end up doing something else that promises to be more interesting or pleasurable . . . Individuals engage in these alternative activities because they are readily available, attractively presented and appear to be more immediately interesting and gratifying than completing the work originally in hand' (Hills and Argyle, 2003). It is likely that most of us who use the Internet would identify with this and would readily acknowledge that we use the Internet on occasions to reduce mild negative emotional states, such as boredom. What is more problematic, in the context of excessive or compulsive Internet use for sexual purposes, is the likelihood not only that the individual is using the Internet to change or avoid negative mood states, but that the material accessed is highly reinforcing, particularly as access often culminates in masturbation (Quayle and Taylor, 2002).

Whilst the primary focus for concern is of course the images, research also suggests that the Internet itself can have an effect on individuals with problematic sexual behaviour, emphasising again the significance of a notion of process in understanding engagement with abusive images and the Internet. For such people the Internet is not just a passive means of communication. We can summarise this by saying that the Internet may:

- Alter mood.
- Lessen social risk and remove inhibitions.
- Enable multiple self representation.
- Show evidence of group dynamics.
- Validate, justify and offer an exchange medium.
- Challenge old concepts of regulation.
- Disrupt and challenge conventional hierarchies.
- Empower traditionally marginalised people and groups.

Abusive images of children seem to serve a variety of purposes for those who collect them. As already emphasised, this seems to be best conceptualised as a process, rather than a state, and an individual may move between different kinds of engagement with child abuse images depending on context. In understanding the function of abuse images for the offender and how this relates to the Internet, we can start to build on a conceptual model that allows us to examine offending activities that relate to abuse images as such a process. This will be examined further in Chapter 3, where we look at a process model of inappropriate Internet use within a cognitive behavioural framework. This is important, because as we noted at the beginning of this chapter, adult sexual interest in children on the Internet embraces both legal and illegal activities. For example, collecting abuse images is illegal, but talking about sexual fantasies or engaging in sexual role-plays with other adults, may not be in many jurisdictions. Similarly, sharing information about encryption software is not illegal, but giving information that allows offenders to have access to children is likely to be. Many offenders move through a variety of offending behaviours, and we need to be open to the possibility that at least some will move away from illegal activities to those that we may consider undesirable, but which are still legal. For example, as we have already noted, the Internet caters for a variety of sexual appetites, and may include images that are not obviously sexual in content for most people, but which for some are highly arousing, such as those of crash victims or birth pictures. While most readers would think of these as being inappropriate sexual stimuli (and indeed they often show what can only be described as repulsive and horrendous images) they do not generally, in the current climate, involve any illegal activity as such.

Galbreath et al. (2002: 190) have emphasised the driven nature of much on-line sexual activity, 'For most persons, Internet sites containing paraphilic materials are usually dismissed as either humorous, bizarre, or even repulsive. However, such Web sites can become riveting for those discovering that their sexual appetites are whetted by such exposure. Some patients have found the process of seeking out, and then collecting, paraphilic images and stories to be akin to an illicit scavenger hunt. Some have spent literally hours on the Internet, compulsively looking for the types of materials that excite and arouse them.' These authors have suggested that the ease of access to material on the Internet has serious implications 'for a subset of individuals whom, but for its advent, might not normally have been inclined to seek them out'. A case study by Quayle et al. (2001) had also described how for some people, the Internet acts as a catalyst for the emergence of dormant sexual interests. Clearly this is not the case for all people, and there are many who access child pornographic images who have a well-established sexual interest in children. What is important in relation to this is that the Internet is not a passive medium for offending but rather an interactive one. People engage with the medium at a variety of different levels and even simple exposure to materials through searching and downloading engages viewers in a world that sees as normal and acceptable the very activity itself. 'Once an individual has discovered that there are others on the Internet with similar interests, they may then begin to rationalise that paraphilic behavior (e.g., masochistic or paedophilic conduct) is acceptable. Chatrooms can provide the opportunity to discuss shared sexual interests, or they can even be used to teach the novice how to become an active practitioner.' (Galbreath et al., 2002: 191).

The anarchic nature of the Internet has meant that there has been little control over content, and it has been suggested by Cooper (1998) that the Internet's 'triple-A engine' of accessibility, affordability and assumed anonymity allows people to explore many sexual desires and interests with little sense of embarrassment and with at times an inflated sense of security. An example of this can be found in a study by Demetriou and Silke (2003). They established a website to examine whether people, who visited for the purposes of gaining access to legal material, would also attempt to access illegal or pornographic material. Over an 88-day period, 803 visitors entered the site and it was found that the majority of visitors accessed those sections purporting to offer illegal or deviant material. The combination of opportunity, ease, perceived anonymity and the immediacy of personal rewards created a situation where such behaviour is 'not simply common, it actually becomes the norm'. However, we might assume that for the majority of the people in this study, such activity did not become all consuming or compulsive, and that while it may have been exciting, funny or about taking risks, some level of self-control would have 'kicked-in' to limit the activity. But as we know in relation to many other activities, for some people self-control is problematic, and in the context of the Internet access to material that is highly reinforcing serves to undermine the person's willingness not to give in to the attraction of immediate access.

From the perspective of the practitioner, the Internet has the capacity to alter the ways that individuals feel, think and behave. For at least some offenders, the exclusivity of their on-line activity means that they limit their exposure to other social contexts which might offer a challenge to their offending behaviour. If the only people you are engaging with are involved in the same illegal activity, it becomes much less likely that you take the risk of disagreeing with what they are doing, even when it may offend some moral sense (Quayle et al., 2001). Galbreath et al. (2002: 193) suggested that 'Some persons who have accessed paraphilic materials over the Internet appear to have done so in association with either depression, anxiety, or stress. Downloading sexually explicit materials, including paraphilic images, may have helped to temporarily palliate their discomfort. Such persons, sometimes troubled and confused by ongoing life events, ordinarily do not manifest a malicious disregard for the wellbeing of others.' The use of the Internet as a means to emotional avoidance or regulation is an interesting and important issue and one which has been largely ignored within the sex offender literature. This will be discussed in more detail in Chapter 6.

Working with offenders

Central to all work with sex offenders is the consideration of reducing the possibility that the person will re-offend. In the next chapter we will examine in more detail the role that therapy has played with regard to this, and the way that the focus has moved from changing some inherent quality of the person in terms of what they respond to sexually, to a notion of managing the likelihood of future involvement in similar offending activity. In the context of the Internet, as with other offending, one issue relates to how we might convince some clients that it is worth engaging with their emotional distress without using the Internet as a means of avoidance. In addition, we are also asking them to forego the immediate pleasure and gratification that comes from accessing and using child abuse images. As we will see, such ideas appear contrary to many of the traditional cognitive behaviour therapy (CBT) approaches that have been adopted in the context of sex offender treatment. Instead of asking people to try and change emotions and thoughts, the focus we will present is on accepting that they are present and rather than struggling with them, focus on what it is possible to change – namely their behaviour. One potentially powerful strategy, that lies at the heart of all such acceptance based treatments, is getting the client to explicitly state their values and to look at how immediate gratification may inhibit their ability to fulfil those values.

Ward (2002: 515) discussed the fact that while the role of values in the rehabilitation of offenders has often been acknowledged, there has been little discussion of the explicit ways in which this should occur. He suggests that '. . . it is necessary for individuals working to rehabilitate offenders to explicitly construct conceptions of good lives for different offenders and to use these conceptions to shape the behaviour change process'. Ward used a study by Maruna (2001) who interviewed offenders desisting from and persisting with lives of crime to illustrate his argument. The major tasks for offenders attempting to live a crime-free life was to 'make good' by working out a different way to live based on a clear set of personal values and a consistent self-narrative. He suggested that, 'This means that therapists attempting to rehabilitate offenders ought to be guided by an awareness of the role that values and primary human goods play in facilitating well-being' (p 524). However, values cannot be pre-packaged, and what is relevant to one offender may be irrelevant for another. 'The reliance on manual-based interventions in the treatment of offenders can add to this problem. Because therapists tend to follow standardised procedures, they may fail to consider the appropriate form of life for a given individual' (p 526).

In the subsequent chapter on emotional avoidance, (Chapter 6), we will consider how acceptance based therapies, such as ACT (Hayes et al., 1999), are values oriented interventions, which focus on valuing as an activity. Quite literally the client is being asked to 'value with their feet', and to begin to experience their life as chosen rather than imposed. An active part of this is the assessment of client values, where the therapist's role is to clarify the direction inherent in what might be fairly concrete valued ends. The therapist also assesses variables controlling the client's statements about valued ends, and should attempt to intervene when the responses are based on 'pliance' (these might be statements controlled by the presence of the therapist, or by the emotional proximity of others such as parents, or that may be culturally desirable values). The assessment of values is followed by the generation of goals and actions that are

relevant to those values, and the examination of private events that act as barriers to moving forward in their life in these areas. Underlying this is the assumption that emotional acceptance is a means to an end, and putting values into action is that end.

Although coming from a very different perspective, such individual operationalisation of values and goals in the context of emotional acceptance would seem to have relevance to Ward's (2002) critique of current Sex Offender Treatment Programmes. With Internet offenders it would allow an exploration of the function of the Internet in terms of individual needs, and how far immediate emotional avoidance and gratification reduced the likelihood of the offender realising his personal values. Isen (1999) has listed some of the possible effects of positive effective states which include: promotes sociability; facilitates the recall of positive material in memory; reduces some elements of risk taking; fosters more complex problem solving; promotes more thorough decision making and promotes more humanistic motivations. While Howell et al.'s (2004) caution is against treating positive affect as simply the mirror image of negative affect, it is apparent that many of the possible effects would be seen as not only congruent with therapeutic goals but facilitative of them. In a similar vein, Middleton (2004: 107) has suggested, 'If the premise is that use of the Internet is a means of altering mood or avoiding negative emotional states such as boredom, depression or anxiety (in much the same way that individuals may resort to instrumental use of alcohol or drugs) then it is clear that any strategies so far discussed will have limited impact unless the individual is able to gain insight into the causes of the behaviour and helped to generate alternative coping strategies. Similarly if the problematic use of the Internet is driven by the need to avoid negative emotional states or personal distress then the practice of downloading and masturbating to abuse images provides a highly rewarding or reinforcing context for further avoidance.'

Over the next chapters we will return to the challenge of determining what factors are important for the particular offender under consideration whose offence includes the use of the Internet. Beech et al. (2003) have suggested that functional analysis may play an important part in the assessment of risk of future offending, '. . . a clinical tool used to investigate the antecedents, behaviours and consequences of the offence. This allows an assessment to be made of the process of the offence and the offence pathway that characterises the offending for that individual. Hence this type of analysis is an important first step to ascertain the type of goals and strategies a sexual offender has towards offending.' Shingler and Strong (2003) have also highlighted the neglect of the behavioural aspect of CBT treatment with offenders. Such an approach emphasises the purposes that the behaviour serves for the person, and places importance on the role that environment plays in causing, controlling and maintaining behaviour. A functionalist approach de-emphasises the form that the problem takes and shifts attention to the purposes that the behaviour might serve for the individual. In the context of how offenders use Internet abuse images this may prove to be an important issue. Behaviour that relates to the downloading of images may be very high rate

and therefore more accessible to analysis, and descriptive functional analysis can also be used as a form of intervention which does not exclude private events (thoughts and feelings) but gives them equal status as observable behaviours (Sturmey, 1996).

The approaches used in this book are designed to encourage the practitioner to consider the function of the behaviours for the individual and how these might change over time and context. We have attempted to embrace some of the earlier principles of behaviour analysis, in particular functional assessment, as well as acknowledging the important role of existing CBT frameworks. We would also encourage practitioners to consider some of the new acceptance based strategies that enable us to consider the values that individual offenders hold and how these might be used therapeutically to enable more effective self-control in the context of the Internet.

Chapter Two

Theories of Child Sexual Abuse and the Role of Cognitive Behaviour Therapy

This chapter provides a background to the literature on why adults sexually abuse children, and the role that cognitive behaviour therapy (CBT) has played in service delivery for this group of offenders. A variety of explanations have been offered as to the aetiology and maintenance of sexual offending, which encompass biological, psychological and sociological theories, all of which purport to explain the onset of deviant sexual fantasies and behaviour. However, as Bickley and Beech (2001) have argued, owing to the heterogeneity of the perpetrators of such abuse and the complex nature of this behaviour, no one theory adequately explains both the motivating factors that lead an adult male to have sexual relations with a child and the sustaining factors that contribute to the continuance of such relations. For the purposes of this chapter and by way of an introduction to the area, we will attempt to briefly describe each of these theories.

Biological theories

The concept of deviant sexual preferences as having an underlying biological abnormality goes back to the medicalisation of sexual problems. The attractiveness of such an idea is understandable as it holds out the possibility not only that these people are 'sick' rather than 'bad', but also that they may be 'cured', or at least managed. This belief has led to the prescribing of many drugs, such as Depo-Provera, centrally active hormonal agents and serotonin-active anti-depressants to control deviant sexual arousal and behaviour (Maletzky and Field, 2003), and the search for a congruent theoretical model to explain how this might work. Authors such as Flor-Henry (1987: 79) have concluded that 'sexual deviations are, overwhelmingly, a consequence of the male pattern of cerebral organisation'. The premise underlying much of the anti-androgen treatments for deviant sexuality is that the male offender's sex drive is out of control because his level of sex hormones (plasma testosterone) is too high. Androgens promote sexual arousal, orgasm,

and ejaculation, as well as regulate sexuality, aggression, cognition, emotion and personality (Rösler and Witztum, 2000; Marques et al., 2000). Sexually violent acts such as rape are thus hypothesised to be associated with aggression and high testosterone levels (Money, 1970; Rada, Laws and Kellner, 1976). Biological theories concerning paedophilia are most often concerned with the role of androgens and androgen-releasing hormones, which are known to be related to physical changes in the male. The hypothalamus and the pituitary control the secretion of androgens, and hormones are carried from the anterior lobe of the pituitary to the testes. The testes play a central role in the body's output of testosterone, which, once released, circulates in the blood. When males reach puberty, there is a major increase in testosterone levels in the testes, and as the sex drive increases dramatically at this time, there is generally believed to be a correlation between testosterone levels and sex drive. This suggests that testosterone is the primary biological factor responsible for normal and abnormal sexual behaviour. Levels of plasma testosterone increase with erotic activity, and this has been measured in males before, during and after they view sexually arousing films (Pirke et al., 1974). However, the results of systematic research in this area remain equivocal and sparse (Lanyon, 1991; Maletzky and Field, 2003) and it seems to be only in the most aggressive or dangerous of offenders that significantly elevated levels of plasma testosterone are reliably found (Rada et al., 1983). Over 20 years ago Berlin (1983) concluded that some people commit sex offences in response to intense, unconventional sexual urges and that although the aetiology of such urges is multiple, biological factors such as hormone levels or chromosomal makeup sometimes play a major role.

Psychoanalytic theory

Psychoanalytic explanations of deviant sexual behaviour have been largely attributed to Freud, who published his *Three Essays on the Theory of*

Sexuality in 1905. The first of these essays considered sexually deviant behaviour, while the following two dealt with infantile and pubertal sexuality. No brief review can do justice to Freud's work and thinking, but for the purpose of this chapter we will consider a simplification of certain key elements. Freud proposed four states of childhood psychosexual development: oral, anal, phallic and genital, where sexual deviance was seen as an expression of the unresolved problems experienced during these stages of development. Unresolved problems were brought about by 'fixations' or hindrances during stages of development, with a consequent distortion of a sexual object or a sexual aim. An example of this was given by Schwartz (1995), where psychoanalytic theory proposes that boys experience what is termed 'the oedipal conflict' during the phallic stage of development. Such conflict is characterised by competition between father and son for the mother's affection. In parallel with this, boys discover the differences between themselves and girls and conclude that girls are actually boys whose jealous fathers have cut off their penises. Schwartz (1995) stated that castration anxiety leads to the oedipal conflict, which is when boys no longer compete with their fathers for their mother's affections. However, if a boy fails to resolve the oedipal conflict, he may develop a permanent aversion to females as an adult if their appearance brings back this fear of castration.

Psychodynamic theory also describes the human psyche as composed of three primary elements: the id, the ego and the superego. All human behaviour is motivated by wishes that exist at a preconscious level. The id is the unconscious domain from which all the instinctual human drives originate (i.e., hunger, sex, aggression, etc.) and is ruled by the pleasure principle that demands instant gratification of these urges. The ego is the conscious part of the human psyche that serves as the mediator between the id and the external environment. Holmes and Holmes (2002) have suggested that this element is primarily conscious and is ruled by the reality principle that accepts that there is a time and a place for everything. It is this aspect of the psyche that interacts with the external environment in order to ensure survival. The final element, the superego, is what we most commonly refer to as the conscience. Thus, the superego is influenced by past experiences that clearly define the behaviours that result in both

punishment and reward, internalised in such a way as to allow for the development of a system of morals. The human psyche is therefore in a constant struggle to fulfil the primal desires of the id and the moral authority of the superego. When applied to offence behaviour, this theoretical model assumes that sexual aggressors are lacking in a strong superego and have become overwhelmed by their primal id. Such explanations were, and still are, important in our understanding of the development of sexual deviance, but 'Contemporary approaches to sexual deviance owe little to classical psychoanalytical or psychodynamic theory or practice' (Laws and Marshall, 2003a).

An important paper by Marshall (1996) described the historical development of psychological approaches to the treatment of sex offenders, suggesting that there was a move from a Freudian conceptualisation, which equated problematic sexual behaviour with a form of deviant personality, to accounts that were more behavioural or 'motivational'. Such accounts also placed significant importance on early sexual development, but suggested that sexual arousal and masturbation when paired with a 'deviant' stimulus (such as another child or a non-sexual object) could in and of itself become the primary sexual context for arousal. This is also discussed by Seto et al. (2001) when examining the importance of pornography and sexual behaviour. The early treatments associated with such theorising were largely behavioural and included the use of aversive therapy. The focus was on eliminating the problem arousal, rather than any assumed underlying cause, or managing the response. It was also assumed that by reducing sexual responsivity to some stimuli this would be sufficient to change the offending behaviour.

Sexual deviance model

Laws and Marshall (1990) presented a theoretical model of sexually deviant behaviour that described how sexually deviant interests may be learned through the same mechanisms by which conventional sexuality is learned. The model described both the acquisition and maintenance processes, and adopted the position that maladaptive behaviour can result from quantitative and qualitative combinations of processes that are intrinsically orderly, strictly determined and normal in origin. Thus, deviant sexual preferences and cognitions are acquired by the same mechanisms by which other individuals learn more conventionally accepted modes of sexual expression. One consequence of learning theory research was the development of behaviour therapy as a treatment for a variety of problems, which was soon applied to deviant sexuality. Laws and Marshall (2003) in their review of early behavioural and cognitive behavioural approaches to treatment, have described how the earliest behavioural approaches to the modification of sexual offending reflected the view that deviant sexual behaviour was a distorted manifestation of desire and that 'The idea that deviant sexual preferences formed the motivation for paedophilia, rape, exhibitionism, or a host of other deviant behaviours became the rationale for the behavioural approach to these problems. Thus, the reasoning went, the optimal treatment for sexual deviates would simply involve reducing their deviant sexual responses'. Procedures such as aversion therapy were then used as a way of reducing arousal.

Marshall and Barbaree (1990) generated a more global theory of deviant sexual behaviour, which suggested that for males, biological factors cause a ready and unlearned propensity for sexual aggression. This propensity has to be overcome by a process of socialisation, which inhibits the expression of such behaviour. The presence of factors such as poor parenting places the male at risk. Secondary risk factors include negative socio-cultural attitudes, an example of which would be exposure to or the use of pornography. Also important are situational factors, which may further serve as disinhibitors for the person who is already predisposed to offend. The model therefore attempted to integrate the four groups of factors, which were thought to be central in causing sex offending; biological, early childhood development, socio-cultural and situational. More recent research has, for example, examined the evidence for elevated non-right-handedness in sex offenders as a measure of underlying developmental or central nervous system abnormalities (Bogaert, 2001). However, Taylor and Quayle (2003: 49) have argued that while such correlations are interesting, they do little to move us away from models emphasising associations between a variety of biological factors and the emergence of behaviour that is socially labelled as deviant. 'They do not establish what 'causes' people to behave differently and

reinforce the 'medicalisation' of such sexual behaviour'.

Treatment approaches

There have been three main theoretical models of sexual offending that link with treatment approaches. These are Finkelhor's (1984) precondition theory, Marshall and Barbaree's (1990) integrated theory and Hall and Hirshman's (1992) model of sexual offending against children. Finkelhor (1984) suggested four underlying factors, which could be used to explain the occurrence of child sexual abuse:

- that sex with children is seen as emotionally satisfying to the offender and therefore has emotional congruence for them
- men who offend are sexually aroused by children
- and men who have sex with children do so because they are unable to meet their sexual needs in more socially appropriate ways (sometimes termed blockage)
- A fourth factor explains why this is expressed as sexually deviant behaviour – these men become disinhibited and go on to behave in ways that are not congruent with their normal behaviour.

These factors are grouped into four preconditions that must be satisfied before the sexual abuse of a child can occur:

- Firstly, that the person must be motivated to sexually abuse a child.
- Secondly, overcoming internal inhibitions (a cluster of conditions which may range from alcohol abuse to social tolerance of sexual interest in children).
- Thirdly, overcoming external inhibitions or conditions that increase the possibility of offending (again ranging from maternal absence or illness through to unusual sleeping conditions).
- Finally, that the adult must overcome a child's resistance to the abuse.

It is hypothesised that these preconditions occur in a temporal sequence with each being necessary for the other to occur. Finkelhor's model is interesting, and as has been indicated by Beech and Ward (2004) 'persuasively argues that child molestation is a multifaceted phenomenon incorporating both psychological and sociological variables.' While sexual motivation is important, it is argued that this might be expressed in more appropriate social ways, allowing contact with children but without sexual engagement. This model emphasises the importance of socialisation, cultural norms and biological factors in offending behaviour. Beech and Ward (2004) have been critical of this model because it utilised theories and constructs from different theoretical positions, and also because if, as Finkelhor suggested, the three motivational factors may operate independently, then it is 'hard to see why these motives result in a sexual offence'.

The model proposed by Marshall and Barbaree (1990) suggested that the sexual abuse of children occurs because of the interaction of a number of historical, or distal factors, with more recent or proximal factors. Early adverse events, such as poor parenting, or physical or sexual abuse, leave the individual vulnerable to the development of distorted cognitive models of relationships, which may find expression in poor social skills and difficulties in behavioural self-regulation. In a similar vein, Burk and Burkhart (2003) suggested disorganised attachment as a diathesis for sexual deviance. According to attachment theory, humans have a propensity to establish strong emotional bonds with others, and when individuals have experienced loss or emotional distress, they act out as a result of their loneliness and isolation. As has already been discussed, the period surrounding pubescence and early adolescence is thought to be critical in the development of both sexuality and social competence. Where adequate parenting has taken place, boys should have by now acquired appropriate inhibitory controls over sexual and aggressive behaviour. The transition from adolescent to adult functioning requires the development of both social constraints against aggression, and also the skills necessary to develop effective relationships with age appropriate partners. Research by Marshall (1989) had indicated that men who sexually abuse children often have not developed the social skills and self-confidence necessary for them to form effective intimate relations with peers. One consequence of this failure is that such men then seek to be intimate with children.

There has been much subsequent research that has attempted to examine this purported difficulty with intimacy problems (e.g., Seidman et al., 1994). Underpinning this research is the premise that sex offenders have deficiencies in social skills. Such deficiencies would include

being able to accurately read social cues, deciding on appropriate behaviour and having the skills to enact such behaviour. Mulloy and Marshall (1999) outlined Bartholomew's four-category model of attachment and on the basis of this suggested that:

- *A secure attachment style is characterised by the individual having a positive concept of both himself and others, and is confident about his ability to make friends and interacts well with others.*
- *An individual utilising a preoccupied attachment style has a negative self-concept but a positive concept of others, and does not feel confident about his ability to deal with problems without the help of others.*
- *The fearful attachment style, where an individual has a negative concept of himself and others, means that the individual is likely to blame himself for the problems in his life and finds it frightening to go to others for help and to trust people around him.*
- *Those engaging in a dismissing attachment style have a positive self-concept and a strong sense of self-confidence. However, this person has a negative concept of others and does not seek out others for help or support, being more likely to say that he does not care what others think of him. Such a person rarely has a strong emotional involvement in relationships.*

Ward et al. (1995) proposed that sexual offenders who have a preoccupied insecure attachment style would characteristically 'court' the child and treat them as a lover. It is hypothesised that such people do not adequately develop (or fail to adequately internalise) self-regulatory skills, and therefore are more likely to rely on externally based ways of regulating their behaviour. Puberty then acts as a biological catalyst, fusing sexual behaviour with aggressive or violent responses, and consolidating pre-existing sexually abusive tendencies. Poor social and self-regulation skills increase the likelihood of problematic encounters with women as a young adult, which in turn may result in feelings of rejection and lowered self-esteem. A consequence of this is an increase in the possibility of strong negative reactions towards women, which may fuel the development of deviant sexual fantasies. Masturbation to these fantasies strengthens them and sets the scene for a cognitive rehearsal of the fantasies. Such individuals may also see children as less threatening than adult women. Within this diathesis stress model, the existing vulnerabilities of the individual interact with more proximal events, such as stress, alcohol use, or the presence of a child. This may increase the likelihood that the individual may act upon their feelings and engage in offending behaviour. The behaviour may be positively reinforced by sexual arousal and ejaculation, and negatively by the change in emotional state from negative to positive mood.

Such dynamic models of offending are important and have been used by other authors, such as Quayle and Taylor (2003) and Davis (2001), to conceptualise the role that the Internet and images may have in offending behaviour. Ward (2002) has, however, criticised Marshall and Barbaree's model because it is general, rather than offence specific, and would have difficulty in explaining situational, as opposed to preferential, offending. The model is also criticised because there is little empirical evidence to support the idea that all offenders have problems with self-regulation. Beech and Ward (2003) were also critical because the model is 'silent' in relation to the development of typologies of offenders, and because they 'mistakenly focus on the way individuals learn to control aggression in the context of sexuality', without sufficiently clarifying the idea of 'fusion'.

A third model is Hall and Hirschman's (1992) theory of offending against children. This model has four components:

- physiological sexual arousal
- faulty cognitions that justify sexually aggressive behaviour
- affective discontrol
- personality problems

The first three of these factors relate to a given state and situation, whereas the fourth is a trait factor (personality) and therefore represents an enduring vulnerability. The relationship between personality disturbance and sexual offending is seen as a dynamic relation and was explored in earlier research by authors such as Groth (1979). It has been suggested that the interest in personality gained new momentum with the publication of a meta-analysis of recidivism (Hanson and Bussiere, 1998), which indicated that the presence of any personality disorder was the only variable to significantly predict sexual recidivism in a category measuring 'Psychological Maladjustment'. In Hall and Hirschman's (1992) model, it was hypothesised that the personality defect becomes activated in some contexts, leading to sexual arousal, emotional changes and distorted or faulty thinking. The other three factors also act as motivational precursors to offending, and may interact with each other to move the person towards the commission of a sexually aggressive act. Hall and Hirschman's model did allow for the development of typologies as it suggests that combinations of these factors characterise different kinds of 'child molesters'. Beech and Ward (2003) have suggested that one of the strengths of this model is its focus on multiple factors and the suggestion that sexual offending may be the product of converging causal pathways. However, they were also critical of the model because it did not represent a true multifactorial theory, it lacked specificity, the distinction between state and trait factors was conceptually confusing, and the notion of primary motivational factors remained vague. These authors proposed instead a pathways model of child sexual abuse, building on existing models, but suggesting that 'the clinical phenomena evident among child molesters are generated by four distinct and interacting psychological mechanisms: intimacy and social skill deficits; distorted sexual scripts; emotional disregulation; and cognitive distortions'. Each of these then depicts an offence specific pathway 'with different psychological and behavioural profiles and separate aetiologies and underlying deficits'.

Cognitive-behaviour theory

The interest in 'cognitions' as being important influences on behaviour led to a massive growth in therapies whose focus was in challenging or changing dysfunctional cognitive processing. While the initial focus of such therapies was in the context of emotional distress, such techniques were adapted in order to moderate other problematic behaviours, such as eating disorders and sexually aggressive behaviour. Marshall and Laws (2003: 97) have argued that, 'this move was at least initially more to do with the sentiments of the time (i.e., a shift in the conceptualisation of human behaviour to cognitively mediated actions rather than resulting from simple stimulus-response connections) than to do with the empirically demonstrated value of cognitive behavioural approaches'. However, what has emerged from this is a generic cognitive behavioural model for the treatment of sexual offenders, which moves the focus from some inherent psychopathology to examining the offence specific cognitions, emotions and behaviours that are deemed to both be part of the aetiology of the offence (underlying schemata) and which also maintain the offending process.

In the context of the United Kingdom, the current treatment model has been adapted from the work of Fisher and Beech (1999) and addresses four components: denial, offence specific behaviours, social inadequacy and relapse prevention skills. The issue of denial is somewhat problematic, as meta-analyses of treatment data does not suggest that it is associated with recidivism (Hanson and Bussière, 1998), but nevertheless it has secured an important place in treatment. Middleton (2004) has suggested that initial work on denial is important because it is inherently logical that a starting place is the acceptance of responsibility for their offending. Another way if conceptualising this (which may be less judgmental) is to use Cautela's (1993) behavioural model of insight. Rather than forcing an admission, maybe what we are helping offenders to acknowledge are the contingencies that maintain their offending behaviour.

Within a cognitive behavioural framework, offence specific intervention largely focuses on cognitive and behavioural processes that are thought to be associated with offending behaviour. These would include 'cognitive distortions' about the offence, fantasy and deviant sexual arousal and distorted empathic responses towards victims. We have previously discussed one of the most influential models that had informed this component (Finkelhor, 1984), which described how people who commit sexual offences against children move through four preconditions. These are: motivation to abuse, overcoming internal inhibitors, overcoming external inhibitors and overcoming child resistance. Finkelhor described two principle ways that offenders overcome internal inhibitors – the use of mood altering substances (such as alcohol or drugs) and through self-talk or cognitive distortions.

Much of the recent psychological research on sex offenders has taken as its focus the role of cognition in sexual aggression. Such cognitive accounts of offending focus on factors such as empathy, social skills and cognitive processes as a way of understanding, and hopefully changing, offender behaviour. It is not so surprising that, as previously discussed, this has provided the

framework for the majority of treatment models in this area. What is implied is that there is something problematic in the way that offenders view or interpret their social world and the way that they respond to it. What lies between the offender and their behaviour is a way of thinking that results from an active, but inaccurate thinking process, rather than a lack of processing activity. Cognitive processing is taking place, but thinking has become in some way distorted. In the sex offender literature such 'cognitive distortions' are most often defined as attitudes and beliefs that offenders use to deny, minimise and rationalise their behaviour. Such distortions have been defined as consistent errors in thinking that occur automatically (Geer et al., 2000). In the context of offences against children, this would include beliefs such as: if children fail to resist advances, they must want sex; sexual activity with children is an appropriate means to increase the sexual knowledge of children; if children fail to report sexual activity, they must condone it; in the future, sexual activity between adults and children will be acceptable, if not encouraged; if one fondles, rather than penetrates, sex with children is acceptable; any children who ask questions about sex really desire it; and one can develop a close relationship with a child through sexual contact (Horley, 2000). A fundamental assumption of such research is that these attitudes and beliefs play a major role in both precipitating and maintaining offending behaviour (Abel et al., 1994).

The final component relates to the social inadequacy that we have noted has been reported in some sexual offenders. This is a conceptually confusing area as it reflects potential inadequacies in a range of areas such as assertiveness skills, self-esteem, difficulties with interpersonal relationships and intimacy, as well as a cluster of problems that relate to 'thinking skills' and difficulties in recognising and generating solutions to problems. Within a more behavioural perspective, it might be suggested that many of these difficulties relate to difficulties with self-control, and this is certainly reflected in many other offence and non-offence related behaviours.

Cognitive distortions

Though sex offenders do not form a homogeneous group of individuals, it has been argued that they show strikingly similar cognitive distortions about their victims, the offences committed and their responsibility for the offences. It is unclear as to whether such cognitive distortions are post-offence rationalisations or whether offenders genuinely believe these altered perceptions of reality (however, it might also be argued that this is a feature of other kinds of offender's views about victims and offending). Some researchers suggest that cognitive distortions are self-serving, and thus, the offender consciously distorts thoughts initially (Abel et al., 1994). However, it is also suggested that the offenders may eventually believe the distortions as they become more entrenched in their behaviour (Marshal et al., 1999). Regardless, cognitive distortions are considered crucial to the maintenance of offending behaviour for both rapists and child abusers because they serve the needs of the offenders to continue in their offending behaviour while reducing feelings of guilt for their actions. Sykes and Matza (1957) have listed five primary neutralisation techniques used by offenders. These include:

- The denial of responsibility.
- The denial of injury.
- The denial of the victim.
- The condemnation of the accusers.
- The appeal to higher loyalties.

It is argued that these techniques are used to minimise, deny and justify the offence. Additionally, it has been suggested that sex offenders often lack victim empathy and show an inability to recognise the level of planning that went into their offences. Several researchers have categorised the types of minimisation and denial shown by offenders (Haywood et al., 1994; Marshall et al., 1998), and these include:

- Complete or partial denial of the offence.
- Minimisation of the offence.
- Minimisation of their own responsibility.
- Denial or minimisation of harm to the victim.
- Denial or minimisation of planning.
- Denial or minimisation of deviant fantasies and denial of their personal problems that led to the deviant behaviour.

Partial denial has been described as including the refutation of a problem (e.g., I am not a sex offender) or the refusal to accept that an act was sexual abuse (e.g., the victim consented). The role of denial as a predictor of future offending activity is controversial and while many practitioners feel that it is important in terms of

treatment, as noted earlier Hanson and Bussiere, (1998) have indicated through their meta-analysis studies that it is not a predictive variable.

Justification for the commission of an offence has been argued to be common in the vast majority of sex offenders, as it assists in allaying remorse and guilt for the acts committed. From an analysis of interviews with 114 incarcerated rapists, Scully and Marolla (1984) described five ways in which they commonly justified their behaviour. These include:

- The victim is a seductress, and she provoked the rape.
- Women mean yes when they say no, or the victim did not resist enough to really mean no.
- Most women relax and enjoy it, and they are actually fulfilling the woman's desires.
- Nice girls do not get raped, and prostitutes, hitchhikers and promiscuous women get what they deserve.
- The rape was only a minor wrongdoing, so the perpetrator is not really an 'offender'.

While this research had as its focus the excuses and justifications of rapists, many of their findings are also thought to be evident in child sexual abusers, who also justify their actions by neutralising their guilt, through claims that they are helping the child to learn about sex, that sexual education is good for the child, that the child enjoys it, that there is no harm being done to the child, that the child initiated the sexual contact and that the child acts older than they are (Terry and Tallon, 2004). One assertion made by offenders is that the child did not resist and therefore must have wanted the sexual interaction. Typically, offenders fail to recognise any other explanations for the child's behaviour, such as fear, uncertainty about what was happening or the idea that the perpetrator is someone that they knew and trusted. Ward and Keenan (1999) have claimed that the cognitive distortions of child sexual offenders emerge from underlying implicit theories that they have about themselves, their victims and their environment. These implicit theories (which have been referred to as schema by other authors) may be summarised as:

- Children as sexual objects, where children like adults, are motivated by a desire for pleasure and are capable of enjoying and desiring sex.
- Entitlement – the desires and beliefs of the abuser are paramount and those of the victim

are either ignored or viewed as only of secondary importance.

- Dangerous world – the abuser views other adults as being abusive and/or unreliable and perceives that they will reject him in promotion of their own needs.
- Uncontrollability – the abuser perceives his environment as uncontrollable wherein people are not able to exert any major influence over their personal behaviour and/or the world around them.
- Nature of harm – the abuser considers the degree of harm to his victim and perceives sexual activity as beneficial and unlikely to harm a person.

It is argued that offenders rarely modify these implicit theories even when faced with evidence (behaviour) to the contrary. Marshall et al. (1998) have also stressed that 'the distorting process thought to be characteristic of sexual offenders does not differentiate them from the rest of us; it is the content of their distortions, and the goals manifested by their behaviours, that differentiates them'. Implicit theories or schemata are not peculiar to the child sex offender – within a cognitive behavioural formulation we all have implicit theories or schemata about ourselves in relation to our social world and these are generated in the context of earlier social experiences. What is relevant is how such schemata influence the way that the individual interprets and makes sense of their immediate social world. What is more difficult to make sense of is the situationally specific element to many of these distortions, which make some of the empathy research, for example, so difficult to interpret. It is also important to note that regardless of what we believe underlies the offending activity; ultimately what we are interested in changing is behaviour. Modification of beliefs is always in the service of modifying activity.

The offence process

Of relevance to this cognitive behavioural perspective is the concept of a cycle of offending behaviours mediated by cognitions. When contemplating the abuse of a child, the abuser must make a series of decisions about the act itself. These decisions may be made over a period of time or on the spur of the moment when the opportunity to abuse presents itself. There are

multiple determinants involved in this cycle, but what is important is that the sexual abuse is a purposeful act. These determinants may include:

- Situational factors (i.e., the opportunity to offend).
- Affective states (depression, anger, isolation).
- Past learning.
- Biological influences.
- Prevailing contingencies of reinforcement (current, unforeseen support or back up).

Beech et al. (2003) have suggested that: 'Currently the most useful framework is probably what is called a Decision Chain' (Ward, Louden, Hudson and Marshall, 1995). This model has tended to supercede earlier frameworks such as Finkelhor's (1994) preconditions or Wolf's (1985) offence cycle. Such a Decision Chain is made up of a sequence of choices, which lead to an offence, where each choice is characterised in terms of the situational context, the thoughts that mediated the situation, and the emotions and actions that arose from these thoughts. Clearly such an analysis can only be made at an individual level and although it is important to, for example, understand typical cognitive distortions or implicit theories, this can never replace an idiographic assessment. Beech et al. (2003) have described the advantages of Decision Chains in that 'they can represent with equal facility offences that spring from negative emotional states and poor coping strategies (as in the Wolf, 1985 cycle) and those where these negative factors are not involved' (see Eldridge, 1998; Laws, 1999; Ward and Hudson, 1996).

Beech et al. (2003) have also drawn attention to how thinking about the offence process can be informed by the work of Ward and Hudson (1998) who have suggested a way of classifying offenders according to one of four different routes to offending, 'These groups are defined by the individual offender's goal towards deviant sex (i.e., avoidant or approach), and the selection of strategies designed to achieve their goal (i.e., active or passive)'. An avoidant goal offender is described as a person with a commitment to restraint, as the overall goal is one of avoidance. However, self-regulation deficiencies ultimately result in goal failure. These may include inadequate coping skills (under-regulation) or inappropriate strategies (misregulation). Consequently, negative emotional states and covert planning are characteristic of the avoidant pathway. Beech et al. (2003) have suggested that this type of pathway can be seen as being similar to Wolf's (1985) description of the offence process. In contrast, with the approach goal offender, positive affective states, explicit planning and the presence of distorted attitudes about victims and offending behaviour are typical of the process leading to offending.

In this model, Ward and Hudson (1998) subdivided the approach and avoidant pathways into active and passive. This is described by Beech et al. (2003) as follows, 'The approach offender who is active is seeking opportunities to offend and actively setting up the situation in which to offend. The approach passive offender however, while motivated to offend only does so when the opportunity presents itself. With the avoidant offender the active pathway is one in which the offender makes an effort to avoid offending while the passive offender would prefer not to offend but does nothing to prevent himself'.

Taxonomic systems

Marshall and Laws (2003) have suggested that the final important development of the 1980s related to the work on classificatory (or taxonomic systems) applied to sexual offending. This was part of an ongoing effort to develop an understanding of characteristics that would allow for classification of sex offenders into specific groups, or typologies. Such schemes utilise offender characteristics and/or victim-choice information, including interpersonal and situational characteristics, to outline a framework for analysis (e.g., Knight and Prentky, 1990). Early research divided people with a sexual interest in children into two main types, according to their level of psychosexual motivation, and excluded those who used violence against children. These were termed child rapists and were seen as qualitatively different from 'molesters'. In addition, child molesters were divided into either regressed or fixated offenders. The former was theorised as having developed age-appropriate sexual and interpersonal orientations, but under particular circumstances could regress to the expression of sexual behaviour with children. The fixated offender was described as one whose primary sexual interest was children, and who never developed psychosexually beyond that level. Such accounts are still very influential and have found their way into emerging typologies of

people who use child images on the Internet (Brookes, 2003). Brookes (2003) suggested that behavioural patterns could be used as a 'benchmark' to begin to categorise offenders that have the same characteristics but specifically use computers as a tool to commit crimes against children. He placed the subjects within his study into four typologies: sadistic predator; introverted; regressed, and fixated/preferential. However, such typologies may be problematic and naïve. For instance, subdividing a rape typology has raised concerns given the expected random variations in what is presumed to be a continuum of normal male heterosexual aggressive sexual behaviour (e.g., Brownmiller, 1975; Scully and Marolla, 1985).

Earlier research had classified offenders based on their motivation for committing sexually deviant behaviour. One such classification scheme was proposed by Groth et al. (1982), who considered two issues: the degree to which the deviant sexual behaviour is entrenched and the psychological needs that were being served. With regard to the first issue, Groth proposed the fixated-regressed dichotomy of sex offending. This was not a dichotomous distinction, but rather existed on a continuum. The fixated offender was characterised as having a persistent, continual and compulsive attraction to children, and would be likely diagnosed with paedophilia, or recurrent, intense, sexually arousing fantasies of at least six months in duration involving pre-pubescent children (American Psychiatric Association, 1999). Finkelhor (1984) had described these offenders as exclusively involved with children to whom they were not related, and are attracted to children from adolescence. According to this model, the offender has not fully developed and shows characteristics of a child. In particular, it is theorised that fixated offenders do not develop past the point where they find children attractive and desirable (Holmes and Holmes, 2002). The fixated offender's actions are typically premeditated in nature and do not result from any perceived stress. In addition, this type of offender is often unable to attain any degree of psychosexual maturity and, during adulthood, has had virtually no age appropriate sexual relationships. Conte (1991) has argued that these offenders develop relationships with vulnerable children (vulnerable in either an emotional or situational sense) and they typically recruit, groom and maintain the children for a continuing sexual relationship.

In contrast, the regressed offenders' behaviour is said to emerge in adulthood and tends to be precipitated by external stressors, such as environmental events and disordered childhood relationships (Gebhard et al., 1965). These two variables are said to interact in such a manner as to leave the offender powerless to control his behaviour, which culminates in an offensive act. When this classification system was created, the authors were unable to specify childhood precursors to offending but there have since been extensive research evaluating the nature of possible stressors. Such stressors can be situational, for example, unemployment, marital problems and substance abuse, or can be related to negative emotional states such as loneliness, stress, isolation or anxiety. Schwartz (1995) has argued that these stressors often lead to poor self-confidence and low self-esteem, and undermine the abuser's confidence in themselves as men. In this context, offending activity with children is not 'fixed', but is a temporary departure from the offender's attraction to adults (Simon et al., 1992), and this type of offender is more likely to choose victims who are female and to whom they have easy access (such as their own children). Simon et al. (1992) attempted to empirically validate the fixated-regressed typology through a sample of 136 consecutive cases of convicted offenders over a two-year period. These authors reviewed pre-sentence information that was made up of case history notes, MMPI results, pre-sentence reports and police report data. However, the analysis of their data yielded a unimodal and continuous distribution of offenders rather than the bimodal (fixated/regressed) distribution, which would have been predicted by Groth's theory. Subsequently, Simon et al. (1992) suggested that Groth's fixated/regressed dichotomy was unable to account for all child sexual abusers and recommended using a modification of Groth's approach which would entail the use of Groth's criteria along a continuum rather than the original dichotomy.

Multidimensional typologies

A more recent attempt to classify child molesters is described by Knight and Prentky (1990) who developed multidimensional typologies of offenders on two axes. Axis I addressed the degree to which an offender is fixated with children and is further broken down to consider the offender's level of social competence. Axis II evaluated the amount of contact an offender has with children and is analysed according to the meaning (interpersonal or sexual) of that contact. This axis also evaluates the amount and type of physical injury involved in the contact. This system, which is known as the Massachusetts Treatment Center: Child Molester Typology, version 3 (MTC: CM3) assigned each offender to a separate Axis I and Axis II typology. Looman et al. (2001) attempted a replication of Knight and Prentky's research with 109 child molesters in Canada. Their sample was classified according to the MTC: CM3 typology, and groups of molesters were compared on a number of meaningful variables, such as number of victims and sexual deviance. All the child molesters, with the exception of the sadistic types, were classified into all subgroups with an acceptable level of reliability. Differences were found between groups on the phalometric assessments using the Penile Plethysmograph (PPG) (a biosignal measure using penile tumescence) with the high fixation-low social competence group having highest levels of deviance on the slide assessment for Axis I. Interestingly, the average deviance indices for all four levels of Axis I indicated at least a failure to differentiate appropriate from inappropriate stimuli in terms of sexual responding. However, the high fixation-low social competence group was the only one that demonstrated a clear sexual preference for children, and was also distinguished by their preferences for male victims and their higher levels of self-reported childhood sexual abuse.

Re-offending and risk assessment

As we have previously discussed, one of the issues that has been the focus of much research in this area is the practitioner's ability to assess what factors are likely to influence the risk of future offending. This issue dominates concerns over typologies, assessment and intervention. Marshall and Laws (2003: 104) have suggested that 'It became apparent that simply providing a post-treatment report on how well a client had done was not sufficient to guide decisions about the release of an offender nor how such an offender should be managed in the community'. Hanson and Bussière (1998) generated a meta-analysis of 61 studies on recidivism that involved a total of 28,972 offenders. On the basis of their findings, the authors subsequently produced a brief risk prediction scale, which was later modified to incorporate clinical judgments (Hanson and Thornton, 1999). The meta-analysis illustrated that the best predictors of recidivism were sexual deviancy as measured by PPG, a history of sex crimes, psychological characteristics, a negative relationship with their mother, failure to complete treatment and the presence of depression and anxiety. Other actuarial assessments had sought to evaluate an individual through the interpretation of standardised scores on various risk assessment instruments, whereas clinical assessments are based upon the practitioner's personal judgment and knowledge. Grubin (1997) has argued that actuarial instruments provide little information pertaining to the causation and management of sexual offending and say nothing about the individual. Equally, Marshall and Laws (2003) have suggested that the limitation of all actuarial instruments concerns the fact that they are based on features of the individual that are static and unchangeable. This clearly does not allow for the modification of risk by factors such as treatment.

Increasingly, these problems have been addressed by the inclusion of dynamic modifiable factors in the assessment of risk (Hanson and Harris, 2001). Hanson and Harris (2000) had provided evidence that dynamic factors could be broken down further into stable dynamic risk factors (those expected to remain unchanged for a substantial period of time) and acute dynamic risk factors (factors that change rapidly). From their study of data from 208 sexual offence recidivists and 201 non-recidivist sex offenders, the authors concluded that stable dynamic risk factors showed the greatest potential in differentiating the recidivists from the non-recidivists. Criminal lifestyle variables were found to be the strongest predictors of recidivism and this is supported by earlier research by Browne et al. (1998) who had found that in a sample of 98 sex offenders, treatment drop out was best predicted by having spent time in prison, having committed a violence-related index offence, having committed non-contact offences, unemployment, substance abuse and delinquent/disruptive behaviour during treatment. Hanson and Harris (2000) concluded that recidivists had poor social support, attitudes tolerant of sexual assault, anti-social lifestyles, poor self-management strategies and difficulties complying with supervision. There were similarities between recidivists and non-recidivists concerning general mood, but the recidivists displayed more anger and subjective distress before re-offending. In recent years, a variety of evaluative instruments have been developed in order to assess the risk of sex offender recidivism, and it may well be that these are equally valid in the context of those whose offences relate to Internet abuse images. Hammond (2004: 95) has suggested that, 'In the area of Internet sex offenders, reliability and breadth of assessment is vital because we are still in a stage of discovery. The fundamental question of whether such offenders may be qualitatively distinct from contact offenders, and the degree of overlap there is between them, depends on the collection and collation of data'.

In their review of behavioural and cognitive behavioural approaches to treatment, Marshall and Laws (2003: 110) concluded by saying that, '. . . cognitive behavioural procedures have developed into a comprehensive approach that is widely shared and appears to be effective. The breadth of treatment targets has progressively increased and research has been implemented to evaluate the basis for these expanded targets'. Cognitive-behavioural treatment has emerged as the principal type of treatment used to modify deviant sexual arousal, increase appropriate sexual desires, modify cognitive distortions and improve interpersonal coping skills (Terry and Tallon, 2004). Nicholaichuk and Yates (2002) have described how this treatment approach is based on the premise that, '. . . cognitive and affective processes and behaviour are linked, and that cognitions, affect, and behaviour are mutually influential'. According to Marshall and Barbaree (1990) treatment typically includes targeting the following:

- Deviant sexual behaviour and interests.
- A wide range of social skills/relational deficits.
- Cognitive distortions, which permit the offender to justify, rationalise and/or minimise the offending behaviour.

As well as attempting to reduce deviant sexual behaviour and interests through techniques such as counter-conditioning, cognitive-behavioural treatment seeks to enhance the offender's interpersonal functioning, through targeting relationship skills, appropriate social interaction and empathy (Marshall et al., 1998). Social problem solving, conversational skills, managing social anxiety, assertiveness, conflict resolution, empathy and intimacy, anger management, self-confidence and the use of mood altering substances are also targeted (Laws and Marshall, 2003). Since the meta-analysis study by Hanson and Bussière (1998), the inclusion of empathy-enhancement in treatment has become more controversial. Such intervention is based on the belief that the attitudes of sexual offenders toward their victims will change if they understand how the victim feels, and will inhibit future sexual abuse.

Cognitive restructuring is an integral part of cognitive-behavioural treatment, regardless of the focus of change. As we have already considered, child sex offenders are said to construct internal rationalisations, excuses and cognitive distortions in order to maintain their sexually deviant behaviour. Marshall and Barbaree (1990) have argued that it is important that an offender's cognitive distortions are challenged so that he can comprehend his faulty thinking and recognise its distorted, self-serving nature. The practitioner facilitates this through challenging beliefs and helping to present more socially appropriate and adaptive views. Within this framework, the benefits of accepting such views are identified. Implicit is the assumption that cognitive distortions are a product of an automatic way of processing information about the world and are amenable to change. It is argued that changing such cognitions will also result in a change in behaviour. Central to this is an assumption that the offender can learn how these cognitive distortions are problematic in achieving a 'good life' (Ward, 2002) and lead the offender to engage in behaviours that make the achievements of such a good life impossible. One of the difficulties of most sex offender treatment programmes is that the practitioner makes the assumption that the offender really shares similar values and these become implicit, but not explicitly stated in any treatment programme. Ward and Brown (2004) have increasingly argued the need to make such values explicit, and one feature of the following chapters is an attempt to do this within a more radical behavioural framework.

Studies on treatment efficacy not only have to consider the changes that take place in the offenders behaviour both during and immediately at the end of treatment, but also how treatment has impacted on behaviour over time. This is difficult to assess, as recidivism is invariably going to be based on statistics derived from future convictions. It would hardly be in the best interest of the offender to acknowledge that they were offending again, although it is possible that this does happen. However, most studies conducted on treatment efficacy focus on the rate of recidivism among offenders, usually comparing those who have been through treatment with those who have not. In itself, it could be argued that this is problematic as there may be differences amongst those who are offered treatment and those who are not. For example, many treatment programmes will only offer therapy to those who 'admit' their offence. Furthermore, in the UK, the current sentencing structure means that many offenders on short prison sentences are unlikely to be offered access to a sex offender treatment programme. However, effects on recidivism can be seen in a follow-up study conducted on 89 sex offenders in Ontario by Looman et al. (2000). They found that those offenders who participated in treatment had a sexual recidivism rate of 23.6 per cent, whereas those offenders who did not participate in treatment had a sexual recidivism rate of 51.7 per cent. Similarly, when 296 treated and 283 untreated offenders were followed for a six-year period, Nicholaichuk et al. (2002) found that convictions for new sexual offences among treated sex offenders were 14.5 per cent versus 33.2 per cent for untreated offenders. Further, during the follow-up period, 48 per cent of treated offenders remained out of prison as compared to 28.3 per cent of untreated offenders.

Time series comparisons of treated offenders and comparison samples also showed that treated offenders re-offended at significantly lower rates after ten years. In reviewing studies pertaining to the efficacy of a particular type of treatment, there is significant evidence that cognitive-behavioural treatment has emerged as the principle type of sex offender treatment targeting deviant arousal, increasing appropriate sexual desires, modifying distorted thinking and improving interpersonal coping skills (Marshall and Barbaree, 1990; Eccles and Marshall, 1999; Marshall and Pithers, 1994; Becker, 1994; Hall, 1995; Abracen and Looman, 2001; Burdon et al., 2002; Nicholaichuk et al., 2002; Craig et al., 2003). Further, Marshall and Anderson (2000) found that cognitive-behavioural treatment programmes that have an internal self-management relapse-prevention component appear to be the most successful in reducing recidivism rates. Studies of the effects of treatment completion on recidivism have also supported the effectiveness of treatment (Hall, 1995; Hanson and Bussière, 1998; Hanson, 2002).

A retrospective study, conducted by McGrath et al. (2003), found that the reduction in the sexual recidivism rate among those offenders who participated in treatment was statistically, as well as clinically, significant. Those who completed treatment were almost six times less likely to be charged with a new sexual offence than were offenders who refused, dropped out or were terminated from treatment.

As previously noted, in the context of the United Kingdom, the accredited treatment model developed for the National Probation Department is adapted from the work of Fisher and Beech (1998) and addresses four key components – denial, offence specific behaviours, social adequacy and relapse prevention skills. Middleton (2004) has suggested that in spite of an absence of research concerning the specific characteristics of the Internet offender group, early analysis of psychometric testing has suggested evidence that these offenders have similar characteristics to those who commit other forms of sexual offending and present along a similar spectrum of high treatment need through to relative low treatment need. Middleton (2004) also concluded that there may be additional treatment targets which will be determined through individual assessment and that these may include the degree to which the offender has exhibited compulsive or obsessive behaviour in pursuing the on-line activity, the importance of community in the offending behaviour, and obsessive collecting activity. Again, Middleton (2004: 110) had emphasised the importance of a specific assessment of the individual and the context in which the behaviour was developed and sustained. He concluded, 'Most human behaviour can be understood as meeting needs for the individual and, in order to be effective, treatment will help the individual to meet these needs in a more appropriate manner'. The focus of the following chapters is looking at the ways in which needs were met through accessing Internet abuse images and how these needs may be met in a more pro-social way.

Chapter Three

The Process of Offending on the Internet

The aim of this chapter is to provide a model of offending behaviour as it relates to child abuse images and the Internet that might enable offenders to gain some insight into their behaviour in terms of how they fit (or do not fit) the model. It is apparent that there is no such individual as the 'Internet offender', but that the people who use the Internet to access abuse images of children are a heterogeneous group who engage in a range of offending behaviours. Such offending behaviours occur in relation to each other (for example, a person is unlikely to trade child abuse images without first downloading them from the Internet), but not all offenders engage in all classes of behaviour. One way of conceptualising offences related to child abuse images and the Internet is to think of them as a process, rather than a series of discrete behaviours. If we take this approach, the focus is on the offending behaviours, rather than some inherent qualities of the offender; it also implies a dynamic relationship between offending behaviours. This is not to see the offender as a passive vessel, but as a person who makes choices (which may be rational, or at least understandable) about his offending behaviours. What might mediate these choices are classes of verbal behaviours, expressed as self-statements, attitudes, and ways of thinking, that increase the likelihood of engagement, sustain the behaviours and allow for movement between behaviours.

Our first therapeutic goal is to enable offenders to identify the types of behaviours that they have been engaging in and to see these behaviours in relation to each other. Many offenders may seek to minimise the seriousness of their offence by seeing it as different to, or less than, the commission of a contact offence. Others will have committed contact offences in relation to, or in addition to, their involvement with the Internet. To present a model of Internet offending as a dynamic process raises issues about where people have come from and where they were potentially moving towards in terms of their offending. It also addresses issues that emphasise factors that interrupted or inhibited movement through the process, as well as those that facilitated or enabled such movement. As part of this chapter, we have included educational material that relates to UK sentencing guidelines for offences related to child abuse images. These may be of value when working with some clients.

The aims of this chapter therefore are:

- To use a process model of offending behaviour to identify the types of behaviours the offender had been engaged in.
- To look at the pathway to offending, and in what way the offence behaviour had progressed.
- To look at the factors that facilitated or inhibited movement through that process.

Background

As discussed in the previous chapter, the theoretical perspective that dominates both our understanding and treatment of adults who are sexually interested in children is a cognitive-behavioural one. In this context, offender differences in empathy, social skills, and cognitive processes have been a major focus for research and therapy (Covell and Scalora, 2002; Geer et al., 2000). Distortions in the way sex offenders think are assumed to reflect attitudes and beliefs which are used to deny, minimise, and rationalise behaviour, and are related to underlying belief systems or schema which play a role in precipitating and maintaining offending (Murphy, 1990). Authors such as Ward et al. (2000) suggested that the problem for the offender can be viewed as partially arising from deficits in one central mechanism: the ability to infer mental states, with the result that the offender has difficulties in being aware of other people's beliefs, desires, perspectives, or needs. Cognitive Behavioural Therapy (CBT) approaches are largely based on such an understanding of offender behaviour and have traditionally been guided by a relapse prevention framework. It has been asserted (Marshall et al., 1998) that the majority of programmes are predominantly derived from the same conceptualisation of treatment and are being increasingly applied to diverse populations.

To date, there has been little therapeutic research that has focused on either the assessment or treatment of people who download child abuse images from the Internet, or who use the Internet in other ways to express sexual interest in children. Earlier research has identified difficulties experienced by professionals who work in this area both in understanding the nature of the offence and accommodating this as part of existing sex offender programmes (Quayle et al., 2000). Related to this, Marshall et al. (1998) and Abracen and Looman (2001) have asked us to consider in what ways do we need to modify our programmes in order to educate ourselves to effectively treat different types of sex offenders. In a similar vein, Hudson et al. (1999: 782) have asserted that '. . . it is frequently observed that sexual offenders are extremely heterogeneous, and therefore to propose that there is a single offence and/or reoffence pathway is, at best, rather unlikely'. Ward et al. (2004) have argued that programmes need to be responsive to individual needs and that the level of fit between the client and the treatment programme should be acknowledged as a critical factor. They suggested that there is a need to distinguish three distinct, although related factors: treatment motivation, responsivity and readiness. At its simplest, in order to be ready for treatment, the individual must recognise a need to change because their offending creates problems for themselves or for others, and go on to make some commitment to change. These authors also suggest that '. . . in most models of behaviour change . . . some level of problem awareness or problem recognition is seen as an important readiness factor' (p665).

Internet addiction

Within the last few years, one way of conceptualising problematic Internet use has emerged in the concept of 'Internet Addiction' (Griffiths, 1998). This is seen as a kind of technological addiction, falling within a subset of behavioural addictions, and involves excessive human–machine interaction, which can be either passive (such as television) or active (such as computer games). Such interaction is thought to '. . . usually contain inducing and reinforcing features which may contribute to the promotion of addictive tendencies' (Griffiths, 2000). A recent confirmatory factor analysis study (Pratarelli and Browne, 2002) suggested that Internet addiction may involve an addictive performance profile which in turn leads to excessive behaviours that

involve the use of the Internet for sexual purposes, and its functional usefulness for a variety of professional and personal goals. The label of addiction has been seen as problematic (Davis, 1999) and diagnostic tools such as DSM-IV (APA, 1994) use instead the term dependence, while others (Cooper et al., 1999) have talked of pathological use. More recently, in the context of excessive downloading of pornography and entering sexually explicit chat rooms, Stein et al. (2001) advocated the use of the label 'Hypersexual disorder'. With regard to many of the people who download child abuse images, none of these labels appear satisfactory, as they seem to suggest both a model of Internet use as an illness, and also relegate it to an extreme end of a continuum of behaviour. It would seem more helpful to think of the downloading of child abuse images as 'problematic', both in terms of content and the amount of time spent on-line (Quayle and Taylor, 2003).

Pathological Internet use

Further research by Davis (2001) has presented a specific cognitive-behavioural model of Pathological Internet Use (PIU) which focused on associated maladaptive cognitions. Davis suggested that PIU resulted from problematic cognitions and behaviours that either maintained or intensified maladaptive responses. The model he presented distinguished between specific PIU and generalised PIU. Specific PIU referred to a condition in which an individual pathologically used the Internet for a particular purpose, such as on-line sex or gambling, while generalised PIU referred to general 'time wasting' activities on the Internet, such as repeatedly checking e-mails and surfing through different web sites. Specific PIU usage was purposive and tended to be content specific, and as such is particularly relevant to the problems associated with downloading child abuse images. Generalised PIU, in contrast, related to multidimensional overuse, resulting in dysfunctional behaviours across a broad spectrum. Davis (2001) in identifying the aetiology of Pathological Internet Use, suggested that it resulted from problematic cognitions that either intensified or maintained the maladaptive response. He presented a model emphasising cognitions (or thoughts) as the main source of problem behaviour. Contributory causes identified in this model were the diathesis (vulnerability) element in the diathesis-stress model, and were described as underlying psychopathology (such as depression, social anxiety and substance dependence); these were seen as a distal (not immediately related in time), necessary cause of Pathological Internet Use. The stressor was identified as the introduction of the Internet or some new technology related to the Internet. The model suggested that proximal (more immediate) contributory causes were the presence of specific maladaptive cognitions, either about the self or about the world.

This model gave a useful starting point to develop thinking about adult sexual interest in children and problematic Internet use. Although it might be argued that in this case the presumed cognitions are highly adaptive in that they enable the individual to gain access to, and use in some way, preferred material, such cognitions are, however, problematic in the sense that they support behaviour that ultimately is exploitative of others who are more vulnerable. The further development of such a model enables us to take a more discriminating view with regard to the offender, and focuses on the behaviours that the offender engages in and the cognitions that support or justify activities. It moves away from thinking about typologies of offenders derived from innate characteristics to thinking about how the offender constructs his world discursively and the impact that this has on behaviour. It allows us to think about what offenders do (Hudson et al., 1999).

Samples of Internet offenders to date are too small and too recent for us to develop meaningful causal relationships, between downloading pornography and the commission of a contact offence, within a quantitative framework. A survey by Langevin and Curnoe (2004: 583) of 561 sex offenders indicated that only 17 per cent had used pornography in a way that was clearly connected to the sexual crime in question, leading them to state that '. . . the mere possession of pornography per se does not lead to the commission of a sexual crime, as 47 per cent had it in their possession prior to their crimes, however only 17 per cent used it for self-stimulation either immediately prior to the crime or during the crime'. However, of this percentage, the majority who had used pornography had done so in the commission of an offence against a child, and one third took pictures of children as part of commercial sexual exploitation. In the context of offences committed through the Internet this may be important for two reasons. Accessing child abuse images is a crime in and of itself, regardless of whether the person goes on to commit a contact offence against a child. Those who produce child abuse images have also committed a contact offence. However, many of the images of children circulating on the Internet would not necessarily be illegal and would not be classified as pornographic. This highlights an important distinction between legal and psychological definitions of pornography.

Model of problematic Internet use

The model proposed in this chapter draws on an ongoing qualitative analysis of offender interviews (see Quayle and Taylor (2002) for a detailed account of the methodology) and facilitates the examination of contexts and cognitions related to offender behaviour and problematic Internet use outside of a pathological framework. In the proposed model, such cognitions support accessing illegal material, sustain engagement with the Internet, and may lead to the commission of further offences. These cognitive distortions are characteristic of a set of attitudes and values that support the legitimacy of sexual interest in relation to children, and in particular, the use of the Internet as a means of meeting this. The model, presented in the materials at the end of the chapter, describes the relationship between various factors that might characterise the *process* of engagement with the Internet: setting events, Internet use, problematic cognitions, and offending behaviour. It acknowledges the criticisms made by Ward et al. (2004: 6) with regard to existing models of sexual offending behaviour that, 'Until recently the models of the sexual abuse process have tended to be of the 'one size fits all' variety, that is, it is assumed that all sexual offenders do not want to offend and only do so in times of stress or where they are feeling bad about themselves'. These authors emphasised that negative emotional states and poor coping strategies are not the only major precursors for offending and that some individuals consciously decide to engage in sexually abusive behaviour. They suggested that instead a comprehensive model of the offence process needs to contain a number of pathways, taking into account different types of goals, varying affective states and different types of planning. They also suggested that it should include an explicit temporal emphasis and to be able to take account of the dynamic nature of the offence process, taking account of the various milestones of the offence process.

Beech et al. (2003) have also argued that any assessment of a sex offender should include a detailed functional analysis to determine the underlying motives and functions for the offending behaviour. Such approaches to behaviour emphasise the purposes that the behaviour serves for the person and place great importance on the part that environmental events play in causing, controlling and maintaining behaviour. This de-emphasises the form that the problem takes and shifts attention to the purposes that the behaviour might serve for the individual (Sturmey, 1996). An example of this approach can be seen in the chapter on emotional avoidance, where one function of Internet images is in the avoidance of adverse emotional states. Functional analysis typically involves obtaining detailed information about the antecedents, the behaviours and consequences of offending, which includes private events (thoughts and feelings) as well as overt behaviours.

One framework, which may help provide information for a functional analysis, is the decision chain (Ward et al., 1995), which is a sequence of choices leading up to an offence. Each choice is characterised in terms of the situation it took place in, the thoughts that made sense of and responded to the situation, and the emotions and actions that arose from these thoughts. As noted in the last chapter, decision chains are useful in that they can represent with equal facility offences that spring from negative emotional states and poor coping strategies (as in the Wolf, 1984 cycle) and those where these negative factors are not involved (Eldridge, 1998; Laws, 1999; Ward and Hudson, 1996). In Ward et al.'s (2004) pathways model, the avoidant goal offender is described as having a commitment to restraint, as the overall goal is one of avoidance. However, self-regulation deficiencies, for example, inadequate coping skills (under-regulation) or inappropriate strategies (misregulation), ultimately result in goal failure. Consequently, negative affective states and covert planning characterise the avoidant pathway. This type of pathway can be seen as being similar to the Wolf description of the offence process. For the approach goal offender, positive affective states, explicit planning and the presence of distorted attitudes about victims and offending

behaviour typify the process leading to offending. Ward and Hudson (1998) discussed the approach offender as actively seeking opportunities to offend and setting up the situation in which to offend. The approach passive offender however, while motivated to offend only does so when the opportunity presents itself. With the avoidant offender the active pathway is one in which the offender makes an effort to avoid offending while the passive offender would prefer not to offend but does nothing to prevent himself. Beech and Ward (2003) have attempted to outline a model of the offence process that links aetiological theories with risk assessment. Their model examines developmental variables, vulnerability (as measured by psychological disposition risk factors and historical risk markers), triggering or contextual events and acute risk factors.

Beauregard et al. (2005) have further drawn our attention to context in understanding sex offender behaviour. In an earlier study of the rational choices made by paedophiles, Proulx et al. (1999) identified a five choice-model. First, they argued that a paedophile has to choose his hunting ground, (the places where he is likely to encounter potential targets). These hunting grounds may be domestic (e.g., victim's or offender's home), occupational (e.g., offender's workplace), or public (e.g., streets, parks, recreational sites). Second, after having chosen the hunting ground, the paedophile has to choose the time when he is going to risk an offence. Children will find themselves in parks or on the street only at certain hours of the day, and are usually at home during the evening. Third, if the paedophile finds himself in a place and at a time where children are present, he has to select his target according to its erotic value (sex, age, physical characteristics), its vulnerability (physical and/or psychological) and its familiarity. Fourth, when the victim has been chosen, the offender has to select a strategy to make initial contact and then to have sexual contact with the victim. The strategies usually used by paedophiles are manipulation, threats, coercive actions, seduction, and money. For every step of the decisional process, there is an assessment of the risk of negative consequences. These may include the probability of someone interfering, of being caught, of being denounced by the victim, of being accused, convicted, and incarcerated. Proulx et al. (1999) concluded by stating that this decision process is related to stable personal characteristics of the offender (e.g., personality disorders, deviant sexual preferences) and to his internal scenario which includes emotional states, deviant sexual fantasies, and cognitive distortions. We can think of the Internet in a similar way as providing a location for offending activities and presenting critical events at which choices are made by the offender (Taylor and Quayle, 2005).

Setting conditions for offending

In the model of offending presented in this chapter, an attempt is made to look at both the distal and proximal setting conditions, the contexts (such as access to the Internet) that set the scene for accessing pornography, the cognitions which act as discriminative stimuli for further offending behaviour and inform choices about future offending, and the reinforcing properties of both access to the social world of the Internet and pornographic images of children. The concept of distal and proximal setting events replaces 'contributory causes' used by Davis (2001) and examples of distal setting events might include early sexualised experience and poor adolescent or adult socialisation, while more proximal events are in relation to an existing sexual interest in children, the commission of a prior contact offence, and dissatisfaction with a current persona. The setting events identified might relate both to Internet use and the development of problematic cognitions, with the decision to go on-line seen as a way of generating solutions to both distal and proximal setting events. The structures and protocols of the Internet itself are also however a factor in this. The presumed anonymity of the Internet is one element, and there is also evidence of disinhibition associated with Internet use. The ready accessibility of material to generate fantasy is a further factor.

Many offenders will have taught themselves how to use the Internet, and gaining access to it brings opportunity to find pornography. While some develop only sufficient skills to help them download such material, many offenders quickly acquire high levels of skill either through chatting to others, reading Internet magazines, or buying or downloading software packages. Long periods of time spent on the Internet provide opportunity for practice that is highly reinforcing. This can be conceptualised as part of the process of engagement, which is facilitated by cognitive and social factors. There may be a rapid increase in

feelings of power associated with being able to find material, by-pass security measures and gain credibility with other Internet users. This is reflected in cognitions that indicate an emergent sense of power and control.

As offenders start to download images, what can emerge is the increasing normalisation of accessing and collecting pornographic material, and cognitions supporting this may make reference to others engaged in similar behaviour. One consequence of this may be an increase in the amount of time spent on-line and a reduction in actual social behaviour – a sense of not wanting to or not needing to move away from the computer in order to be with people. This might be more clearly seen where offenders move from picture to text-based material and where they seek out 'chat' with others through Internet Relay Chat (IRC). Cognitions reflect the difference between the social world off-line and the more exciting on-line environment, but may also increasingly make reference to 'addiction' as one way of explaining continuing and escalating engagement with the Internet. Such cognitions are used as a way of rationalising staying on-line and looking for child abuse images, and engaging in other forms of sexualised activity. In talking about addiction, downloading behaviour is seen as a form of illness over which the offender has little or no control. One important point to note in relation to the Internet is that there are few external controls, by way of people or situations, which are going to influence this behaviour. Once on-line, downloading pornography is not censured but is reinforced by the community engaged in similar behaviour.

Internet offending behaviour

In terms of the present model, the processes identified result in either offending behaviour and/or behaviour related to this, but which is legal. The model proposes five forms of offending behaviour. The first two relegate the child subject to an image; the next three involve either real or surrogate involvement and contact with a child, which can only occur within a suitable facilitating environmental context:

- *Downloading*. Spending time on-line is associated with an increase in the number of images downloaded and a corresponding expansion and/or focus in collecting. Such collecting behaviour generates cognitions that appear to distance the respondent from the content of the collection and objectifies the children within such images. For many offenders this will involve downloading large numbers of images and then sorting and cataloguing new images. Some offenders may look for images to complete a series, and keep the series name, others like to complete a series but change the name to either suit the child or a particular fantasy. Being able to access images at will for the purposes of masturbation can also be accompanied by feelings of control, often absent in real-life relationships.

• *Trading.* Offenders who communicate with others may find that the relationships formed assume importance and are selective, and access to both material and relationships are often through a carefully policed private channel. Offenders may also contact people they meet through the Internet and arrange to meet them physically. The 'reality' of the relationship is important in legitimising and normalising their interests, and for those who engage in any social interaction, the process of sustaining that engagement requires the offender to have credibility. Credibility and status can be achieved through the size of the collection of photographs or through the exchange or trade of new or 'rare' material such as pictures or text. The latter may consist of fantasy stories, or talk of previous 'contact activities'. Again, cognitions that support such behaviour tend to emphasise the feeling of importance gained from owning and distributing such images, while at the same time equating the pictures with more socially desirable commodities, such as works of art. It appears that there has to be 'input' of some sort both to engage in such relationships and to sustain them (in a similar way to real life relationships).

For people who trade, or distribute, images, the notion of images as currency often appears to be important. They are currency in terms of trading for new material but they are also currency in maintaining existing on-line relationships and giving credibility. The notion of a community of collectors again serves to normalise the process of collecting but also legitimises the downloading and saving of images that in other contexts may have been aversive to the offender. For example, someone may not find torture images arousing but keeps them because they are aware that others will and that they can be traded for more desirable images.

• *Production of child abuse images.* The production of child abuse images necessarily involves a contact offence. Self-statements that support such production lean heavily on the legitimacy of the behaviour, possibly because it is a copy of what had been seen on-line. Such justifications share many of the same qualities as those that accompany downloading, raising issues about the relationship between downloading and contact offences. Anecdotal evidence suggests that the production of pornographic images for personal use is not unusual. However, the production of pornographic images is also seen in the context of trading, where having new material to trade facilitates the acquisition of highly desired and preferred other images. Within the community of the Internet, having private pictures to trade also brings with it status and power.

• *Commission of a contact offence.* For some offenders, the commission of a contact offence without production of child abuse images might be argued to be an extension of on-line behaviour, where the fantasies engaged with on-line are acted out in real life. The cognitions that support contact offences often make reference to the pictures reflecting the fact that others have engaged in similar behaviour, along with passive acceptance by the child.

• *Engagement with Internet seduction of children.* Chat rooms, email, IRC, peer-to-peer are all possible Internet media that facilitate the seduction of children. It is important to note that, unlike producing child abuse images and committing a contact offence, this form of offending does not necessarily involve immediate direct contact with a child. It is a form of offending mediated by Internet protocols, and the facilitating environmental context that enables this is different from that involving direct contact. However, the migration of such behaviour from the on-line to the off-line world may then result in the commission of a contact offence.

Non-offending behaviour

The model presented in this chapter reflects the fact that not all people who engage in problematic Internet use either go on to commit an offence through downloading child abuse images or attempting to seduce children through the Internet. There is also evidence of a movement between pornographies and of using the Internet to further adult sexual relationships. This is often expressed in terms of boredom or satiation, so that cognitions that support accessing new material are in relation to increasing the levels of sexual stimulation. For some people, the focus of collecting might be erotica, rather than material that would meet the legal definition for child abuse images. This appears to function in the same way as child abuse images (as a sexual stimulus, as a collectible item, as a means of exchange, and so on), but could be justified by the offender because it does not constitute pornography, and is often described as 'artistic'.

This model of problematic Internet use and sexual interest in children might serve several functions. It enables us to think of sexual offences against children that arise out of Internet use as being part of a complex array of behaviours, rather than any single activity. Such behaviours occur in relationship to each other, although because of the process of offending, not all people who use the Internet will engage in offence-related behaviour to the same degree. For example, the person who downloads child abuse images as part of an array of pornographies, but who does not communicate with others, trade, or produce material, may be qualitatively different from the person who adventitiously uses children within their social world to produce images to trade on the Internet. The latter has necessarily committed a contact offence against a child in the production of material, but has also had prior engagement with the Internet pornography world that necessitated the production of pictures. It is also evident that while there are people who have a previously acknowledged sexual interest in children, for whom the Internet becomes a medium for meeting their expressed preferences, there are equally those who seem to have had no prior knowledge that the images might be sexually arousing for them. In the latter case, we do not know whether such 'dormant' interests might ever have found expression without the Internet. This model also allows us to look at the cognitions or 'self-statements' that people generate in relation to their activities, which enable them to behave in ways that bring them into conflict with the law.

In developing such a model, three issues seem important. The first is to note that adult sexual interest in children on the Internet embraces both illegal and legal activities. Collecting child abuse images is illegal, but talking about fantasy, or

engaging in sexual role-plays may be inappropriate but are not necessarily illegal. Sharing information about computer security is not illegal, but sharing information about access to children is illegal in many jurisdictions. Furthermore, as we have noted, not all pictures that are attractive to, and collected by adults with a sexual interest in children are necessarily illegal (Taylor et al., 2001). Any model of behaviour in this area, therefore, must embrace not only clear offending behaviours, but other related but not necessarily illegal activities.

The second issue is to emphasise the notion of process, as a key element in understanding the expression of the behaviours with which we are concerned. Offending is a dynamic, rather than static process, with individuals moving along a range of potential continua, related to satiation of sexual arousal, processes of engagement with both collecting and communities, and the exploration of different on-line personas. Previous history of contact offences, personal circumstances and opportunity are also critical elements.

The third issue is to note that the use of the Internet for sexual purposes extends beyond the relatively narrow confines of our concern with child abuse images to embrace many other forms of sexual interest. What is referred to as Cybersex is a major part of many people's experience of the Internet, (Cooper et al., 2000) and for some that experience may well have problematic qualities. In particular, a number of authors have made reference to its compulsive and addictive features. The use of the Internet for sexual purposes, therefore, is not unique to the paedophile community, and the more general problematic qualities of Cybersex may well find their parallels in paedophile behaviour and activity.

However, the model proposed here is a first step to increase understanding of the role that the Internet may play in offending behaviour in general, and in particular, offences related to the abuse of children. Such an understanding may be important in helping the offender both understand the factors that enabled him to offend, and may be similar to ideas about insight. Cautela (1993) suggested that insight does not necessarily imply belief in the existence of the 'unconscious mind'. Behavioural insight consists of making the client aware of the antecedents and consequences of target behaviours and may provide a springboard for change.

Points of concern

- People whose offences relate to Internet abuse images are a heterogeneous group, which includes people with a history of prior sexual offences as well as those who may have no previously acknowledged sexual interest in children.
- It would be naïve to assume that all offenders are distressed by their offending activities. For at least some offenders, the approach to offending is associated with a positive affect. As yet, there is little to inform us as to the number of offenders who use Internet abuse images who may fall into this category, but this must be part of any assessment approach.
- Any model of offending allows a collaborate approach to understanding the context for the offending behaviour, and the behaviours, cognitions and emotions which are part of the chain of responding.
- Such a model allows for the possibility that some offenders will have moved from illegal to legal activity.

Working with the client

The model below illustrates in diagrammatic form a process of engagement with the Internet resulting in offending behaviour related to child abuse images (Quayle and Taylor, 2003). It emphasises five classes of offending behaviours:

1. Downloading.
2. Trading.
3. Distribution and production.
4. Engagement with Internet seduction of children.
5. Contact offences.

The classes are not discrete and each requires particular conditions for expression. For example, the production of child abuse images necessarily involves the commission of a contact offence, but the latter does not automatically imply the former.

This model does not imply that the person who engages in the downloading of child abuse images will automatically go on to commit a contact offence against a child. But there is evidence to support the view that where there are facilitating factors (environmental, such as access to children, as well as those pertaining to the individual, in terms of past history, etc.), which increase the likelihood of it being the case. There

is clearly considerable evidence to support the suggestion that there is a relationship between pornography and sexual aggression, but as yet it is unclear as to what that relationship might be.

A critical issue is for the therapist to identify with the client their route to offending, and to help the client understand some of the processes associated with the Internet that can facilitate increased involvement with problematic Internet behaviour.

The following are activities that should help the client to gain increased awareness of their behaviour. It is important to note, however, that in discussing and working with a client, they may present with case material that can be better used in developing individual exercises. We have also included material for the practitioner on the legal position in relation to Internet offences. This may be used educationally with clients.

Exercises

1. As with any CBT approach, the goal initially is to identify the relationships between mood, cognition and behaviour.
   - Give a copy of (or display on a board/flipchart) the **model of offending behaviour** to the client and discuss it with them. Ask the client to identify their offending behaviour, using the **worksheet format**.
   - Each offender should be asked to explore each step in the process that resulted in the offences committed, and give a detailed written description of the same.
2. Use the **history recording form** to get the client to identify what they see as important issues in relation to their offending behaviour.
3. Examine with each client the cognitions that justified each stage in the offending process and the environmental factors that facilitated this.

Completion criteria

By the end of this unit the client should have:

1. Used the model of Internet related offending to identify their offending behaviour and given a written description of the same. The description should accord with that provided by the police, forensic or probation report.
2. Given a written account of each of the steps taken which moved them further down the offence process.

3. Described any distant factors that enabled a context for offending.
4. Identified problematic self-statements that facilitated the offending.
5. Described what environmental factors, if any, supported the offence behaviour.
6. Described what factors helped limit the offending behaviour.

Legal position
The sentencing guidelines
(Sentencing Advisory Panel, 2002)

The two primary factors determinative of the seriousness of a particular offence are:
(a) The nature of the indecent material.
(b) The extent of the offender's involvement with it.
The nature of material is categorised by reference to five levels:

1. Images depicting erotic posing with no sexual activity.
2. Sexual activity between children, or solo masturbation by a child.
3. Non-penetrative sexual activity between adults and children.
4. Penetrative sexual activity between children and adults.
5. Sadism or bestiality.

In terms of the nature of the offender's involvement with the material, the seriousness of an individual offence increases with:
(a) The offender's proximity to, and responsibility for, the original abuse.
(b) Any element of commercial gain will place an offence at a high level of seriousness.
(c) Swapping of images can properly be regarded as a commercial activity, albeit without financial gain, because it fuels demand for such material.
(d) Widescale distribution, even without financial profit, is intrinsically more harmful than a transaction limited to two or three individuals, both by reference to the potential use of the images by active paedophiles, and by reference to the shame and degradation to the original victims.
(e) Merely locating an image on the Internet will generally be less serious than downloading it.
(f) Downloading will generally be less serious than taking an original film or photograph of indecent posing or activity.

Sentences

(a) A fine will normally be appropriate in a case where the offender was merely in possession of material solely for his own use, including cases where material was downloaded from the Internet but was not further distributed, and either the material consisted entirely of pseudo-photographs, the making of which had involved no abuse or exploitation of children, or there was no more than a small quantity of material at Level 1.
(b) A conditional discharge may be appropriate in such a case if the defendant pleads guilty and has no previous convictions. But a discharge should not be granted for the purpose of avoiding the requirement of registration under the Sex Offenders Act 1997.
(c) Possession, including downloading, of artificially created pseudo-photographs and the making of such images, should generally be treated as being at a lower level of seriousness than possessing or making photographic images of real children. But there may be exceptional cases in which the possession of a pseudo-photograph is as serious as the possession of a photograph of a real child: for example, where the pseudo-photograph provides a particularly grotesque image generally beyond the scope of a photograph. It is also to be borne in mind that, although pseudo-photographs lack the historical element of likely corruption of real children depicted in photographs, pseudo-photographs may be as likely as real photographs to fall into the hands of, or to be shown to, the vulnerable, and there to have equally corrupting effect.
(d) A community sentence may be appropriate in a case where the offender is in possession of a large amount of material at Level 1 and/or no more than a small number of images at Level 2, provided the material had not been distributed or shown to others. For an offender with the necessary level of motivation and co-operation, the appropriate sentence would be a community rehabilitation order with a sex offender programme.
(e) The custody threshold will usually be passed where any of the material has been shown or distributed to others, or, in cases of possession, where there is a large amount of

material at Level 2, or a small amount at Level 3 or above.

(f) A custodial sentence of up to six months will generally be appropriate in a case where (a) the offender was in possession of a large amount of material at Level 2 or a small amount of material at Level 3; or (b) the offender has shown, distributed, or exchanged indecent material at Level 1 or 2 on a limited scale, without financial gain.

(g) A custodial sentence of between six and twelve months will generally be appropriate for (a) showing or distributing a large number of images at Level 2 or 3; or (b) possessing a small number of images at Levels 4 or 5.

(h) In relation to more serious offences, a custodial sentence between twelve months and three years will generally be appropriate for (a) possessing a large quantity of material at Levels 4 or 5, even if there was no showing or distribution of it to others; or (b) showing or distributing a large number of images at Level 3; or (c) producing or trading in material at Levels 1 to 3.

(i) Sentences longer than three years should be reserved for cases where (a) images at Levels 4 or 5 have been shown or distributed; or (b) the offender was actively involved in the production of images at Levels 4 or 5, especially where that involvement included a breach of trust, and whether or not there was an element of commercial gain; or (c) the offender had commissioned or encouraged the production of such images. An offender whose conduct merits more than three years will merit a higher sentence if his conduct is within more than one of categories (a), (b) and (c) than one where conduct is within only one such category.

(j) Sentences approaching the ten-year maximum will be appropriate in very serious cases where the defendant has a previous conviction either for dealing in child pornography, or for abusing children sexually or with violence. Previous such convictions in less serious cases may result in the custody threshold being passed and will be likely to give rise to a higher sentence where the custody threshold has been passed. An extended sentence may be appropriate in some cases, even where the custodial term is quite short: see *R v Nelson* [2002] 1 Cr App R(S) 565.

Aggravating factors

There are specific factors which are capable of aggravating the seriousness of a particular offence. These are:

1. If the images have been shown or distributed to a child.

2. If there are a large number of images. It is impossible to specify precision as to numbers. Sentencers must make their own assessment of whether the numbers are small or large. Regard must be had to the principles presently applying by virtue of *R v Canavan, Kidd and Shaw* [1998] 1 Cr App R 79.

3. The way in which a collection of images is organised on a computer may indicate a more or less sophisticated approach on the part of the offender to trading, or a higher level of personal interest in the material. An offence will be less serious if images have been viewed but not stored.

4. Images posted on a public area of the Internet, or distributed in a way making it more likely they will be found accidentally by computer users not looking for pornographic material, will aggravate the seriousness of the offence.

5. The offence will be aggravated if the offender was responsible for the original production of the images, particularly if the child or children involved were members of the offender's own family, or were drawn from particularly vulnerable groups, such as those who have left or have been taken from their home or normal environment, whether for the purposes of exploitation or otherwise, or if the offender has abused a position of trust, as in the case of a teacher, friend of the family, social worker, or youth group leader.

6. The age of the children involved may be an aggravating feature. In many cases it will be difficult to quantify the effect of age by reference to the impact on the child. But in some cases that impact may be apparent. For example, assaults on babies or very young children attract particular repugnance and may, by the conduct depicted in the image, indicate the likelihood of physical injury to the private parts of the victim. Some conduct may manifestly (that is to say, apparently from the image) have induced fear or distress in the victim, and some conduct which might not cause fear or distress to an adolescent child, might cause fear or distress to a child of, say, 6 or 7.

Mitigating factors

So far as mitigation is concerned, some, but not much, weight should be attached to good character. A plea of guilty, by virtue of section 152 of the Powers of Criminal Courts (Sentencing) Act 2000, is a statutory mitigating factor. The extent of the sentencing discount to be allowed for a plea of guilty will vary according to the timing and circumstances of the plea. The sooner it is tendered, the greater is likely to be the discount: see, for example, *R v Barber* [2002] 1 Cr App R(S) 548. These kind of offences very rarely result in the prosecution or cautioning of offenders under the age of 18. When such a person has to be sentenced, the appropriate sentence is likely to be a supervision order with a relevant treatment programme.

Materials for Chapter 3

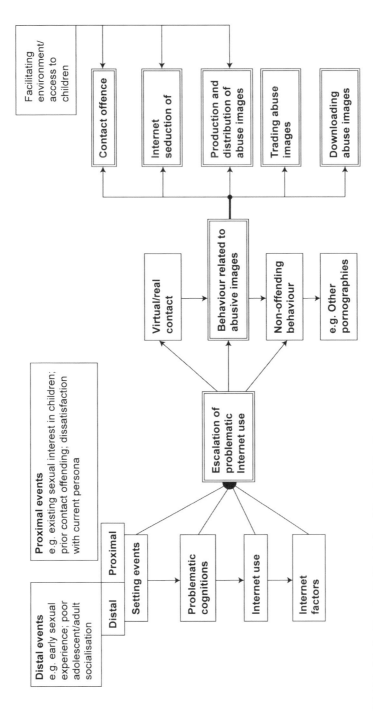

Figure 3.1 Materials for Chapter 3: Model of problematic Internet use

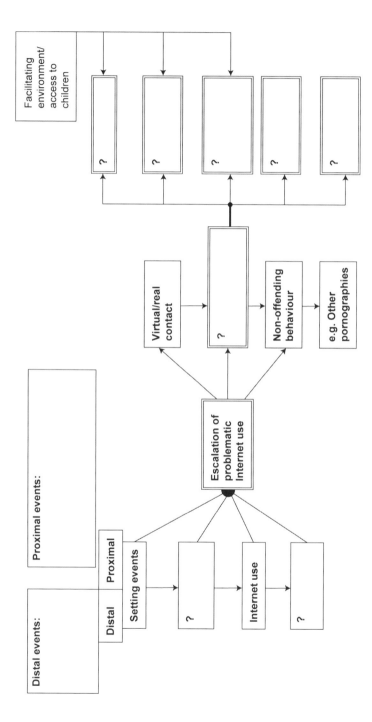

Figure 3.2 Materials for Chapter 3: Model of problematic Internet use worksheet – complete using model as guide

History of offending form

Name: ....

Age: ....   Date: ....

Place: ....

In this exercise, you are being asked to think about the offences you committed as part of a chain of events. It is important to explore where you started from, and what moved you through each step in the process. You will discuss what you have written with your practitioner, and have opportunity to re-examine what you have written. If there is insufficient space allowed on the form, please use an additional piece of paper. This is not a test and there are no right or wrong answers.

1. Can you identify any factors (actual events/the way that you were thinking/the way that you felt) that pre-dated your current offence and which you think might be important? These may have occurred in the distant past (for example, childhood) or more recently?

2. What made you decide to use the Internet?

3. Did the Internet change the way you were thinking? In what way?

History of offending form *continued*

4. At what point did you start to look for child abuse images on the Internet?

5. At any time did you feel what you were doing was a problem to you?

6. What was the effect on the way you were feeling when you found child abuse images?

History of offending form *continued*

7. What was the effect on your sexual fantasies?

8. What was the effect on your life off-line (in the real world)?

9. How would you describe your life on-line (when using the Internet)?

History of offending form *continued*

10. How important were on-line social relationships and friendships?

11. Using the list below, describe the offending behaviours that you engaged in:
    (a) Downloading child abuse images.
    (b) Trading child abuse images.
    (c) Distributing and producing child abuse images.
    (d) Engaging with Internet seduction of children.
    (e) Committing contact offences with children.
    For each offence, list what was going on in your life that made the activity possible, and describe the way that you were feeling. Try also to identify the thoughts that routinely went with each activity.

History of offending form *continued*

12. What influenced your decision to go one step further along the offending process?

13. Have you at any time tried to stop using the Internet to access child abuse images? If so, how many times did you try and stop the usage? Why do you think you were not successful? Does this affect the way you feel about your ability to control using in the future?

Chapter Four

Images *Are* Children

The aims of the material presented in this chapter are to:

- Confront the offender with the reality of the pictures as being evidence of abusive relationships.
- Help the client empathise with the experience of such children.
- Look at the offending process that lies behind such victimisation.

Background

We have noted that research into the nature and extent of abuse images is limited, in part because of its emotive nature, and also because possession is in the main illegal. Such published material that there is tends to be primarily from law enforcement perspectives, meeting rather narrow ends and tending to focus on somewhat limited empirical findings. As further noted in earlier chapters, the lack of relevant research makes it difficult to speculate about the relative importance of traditional factors, such as empathy, in offending that relates to the Internet. It may be that there are parallels to be drawn between different offending activities, both on-line and off-line, but there is very little evidence as yet to support this. However, from the limited evidence that is available, it is possible to surmise that for at least some offenders, the ability to either emotionally or cognitively see the relationship between photographs of children and the commission of an offence is limited (Quayle and Taylor, 2003; Quayle et al., 2001). This chapter will endeavour to examine the research on empathy in sex offending as well as the few studies existing that relate to the victim's experience of being photographed. We then suggest how this may be used to work with offenders to help them both emotionally and cognitively accept that the victimisation of children through the production of images equates with sexual abuse.

An important if obvious starting point when thinking about an Internet offender is that there may be no necessary direct link between the viewer and the child; if the viewer is not the producer, they are necessarily distanced in place, and time, from the person photographed. Unlike the photographer, the viewer therefore does not engage in the particular sexual behaviour portrayed, other than in their imagination. We do know of course that viewing abuse images can be associated with sexual behaviour of the viewer, notably masturbation, and that for adults with a sexual interest in children abuse images serve an important function in generating and sustaining masturbatory fantasy. Thus, even at this level, viewing abuse images is not a passive act, and usually involves sexual behaviour. In general, however, that behaviour is solitary, and confined only to the viewer. However, in addition, we do know that abuse images can also play a part in sexual behaviour in other ways as in, for example, a part of the grooming process used by paedophiles to become close to and sexually desensitise children (Durkin, 1997; Healy, 1997). Tyler and Stone (1985) have suggested that child molesters who possess abuse images in any form use such material to facilitate the seduction of new victims. A child might be shown abuse images as part of the process of breaking down inhibitions, or further developing relationships. This is not uniquely related to abuse images, however, as adult pornography may also be used in the same way.

Defining empathy

Central to much sex offender research and practice is the premise that, '. . . as long as sexual abusers can dismiss the feelings, thoughts, and humanity of others, their potential to execute acts of destruction remains' (Pithers, 1999: 258). Empathy has been defined by Jolliffe and Farrington (2004) as a cognitive process (i.e., the ability to understand another's emotional state) and an affective capacity (i.e., the sharing of the emotional state of another). Empathy, or the lack of it, is presumed to play a major role in the aetiology and maintenance of sexual offending, and earlier work by Finkelhor and Lewis (1988: 76) had suggested that various aspects of male socialisation can block empathy towards children and that an absence of empathy allows sexual exploitation. These authors assert that absence of empathy plays a role in 'all forms of sexual coercion'. The importance of empathy is centred on the idea that aggression is inversely related to empathic responding and that a lack of empathy allows the offender to eliminate anxiety, guilt and loss of self-esteem. Implicit in this is the notion that were the offender able to empathise with children, this ability would inhibit his abusive behaviour (Covell and Scalora, 2002). Empathy, therefore, can be thought of as an individual protective factor, decreasing the possibility of certain types of criminal behaviour, while a lack of empathy is assumed to have a facilitating influence or offending (Jolliffe and Farrington, 2004).

However, while it appears that most researchers and practitioners endorse the notion that sex offenders are deficient in their capacity for empathy, the empirical findings are inconsistent (Covell and Scalora, 2002). Pithers (1999) has suggested that there are problems with empathy research, which would include the following:

1. Operational definitions are not consistent.
2. Measurement techniques vary.
3. There is a reliance on self-report, along with a transparency of questionnaire items.
4. There is a neglect of the potential importance of the circumstances under which subjects complete self-report measures.

Pithers (1999: 259) added, 'It is irrational to expect that the mean empathy score of a large sample of abusers will depart significantly from the test norms unless one assumes that sexual abusers are, as a class, monsters who are consistently cold and predatory. If abusers manifest empathy deficits, they most likely may be found during those moments in time when their emotional precursors to abuse are active (e.g., exacerbated anger, acute anxiety, or profound loneliness)'. What arises from this is that 'trait' notions of empathy may be problematic, and that we need to give greater consideration to the contexts in which empathy is both expressed and measured. The need to move from global empathy measures to those which are victim and abuse specific has been emphasised by other authors (e.g., Simons et al., 2002).

The suggestion that offenders may not be generally deficient in empathy emerged in an analysis of measures by Fisher et al. (1999: 489). In their sample, the differences between child molesters and non-offenders was relatively small

and did not support the notion that child molesters were lacking in empathy generally. Their results were seen as supporting the possibility that many offenders express empathy appropriately but show deficits where their own victims are concerned. Fisher et al. concluded that, 'General empathy itself does not seem to be directly related to empathy for one's own victim, and the presence of cognitive distortions is only significant in high-deviancy child molester'. In a similar vein, Geer et al. (2000) have suggested that research indicates that in fact some offenders are quite capable of being empathic and that reliance on global, trait like measures might obscure any potential differences in empathic responding. It has also been suggested by Elliott et al. (1995) that a significant proportion of child abusers accurately perceive the needs of potential victims and misuse this information to identify vulnerable children. A meta-analysis by Jolliffe and Farrington (2004) concluded that empathy and offending were negatively related, but that the strength of the relationship appeared to be mediated by a number of factors. The most important finding of this analysis was that when intelligence was controlled for, the differences in empathy measures between offending and non-offending populations disappeared.

It is likely that the equivocal findings in relation to empathy are a result of the difficulties in precisely defining the construct itself (Covell and Scalora, 2002). Empathy has been largely understood as a fixed trait, consistent over time and across individuals and situations, with one or two components: a perspective taking or cognitive component, and/or an affective component. Covell and Scalora instead suggested a multifactor definition of empathy which considers the interplay of affective, cognitive and behavioural domains. Viewing empathy in such a way may also account for offenders who appear to utilise empathy to facilitate their offences, 'For instance, paedophiles have frequently been noted to identify children that are isolated, outcast, or abused and in need of emotional support and approval and then manipulate these needs so that the child will capitulate to a sexual assault' (p 254). If empathy is thus viewed as a context or person-specific state, rather than a stable trait, deficits may occur after a 'triggering' event, where empathy is appropriate most of the time and only becomes deficient in response to a specific event.

Model of empathy

Marshall et al. (1995) contended that empathic responses might vary as a function of situation, victim characteristics and post-hoc attempts to rationalise socially unacceptable behaviour. These authors developed a process model of empathy, which suggested four sequential processes:

1. Emotion recognition (discerning the emotional state of another).
2. Perspective taking (putting oneself in another's position).
3. Emotion replication (experiencing the same emotion).
4. Response decision (how to act based on prior information).

The first stage was seen as a prerequisite to subsequent stages, although Pithers (1999) has suggested that the ability to anticipate another's emotional response based on the assimilation of the other's perspective is more relevant than recognition alone. Marshall et al. (1995) also proposed that offenders may not be deficient in the first three steps of the empathic process, but may still decide to continue in their aggressive actions, reflecting 'a flaw in their decision making abilities' (Geer et al., 2000: 103). This model appears to fit very well into a cognitive behavioural framework.

Empathy and treatment programmes

Despite the controversy about the importance of empathy in the offending process, it is seen as an essential component of most sex offender treatment programmes. In a treatment survey, Knopp et al. (1993) found that 94 per cent of programmes reviewed included some aspect of empathy training. Covell and Scalora (2002: 264) summarised such programmes as '. . . training typically involves a clear description of known harmful effects on victims of sexual abuse, having the offender write a letter of apology to the victim explaining his responsibility for the offence, and having the offender read victim reports or view videotapes of victims describing their assault . . .' Defining the 'harmful effects' of the crime is presumed to induce perspective taking on the part of the offender, while viewing or reading about victim suffering is thought to simulate a vicarious affective response. Many authors have argued that most programmes place an emphasis on the cognitive aspects of empathy, rather than

helping offenders learn to evoke emotional empathy, and suggest that in empathy training, information alone may not be adequate to motivate behavioural change (Pithers, 1999; Regehr and Glancy, 2001). This in itself may be a function of the perceived difficulty in assessing emotional responses, being highly reliant on self-reports. It is also the case that it has been difficult to assess the impact of changing empathic responses, as most treatment programmes include empathy training as part of a package of cognitive behavioural interventions.

As yet, there is no research that relates directly to empathy in Internet offenders. For practitioners working with offenders who may have collected many thousands of abuse images of children, it may be difficult to understand how traditional empathy training may be of relevance. Of particular concern is that the children within the images may be seen as 'objects' or artefacts, rather than people and that this may negatively impact on the offender's willingness to exert control in the context of exposure to Internet access. Of relevance here is research by Hanson et al. (1995) who suggested that the most serious threat to empathy is the existence of an indifferent or adversarial relationship. Internet images, other than through the offender's fantasies, offer no other contextualised information about the child that enables the offender to 'relate' in some way to that person.

Victimisation

If there is little research to inform our understanding of the role of empathy in the offending process in relation to the Internet, there is even less that relates to victimisation through the production of abuse images. Indeed, the few studies that have been conducted in this area predate the Internet. This is an important issue, as empathy training requires both a cognitive and emotional understanding of victimisation. In the absence of anything more substantial we have to draw on the findings of pre-Internet studies and extrapolate their significance for children who are victims of abuse images. One of the fundamental problems in understanding the consequences of victimisation through the production of abuse images relates to our ability to distinguish the effects of that from the consequences of other sexually exploitative practices. In part this is problematic because of the close connections between abuse images, intra and extra-familial abuse and studies of ritualised abuse. It is also the case that the little data we have to draw on comes from a variety of sources and is analysed through different methodologies. What we can conclude is that there is no single response pattern to sexual abuse and that this is likely also to be the case for the consequences of image victimisation.

In the context of abuse images, there are four substantial studies (all of which predate the Internet), which have sought to examine the impact of abuse images of children:

- Burgess et al. (1984) examined the involvement of children in pornography and sex rings.
- Silbert (1989) examined child abuse image production in the context of child prostitution.
- Svedin and Back's (1996) sample was drawn from a group of children exposed to both the production of pornography and intra and extra-familial abuse.
- Scott's (2001) study was in the context of ritual abuse.

As can be seen, the populations in each of these studies vary. However, all four studies are broadly similar in the accounts that they give of the symptoms the children displayed during the abuse. Again it is difficult to disentangle the consequences of the abuse per se (physical symptoms, such as urinary infections and genital soreness, as well as behavioural symptoms such as sexualised behaviours) from the consequences of being photographed. However Svedin and Back (1996) gave details amongst their sample of restlessness, depression, hunger, exhaustion, concentration difficulties and aggressive behaviours, which are not immediately associated with sexual exploitation. Silbert's (1989) study also suggested that children who were exposed to longer periods of exploitation suffered more intense emotional reactions, such as feelings of isolation, fear, anxiety and emotional withdrawal.

What is apparent from these studies is a pattern of enforced silence. The children in Svedin and Back's (1996) study were reluctant to disclose the abuse and these authors suggested that the recording of the abuse exacerbated, and in some cases prevented, disclosure. Even when confronted with the visual evidence of their abuse, children continued to limit disclosure, telling people only what they thought they already knew. Silbert (1989) had earlier coined the phrase 'silent conspiracy' to describe this silence.

It is unclear as to whether the sense of shame and humiliation, often reported in these studies, relates to the photography itself or the fact of disclosing it to others. It may also be that children fear being thought to be complicit in the abuse or photography through the evidence of, for example, their smiling faces. Scott (2001) reinforced this idea in the description of how abusers had shown children films they had made of them as a way of demonstrating their level of engagement and enjoyment.

Silbert (1989) made reference to the long-term effects of being photographed as being more debilitating than those in the short or medium term, and that these are compounded when children are involved in more than one form of sexual exploitation. This may also be exacerbated by the knowledge that others may see or distribute the films. One account by a victim of abuse images talked of feeling fearful every time the mail arrived, overwhelmed with anxiety that the photographs would be in the post and that her mother would see them (Collins, 2003). Silbert (1989) described such feelings as 'psychological paralysis'. This is also accompanied by the knowledge that such photographs may be used to exploit other children (Svedin and Back, 1996).

Implications for victimisation through abuse images

This research clearly has implications for children involved in the production of Internet abuse images. They are confronted by the knowledge that the images can never be destroyed and that they may continue to be viewed and used by many thousands of people. The age of the child at the time of the production of the abuse images may also be relevant. In an interview by the authors with a now adult victim, it became apparent that the images of her, which spanned a time period up to when she reached pubescence, had now been scanned and distributed through the Internet. As an adult woman, she was probably still identifiable from these images. It may be that when images are taken of very young children, the radical physical changes that take place as a result of growth and physical development offer at least some protection from future identification when such children reach adulthood, though how far this possibility enters their awareness or mediates their experience is unclear.

An analysis of offender accounts has also allowed an examination in detail of what actually happened to children who were photographed (Taylor and Quayle, 2005). Through this analysis it emerged that in relation to the Internet there were different levels of victimisation through photography that related to the degree of involvement of the child in the process. Expressing this was thought to be important because it enabled a focus on issues additional to, or perhaps compounding, the actual sexual abuse. We can think of such engagement as occurring on several levels:

- *Level One*: a child is photographed without their knowledge (for example on a beach, at a swimming pool, children's playground). Here the child is not aware of being photographed, and there is no direct engagement in the process. In a sense, therefore, there is no knowledge by the child or its caretakers of victimisation, unless they become aware of the presence of these images on the Internet. Photographs of this kind are extensively distributed through the Internet and used for sexual purposes. In this sense, therefore, they are clearly abusive, even if the particular child has no knowledge of the event, and cannot be identified.
- *Level Two*: a child is sexually abused and the act is surreptitiously photographed. These images again may be distributed through the Internet, but these are 'hidden' photographs and the child has no knowledge that they have been taken. Sexual victimisation may have taken place of which the child was aware, but the child may have no awareness at all of the added photographic element involving distribution to other adults.
- *Level Three*: a child is sexually abused and openly photographed during that abuse. They are shown images of the abuse, as a means of further engagement, or entrapment, or perhaps as a form of blackmail. However, the child is not involved in the distribution of these images and may have no awareness of the images being shown to other adults.
- *Level Four*: a child is sexually abused and photographed during the abuse. The child is aware of being photographed and is shown the images; the child is also involved in the creation of further images, the distribution of the same through the Internet and the selection of which images to send and whose 'commissions' to respond to. In this case, there is a sense in which the child is placed in a position of an active, rather than passive

participant in the photographic activities. This of course may also implicitly be the case in Level 3 situations, but in this case the child is explicitly engaged in the process not only of the abuse, but also of distribution and perhaps contact with other adults.

As yet we have no empirical knowledge of the implications of such kinds of involvement for these children. It might be argued that in Level One there is no victim, because the child is not aware of having been photographed. Yet the reality is that such images are used in exactly the same way as are the other images. They are used for masturbatory purposes and may form part of collections of abuse images. There is also the possibility that at some point in the future these children become aware that their photographs have been distributed and used in this way. The specific psychological sequelae of the other levels of victimisation, if they exist, are not understood. However, at an intuitive level, these levels seem to represent an increasing degree of victimisation with long term more likely negative outcomes. The evidence we have to date suggests that any psychological sequelae may also be related to the age of the child when abuse takes place *and* also when disclosure occurs. We know that the emergence of such sequelae to victimisation may be distant in time from the actual event; involvement in photography may be an exacerbating factor in this.

Points of concern

- For viewers of any kind of pornography, there is no necessary relationship between the viewer and individuals in the photographs or videos. The viewer is in all probability distanced both in time and space.
- The empirical evidence for links between lack of empathy and sexual offending is inconsistent.
- However, if empathy is seen as a context or person specific state, rather than a stable trait, deficiencies in empathy may occur after a triggering event in response to a specific event.
- The impact of involvement on the child of involvement in the production of abuse images remains unclear. One important reason for this is our inability to adequately distinguish between the effects of involvement in producing abuse images, and other sexually exploitative practices.

- It seems likely, however, that the long-term effects of being photographed are more debilitating than the short or medium-term effects, and that these are compounded when the child is involved in more than one form of sexual exploitation, and when the child plays an active part in the production of images.
- Significant further negative factors include:
  - Images once made available on the Internet can never be destroyed, continue to be in principle always available, and can be reproduced *ad nauseam* without loss of quality.
  - Age of the child at the time of production both in terms of severity of effects and the potential to be recognised.

Working with the client

As we have noted above a common problem for many users of abusive images is the sense in which the photographs or videos they have collected and fantasised over are thought of as representations of children as sexual objects, rather than real living individuals. One way in which clients can be encouraged to think about the nature and qualities of victimisation in abuse images is to explore with them the different kinds of photographs they have accessed, and how that victimised the children. The exercises below may help you to address these issues. This is likely to be a difficult and challenging process for offenders who may have protected themselves, emotionally, from acknowledging the reality of their behaviour by avoiding this understanding of the material they possess. Whilst, therefore, much of what follows may seem to address 'common-sense' understandings for us as professionals, the same sensitivity and awareness in working with this unit will be required as when working with any other distorted thought processes with your client.

Changing behaviour

The exercises that follow in this chapter are designed to engage the offender in both a cognitive and emotional appraisal of what might be happening to the children in the images collected. In part this is motivated by a desire to help the offender understand that abuse images are not a victimless crime, and to understand the context of their engagement with the Internet that possibly facilitates a change or suspension of

empathic response. However, it might be that all that is achieved is an awareness or acknowledgement that there is a child in the image itself.

The material in the following exercises builds on existing empathy work to look at what lies behind the photograph, to challenge the notion of 'the smiling child', and to consider the impact on the child of being a victim of abuse images. It is likely that at least some offenders see their offences as essentially a 'victimless crime', or at least the downloading and trading aspects as being such. It is also possible for offenders to confuse or blur the nature of the material, saying that the pictures were not really sexual ones, or that they did not realise that they were illegal. A further possibility is that offenders equate adult pornography with abusive images of children, and so minimise or dismiss the non-consensual nature of the material. In the context of treatment for Internet offenders, Middleton (2004) has suggested the use of Marshall et al.'s (1995: 106) four-stage process as an effective way of identifying empathy deficits. He suggested that, 'By seeing that all four stages of empathy are important, offenders can be helped to see the necessity of moving beyond their sense of being helpless victims of their own needs, and into a state of being where they can completely control whether or not they choose to harm others'.

A central element to intervention is addressing the way in which many Internet offenders distance themselves from other clients on a sex offender treatment programme by presenting themselves as different to, or better than, other sex offenders. Indeed it is quite common that the label of sex offender is rejected altogether by Internet offenders, common reasons being given as:

- They were only downloading pictures.
- They haven't produced pictures, and they were there anyway.
- The children are smiling and clearly enjoy the experience, so why is it a problem.
- They had no direct contact with the child, and therefore have no responsibility for the events portrayed.

It is difficult for many offenders to understand and accept that even downloading images provides a context for the production of more images and the necessary abuse of children.

Exercises

The child's perspective

The goal of these exercises is to help the client to think about what a photographed child might think or feel about the experience. In the introduction to this chapter we have reviewed some of the findings from four of the few studies that have attempted to look at this from the child's perspective. However, none of these studies specifically relate to the Internet. We have therefore constructed theoretical case studies (see Rosie's story below), drawn from unpublished data from the COPINE project that can be used in discussion. **This material should be used with caution.** For some offenders the material contained in the vignettes may be highly arousing. On the basis of your assessment of the client and their readiness to engage appropriately with the material at this point, you may feel that either this material is not acceptable, or that the possibility of the material having an arousing effect needs to be discussed, and ways to avoid or minimise that possibility explored at the outset. There may also need to be a 'debriefing element' to the session before it is concluded.

Exercise 1

(a) Ask the client to list how a child might behave/think/feel **during** exploitation (it is important to note that taking photographs occurs within sexual abuse, rather than outside of it). An area to focus on might be the image of the smiling child, and the reality that may lie behind that, in terms of emotional and physical blackmail, and distortions of responsibility. It is also important that clients who have largely erotic photographs in their collection (pictures that are posed and may include nudity but are not specifically showing sexual behaviour) do not use this as a way of avoiding the content of this exercise. For them to have been convicted requires that they have downloaded and saved pictures which were clearly abusive images of children. In these cases explore how the client's fantasy might have exploited and victimised the child in the images. Use the recording sheet at the end of this chapter, and then compare that with what you know from your experience and that given in the therapist notes, which were derived from the published literature.

(b) Ask the client to list how a child might behave/think/feel **during** the **disclosure** of the abuse. As well as exploring the psychological impact of abuse, what particular issues might relate to the Internet, in terms of, for example, the continuing presence of photographs. Use the second scoring sheet and compare with the information given and what you know about disclosure of sexual abuse.

(c) Ask the client to list how a child might behave/think/feel **following** exploitation. What particular issues might relate to the Internet, in terms of the continuing presence of photographs. Use the third scoring sheet and compare this with what you know from your experience and studies of the consequences of sexual abuse.

Exercise 2

Rosie's story. At the end of this chapter are a number of composite case histories (listed under Rosie's story), and these may be used where the client has difficulty in identifying with an actual child. The above exercises can be repeated using the same scoring sheets. **Please use this material with caution.** We are aware that for some offenders the material contained in the vignettes may be highly arousing. On the basis of your assessment of the client you may feel that either this material is not appropriate or that there needs to be a 'debriefing element' to the session before the client leaves the room.

Exercise 3

Who is directing the action and why? Ask the client to visualise a child in a photograph, and then to extend the image to include the room where it is happening, the person taking the photograph, the instructions being given. Focus particularly on who is taking the photograph and why they are taking it. What cues are they ignoring in the child's behaviour? What are they telling themselves in order to justify taking the photograph? What do they plan to do with the photograph after it has been taken?

Exercise 4

The relationship between looking and arousal. Present a simplified learning model of the relationship between viewing and arousal that emphasises how masturbation to pornographic images influences subsequent levels of arousal and sexual interest (an example is provided at the end of this chapter).

Exercise 5

The focus of this exercise is to get the abuser to identify the distorted thinking in relation to the images that accompanied his on-line activity. Ask the abuser to:

(a) Identify the distorted thoughts that were associated with the images.
(b) List the reasons he thought his offence was 'victimless'.

Completion criteria

By completing the exercises in this chapter, the client should have:

1. Completed the recording sheets at the end of the chapter and have compared these with feedback given by the therapist.
2. Repeated the exercise with a case vignette and compared the results with the responses from the first exercise.
3. Written a brief account of who is directing the photograph and why, paying attention to the experience of the child in the photograph.
4. Been able to describe what they now understand about the relationship between viewing, arousal and masturbation and why this might be problematic.
5. Identified the distorted thinking that was associated with the images and listed the reasons why the offence was thought to be 'victimless'.

Materials for Chapter 4

Exercise 1: Therapist notes

There are four studies that are commonly referred to in the context of the effects of abuse images on the child victim:

- Burgess et al. (1984) examined abuse images in the context of sex rings.
- Silbert (1989) had child prostitution as its focus.
- Svedin and Back (1996) examined pornography in the context of intra and extra-familial abuse.
- Scott (2001) looked at intra and extra-familial ritual abuse.

None of these studies take as their focus Internet abuse images, but they are the only material we have available that may help us understand some of the sequelae of being photographed.

During the abuse

The information gained as to the psychological consequences of being photographed during abuse are difficult to disentangle for those of the abuse itself, but include:

1. Physical symptoms, such as urinary infections and soreness around the genitalia or anus, headaches and vomiting.
2. Behavioural problems, such as sexualised behaviour evidenced in levels of interest, overt behaviour and sexualised language, acting out behaviours and difficult peer relationships.
3. Emotional or psychological symptoms, such as depression, tiredness, concentration difficulties, nightmares, aggression, bullying etc.

During disclosure

There appear to be discrete patterns of disclosure that relate to abuse images, typically marked by silence and reluctance to talk about the abuse. This would suggest that the recording of the abuse through photography can increase the fear of disclosure and effectively silence many children. Disclosures when eventually made are often:

1. Limited, with the child only telling as much as they feel the practitioner already knows.
2. Marked by feelings of shame, humiliation and helplessness.
3. Accompanied by the anxiety that the photograph is evidence of complicity by the child.
4. Accompanied by fear that the fact that the child was smiling may be seen as evidence that they were enjoying the experience.

Long-term sequelae

All four studies would suggest that the long-term effects of having been photographed are more profound than in the short-term. These include:

1. Negative emotional effect, such as negative self-concepts, sustained feelings of shame, hopelessness, an inability to feel anything and 'psychological paralysis'.
2. A distressing awareness that even though the abuse has stopped, others may still be able to access their photographs, and that there is nothing they can do about it.
3. Worry that the photographs may act as a context for the further abuse of children.

Exercise 2

Rosie's Story

Rosie was four when her step-father moved into the family home. She had a brother called Peter who was two years older than she was. Her own father had left the family home shortly after she was born and there had been no contact or support from him. She had not known her step-father before this, but he seemed a nice man, was very friendly, paid her and her brother Peter a lot of attention, and for once there was enough money in the house. Shortly after he moved in, Rosie's mother told them that she was going to have another baby. Dave, Rosie's stepfather, talked a lot to them about the baby and used this as an opportunity to discuss sexual behaviour and reproduction. He used Rosie's body to demonstrate female genitalia and responded to questions about male genitals by showing her his penis. At this time Rosie's brother Peter refused to take his clothes off. During the pregnancy, Sue (Rosie's mother) was not feeling well and was happy to leave Dave to look after the children. He told her that he was giving them sex education lessons, and she thought this was a good idea. The lessons were always followed by sweets and television.

For the next few months, Rosie, Peter and Dave played lots of 'games' that included removing clothes and genital contact. Dave had a Polaroid camera and would take photographs of both children, but particularly of Rosie. Some of these he would show to his wife, but the rest were kept in a filing cabinet, which he locked. The games were now happening on a daily basis, always when Dave was on his own with the children, and they were always photographed. Sue was very pre-occupied with the new baby and was glad that Dave seemed so engaged with the children. They appeared to like him and did not object to him looking after them. Rosie occasionally wet the bed, but Sue thought that this was her adjusting to the baby and didn't think anything more of it.

Over the next four years, Dave regularly photographed Rosie and Peter, although Peter was not always willing to join in. He would show them the photographs and occasionally they would look at adult pornographic videos together and Dave would make them both practice what they had seen. Rosie and her brother were told that they were not to talk about the 'fun' they had

together, because some people might use it as an excuse to get Dave into trouble, and then he would not be able to look after them.

Sue never questioned Dave's relationship with the children. She was depressed after the pregnancy and this went undiagnosed for quite a long time. Dave was very supportive. He did not make any demands sexually and was happy to look after the children full-time, dealing with problems at school or fights with neighbouring children. She was glad to have someone there to depend on, and who would look after her. He had had to give up his job to look after the kids, but they managed and his mother would help if they were ever stuck financially.

Dave decided that a computer would be a great help to the children's education, and he persuaded his mother to lend him the money to buy one. Sue also thought this was a good idea. He decided to get a package, which included a digital camera and a scanner, as it was such good value. His mother thought that it was a lot of money, but she was impressed by how much Dave appeared to know already about the equipment, and agreed to finance it. By now, Dave had been buying computer magazines on a regular basis and was quite knowledgeable. It also appeared to make sense to connect with the Internet, so that they could maximise what they could get out of having the computer.

Within two days of going on-line Dave had found out how to get child abuse images from the newsgroups and was downloading them on a regular basis. Rosie was always around during these sessions, as was sometimes her brother, and would look with Dave at the pictures each evening. Dave was now using his digital camera, instead of the Polaroid, to photograph Rosie, and discussed with her how much prettier she was than most of the children in the downloaded photographs. He persuaded her to pose for some photographs and to post these to one of the newsgroups. Rosie chose which ones she liked best. At this stage her brother Peter was reluctant to be photographed, but he sat with them both while they looked at the downloaded images and video clips.

The response to Rosie's photographs surprised all of them. There were lots of postings asking for more and initially Dave responded by taking more and letting anyone have them. Quite quickly, however, he realised that he had a very valuable commodity to dispose of, and he was now much more selective in who he allowed access to Rosie's photographs. He still was not very security conscious however, and communicated by email with a few people, who wanted to commission photographs from him. These were specific requests for Rosie to pose in certain ways, alone or with her brother.

There were also requests for pictures of Dave having sexual intercourse with Rosie. He had never attempted this before, but he decided to persuade Rosie to try. He said he would stop if Rosie got upset or started to cry. Each occasion was photographed and some of the images were traded with others sexually interested in the material. Dave occasionally received large sums of money for some of the more abusive images. Rosie and her brother were given some of this money and were allowed to play games on the computer.

Rosie never talked about what was happening. She had very few friends and had never been encouraged to invite anyone home. Her bed-wetting meant that she would never have wanted to sleep at anyone else's house. She wasn't very good at school, although she always managed to stay out of trouble. Her brother got into quite a few fights with other local children, but Rosie was very much the loner. She was often tired during the day, because both she and her brother went to bed very late. When Dave was arrested and his computer seized, she was very upset. She said nothing about being photographed. Even when a social worker told her that they had seen pictures of her taken by Dave she would not talk. She has now been going to a counsellor for the past three months, but most sessions she sits and says nothing. Sometimes she draws pictures.

Mary's story

Mary was 11 when the abuse started. Her father would sit for hours each evening at his computer. She wasn't allowed to see what he was doing and he became very cross and shouted at her if she came into the room. Her mother worked at a local supermarket and stocked the shelves at night. This meant that she often was not home until after midnight. The first night that the abuse took place was when her mother was out at work. Mary and her younger brother had gone to bed when she heard her father come into the room. He didn't put the light on, but came up to the bed and put his hands under the covers and touched her. Mary pretended to be asleep and hoped that he would go away. She was frightened of him

because he had a terrible temper. Over the next few weeks he continued to touch her when she was asleep, slipping his hands under her nightdress. She started to leave her underwear on when she went to bed.

Taking photographs of her started when he got a digital camera. At first he took pictures of them all and it seemed a lot of fun. One night, when her mother was out at work and Mary was in bed, he came into the bedroom and woke her up, saying that he wanted to take some more pictures of her. She did not want to, especially when he asked her to take off her nightdress. He was taking pictures all the time and didn't seem to notice that she was crying – that she had her nightdress over her face and was crying for him to stop. He never mentioned what had happened and Mary was too ashamed to tell her mother. Her father said nothing. He didn't have to. He didn't notice that Mary avoided him when she could. That she begged her mother not to go to work. That she hated having her photograph taken.

John's story

John was nine and his sister was seven. His parents were separated for the past two years. Every other weekend he and his sister would go and stay with their father, who had access to them. John's mother and father hardly talked to each other – she didn't even come to the door when he came to collect them. He liked going to his father's house because they were allowed to stay up for as long as they liked and were able to watch TV and play on the computer. They didn't have a computer at home, but his father did and he had access to the Internet and lots of computer games.

John was aware that his sister often slept in the same bed as his father, rather than in the bedroom they shared together. His father said she felt frightened at night and wanted to climb in with him. John felt curious about this, but didn't say anything. He thought about getting in to bed with them, but didn't. Sometimes his sister talked to him about the 'games' they played in bed together. She offered to show him how to play as well. One of the games included taking pictures. His sister was allowed to use the camera as well.

One weekend John's father showed John some pictures of his sister on the computer. She had very few clothes on and was lying on the bed. He asked John if he would have some pictures taken as well. If he agreed he could play with the new computer game that they had bought that morning. Over the next few weeks his father took lots of photographs of John and his sister. In most of them they were undressed. John was given instructions about what to do in the pictures, including how to touch his sister and how to touch himself. His sister seemed to think it was funny, but he felt uncomfortable and thought that what they were doing was dirty. He wasn't sure what his father was doing with the photographs and felt frightened that his mother might get to see them.

John started to feel more and more anxious each weekend and dreaded his father taking any more photographs. He became quite withdrawn, unable to tell his mother or his friends what was troubling him. He felt that he should do something about the situation, but was not sure what to do. He thought that his mother would blame him for what was happening, particularly as it involved his sister. He made excuses each weekend not to go to his father's house, but his mother would get very cross because she had made arrangements to go away and would not be able to look after John. His work at school was deteriorating because he couldn't concentrate.

John took ten of his mother's sleeping tablets. He couldn't think what else to do. He must have said something about his father when he was taken in to hospital, but he has no real memory of this. All he remembers was waking up to find a lady from the hospital saying that it was going to be all right.

Exercise 3: Learning model of pornography and sexual aggression

(a) Pornography is used as an aid to masturbation.
(b) When the person looking at it masturbates to ejaculation, this reinforces their sexual response to the content of the pornography.
(c) This in turn increases the likelihood that the behaviour will be repeated.
(d) As the person looking at and masturbating to the pornography habituates (gets used to) to the content, the pornography may cease to have the same effect.
(e) Viewers may then seek out more 'intense' content (such as younger children or more abusive images), or may change category (e.g.) start to look at adult torture images.

Materials for Chapter 4

1. Recording sheet

Try and describe how a child might be feeling during **the sexual abuse** (taking photographs always occurs within an abusive relationship).

1. What may be happening to the child physically?

2. What may the child be thinking?

3. What may the child be feeling?

Materials for Chapter 4 *continued*

2. Recording sheet

Try and describe how a child might feel **when they disclosed** the abuse

1. How might the disclosure have come about?

2. What may the child be thinking?

3. What may the child be feeling?

Materials for Chapter 4 *continued*

3. Recording sheet

Try and describe what the long-term consequences of the abuse may be for the child. **What role did the child play within the particular activity being photographed?**

What impact do you think being photographed had on the child's behaviour? Answer this in terms of the short-term and the longer-term.

1. What may the child be thinking?

2. What may the child be feeling?

Chapter Five

Fantasy and its Escalation

Whilst many clients may have worked on issues to do with fantasy in their offending if they have attended a Sex Offender Treatment Programme, this chapter addresses particular problems that might specifically relate to the Internet. The aims of this chapter are to:

- Review the literature related to the role of fantasy in sexual behaviour in general, and specifically related to adult sexual interest in children.
- Offer strategies to explore the role of Internet abuse images (and perhaps pornography in general) in the escalation of fantasy with adults with a sexual interest in children.
- Help such clients gain some understanding of the role of Internet based fantasy in their sexual behaviour.
- Assist in the development of self-help strategies to control problematic fantasy.

Background

The Internet provides a unique opportunity to access child sex material such as images and text, and enables the user to make contact with other people with a sexual interest in children, in a way that would have been impossible only a few years ago. For the last 30 years, abuse images have been illegal in most jurisdictions, and obtaining such material would have brought with it considerable risk as well as financial cost. Now, as with other pornographies, abusive images of children can be obtained with relative ease and at no cost from the Internet. In addition, such material is available in the privacy of one's own home. Galbreath et al. (2002: 189) have suggested that, 'For those with Internet capabilities, this ease of accessibility has streamlined the ongoing discovery, and potential enactment of one's sexuality, into a 'point and click' process'.

The relationship between access to material and enactment of sexuality is complex and will be examined in some detail. Implicit in this, however, are several assumptions:

- There is a relationship between pornographic materials and fantasy.

- Discovery of materials may lead to a sexual engagement with them.
- Such engagement may be solitary (through masturbation).
- Engagement may also be through the commission of a contact offence.

The Internet has brought with it access to a considerable array of pornographic materials, the majority of which would not have been readily available to those curious or interested. With very little effort or knowledge, people can find material which would in other contexts have been considered 'paraphilic' in content, even if they were not illegal. What will be considered in this chapter is the way in which the Internet may facilitate an 'escalation' in the fantasies that are associated with such images, and in particular those which relate to sexual activity with children.

Sexual fantasy

The research on sexual fantasy in offenders overlaps considerably with findings concerning fantasy in non-offending populations, and draws our attention to the subjective nature of sexual stimuli and human responses. In a key paper in this area, Leitenberg and Henning (1995: 469) stated, 'Certainly it is by now a truism that one's brain is at least as important a sexual organ as one's genitals. What humans think about can either enhance or inhibit sexual responsivity to any form of sensory stimulation, and, in the absence of any physical stimulation, sexual fantasy alone is arousing'. This point is often missed in offender research, particularly in the context of the selection of sexual stimulus materials (Howitt, 1995), where it is assumed that all child related materials are arousing for the person with a sexual interest in children. Many cues can trigger sexual fantasies, and these can be internal as well as external cues such as images, and fantasies can be used to stimulate arousal as well as being a function of the arousal itself. Leitenberg and Henning's (1995: 470) research emphasised, however, the deliberate quality to fantasy, '. . . most sexual fantasies appear to be deliberate patterns of thought designed to stimulate or enhance pleasurable sexual feelings regardless of whether the fantasies involve reminiscing about past sexual experiences, imaginary future sexual activity, engaging in wishful thinking, or having daydreams that are exciting to imagine without any desire to put them into practice'. What is emphasised here is the deliberate attempt to control in imagination what takes place, which may also include an altering of past reminisces to enhance arousal. This point may be of particular relevance to the Internet where people can select particular images to fit their own sexual script and can, where necessary, alter such images to fuel a given fantasy.

Factor analysis studies of fantasy content in the general population have suggested four overarching content categories for both men and women (Leitenberg and Henning, 1995).

- Conventional intimate heterosexual imagery with past, present, or imaginary lovers who are usually known to the person.
- Scenes intimating sexual power and irresistibility (including seduction scenes, multiple partners etc.).
- Scenes involving somewhat varied or 'forbidden' sexual imagery (different settings, positions, practices, questionable partners etc.).
- Submission-dominance scenes in which some physical force or sadomasochistic imagery is involved or implied.

What is apparent from this research is that many 'normal' people engage in fantasies that if acted upon would be seen as deviant. In this sense we need to differentiate between thoughts and fantasies. The latter are purposefully internally generated, whereas thoughts might be considered to be spontaneously triggered by an external event. A study by Byers (1998) attempted to differentiate between unwanted intrusive sexual thoughts and sexual thoughts and fantasies that were experienced as positive and personally acceptable. Within their sample of 171 students, 84 per cent had experienced unwanted sexual intrusive thoughts, although the response to these thoughts was highly idiosyncratic.

Deviant sexual fantasy

Therefore if such sexual thoughts and fantasies are frequently experienced, what, if anything, makes them deviant? Leitenberg and Henning (1995: 146) have posed a series of uncomfortable

questions in relation to this, 'Those fantasies that are simply statistically the most unusual, or those that are associated with socially unacceptable behaviour even if they are not all that unusual? If the latter is the case, does there have to be a causal association in which it is demonstrated that the fantasy significantly increases the likelihood that the socially unacceptable behaviour will occur? Or is a similar content between a fantasy and an unacceptable behaviour sufficient to call the fantasy deviant even if the behaviour never occurs.' Grubin (1999) has also drawn our attention to the fact that even though many people fantasise about, for example, sadistic sexual acts, for the vast majority this does not lead to sexual offending. He gives as evidence of this the number of specialised sadomasochistic magazines available in the US. This in itself is interesting, as one of the major difficulties with fantasy research is its inevitable dependence on self report. Pornography consumption is used by Grubin (1999) as an indicator of sexual fantasies, which is not reliant on self-report measures. This is an important assumption in relation to Internet pornography, which is often seen as a visual representation of fantasy (Taylor and Quayle, 2003).

Fantasy, pornography and offending behaviour

The relationship between fantasy, pornography and behaviour is unclear, but we know that the primary function of pornography is as an aid to sexual fantasy. In their work on the content of sexual fantasies for sex offenders, Gee et al. (2004) described the relationship as '. . . deviant fantasies can be construed as imaginative processes accompanied by a withdrawal from the immediate demands of the external world and a narrowing in focus of an individual's internal world. Such processes allow an individual to create an elaborate, emotionally anchored, mental picture which has its origins in daydreaming, and involves erotica that creates or intensifies sexual arousal . . .' Authors such as Looman (1995) have argued that there is little doubt that child molesters as a group are much more likely to become sexually aroused, when shown slides of nude or semi-nude children or when asked to listen to audio taped depictions of sexual activity with children, than are those who have no history of offending. However, Knight and Prentky (1990) based on their typology, have suggested that not all child molesters fantasise about children and show deviant arousal.

Underpinning this is the assumption that at least some offenders offend for reasons other than deviant sexual interests. Looman's (1995) study suggested a relationship between fantasy and negative mood state (which we will return to in Chapter 6) and concluded that, 'Thus, a self-perpetuating cycle develops, in which negative mood leads to deviant fantasies, which lead to further negative mood, which in turn lead to further deviant fantasies . . . The more the child molester engages in deviant fantasies, the more likely he is to do so in the future, because the act of fantasizing creates the conditions necessary for it to occur'.

Most Internet offenders will agree that they were sexually aroused by some, if not all, of the images they saved (Quayle and Taylor, 2002), and that this arousal usually culminated in masturbation. This is important in the context of the Internet, as the capacity to obtain large quantities of material and the social engagement that may follow on from this, means that we cannot assume that all of the images kept by offenders are for their own sexual purposes; rather it is probable that at least some of the images serve as a means of exchange with others for whom the material was part of a preferred sexual script or fantasy. What is equally apparent is that downloading behaviour, and the fantasies that it fuels, rarely remains a static response. If nothing else, offenders may get bored by the images they have downloaded and find that they lose the capacity to create sexual arousal. Marshall and Marshall (2000) discussed a similar issue in relation to developmental origins of sexual offending. Within this context they suggested that the higher the frequency of masturbatory activities during adolescence, the greater the likelihood that sexual offenders will incorporate other elements, such as forbidden sexual acts, power and control and sexual aggression, into their sexual fantasies. Given the endless availability of pornographies on the Internet, one natural consequence of this may be to seek more arousing images which may include sexually more explicit or violent pictures, or images that depict younger children (Quayle et al., 2001).

Clearly we cannot police fantasy, and many clients who have not been convicted of contact offences might well argue that the Internet provides a safe outlet for fantasy, that might otherwise lead towards contact offences. Whatever the situation, interaction between an offender and the Internet provides an opportunity for fantasy escalation, fuelling a market for more extreme abusive images and leading to a possible 'leakage' between on-line and off-line activities. Other authors have also discussed this process, describing how offenders might become bored with one type of image and move on to gradually more and more explicit material (Sullivan and Beech, 2004).

There are therefore two important issues in relation to sexual fantasies and offending through the Internet. Given the volume of sexually explicit material available (both legal and illegal), we can assume that there must be a market place in relation to such images. We also know from police operations such as Candyman (Innocent Images, 2002) that there are many people who have large volumes of images on their seized computers and that many offenders are constantly searching for new or different images (Quayle and Taylor, 2003). Here, the possession of images moves out of the realm of private fantasy, as the production of such images requires a child to be photographed, and therefore a criminal offence to have taken place. What is more, the demand for new images requires the production of more material and the potential for more children to be sexually abused and photographed. The 'meeting a private fantasy need' in fact may contribute indirectly to the abuse of children. This is not to say that all people who view images will go on to commit a contact offence, but that the viewing of images supports an offence network. The second issue is to do with the relationship between viewing images as part of fantasy and the actual commission of a contact offence against a child. As suggested by Grubin (1999), 'The missing link that encourages the translation of fantasy into behaviour, and behavioural practice into escalation and offending, has remained elusive. It is an important part of the puzzle for those who rely on clinical assessments of risk, but it is unlikely to comprise any single factor'.

Gee et al. (2004) have suggested that we need to move away from notions of deviant fantasy and instead look at the distinction between offence specific and non-offence specific fantasies. From their data analysis, they concluded that, 'For those offenders who report engaging in offence-focused fantasy, non-specific offence fantasies may be an important stepping-stone in the process of sexual offending'. These authors proposed that in a similar way to the disinhibiting effects of pornography, the recurrent use of non-specific offence fantasy may provide the offender with a way of desensitising himself to the offence themes present within the fantasy, increasing the likelihood of offending. Wright and Schneider (1999) have also suggested that sexual fantasies are a primary source of cognitive distortions used by offenders to justify and maintain sexual offending. These cognitive distortions, then, feed back into the processes that lead to sexual offending and are elaborated further during masturbatory fantasies.

Abuse images and sexual offending

The role of abuse images in sexual offending against children draws on the broader, and fragmented literature related to adult pornography and sexual aggression. For over a quarter of a century there have been public and academic debates about the harmful effects of pornography and its relationship to violent or sexual offending. The context to the debate is the sexual victimisation of women and children. A large-scale survey by Finkelhor et al. (1990) in the United States suggested that approximately 27 per cent of females and 16 per cent of males have experienced some form of sexual abuse as children. More recent studies (e.g., Finkelhor and Jones, 2004; Jones and Finkelhor, 2003) would suggest a welcome decline in these figures over the following decade. However, while there has been much outrage voiced about abuse statistics, it has not stopped the growth of the pornography industry, with an increase of sales of sexually explicit videos, magazine, telephone sex, CD-ROMs and Internet services. The public face of our society shows disapproval of the expression of sexually aggressive or demeaning acts against women and children, yet it is supportive of an industry that represents all of these, albeit vicariously (Kleinhans, 2004).

Advances in technological sophistication have led to an increase in the amount of high quality pornography available, along with relatively easy access. Research by Barron and Kimmel (2000), in the context of adult pornography, measured the sexually violent content in magazine, video and Usenet (Internet newsgroup) pornography. Their results indicated a consistent increase in the amount of violence from one medium to the next, although the increase between magazines and

videos was not significant. Their analysis also indicated that while magazines and videos portrayed the violence as consensual, with women as 'victimisers' more often than men, the reverse was true for Usenet. It is perhaps not surprising that such findings have fuelled the debate about the relationship between pornography and sexual aggression.

Several theories have been put forward to elaborate on the possible relationship between the two, and these will be examined briefly below. One of the most influential has been the application of behavioural (classical and operant conditioning) theories to the role of pornography in offending (Laws and Marshall, 1990). It is largely based on the proposition that pornography is used as an aid to masturbation. When the viewer masturbates to ejaculation, this reinforces their sexual response to the content of the pornography. This in turn increases the likelihood that the behaviour will be repeated. As the viewer habituates to the pornography, they seek out more 'intense' content (such intensity might be along any continuum, such as increasing violence, or decreasing the age of the child). Marshall and Marshall (2000) have suggested that any repeated content, whether sexual or non-sexual, of masturbatory fantasies is likely to become entrenched as a result of the negatively reinforcing effects of escape from distress and the positively reinforcing properties of the pleasurable experiences of sexual arousal.

Conditioning theories would predict that the arousing effect of pornography increases as the viewer masturbates to ejaculation, and that the explicitness and content of pornography changes over time as the viewer habituates. One implication of this model is that sex offenders might use more unconventional pornography than non-offenders (or more offence related pornography). However, the results of studies that have examined the use of pornography by offenders do not lend strong support to this. Indeed, studies of identified offenders, using largely self-report measures, found that sex offenders reported less frequent exposure to pornography than comparison groups of non-offenders (e.g., Condron and Nutter, 1988). However, when rapists were compared to child molesters (Carter et al., 1987) the latter used more pornography than rapists and were more likely to incorporate it into their sexual offending. What this does not address is the types of pornography used; rather, these studies, as does much of the literature, treats pornography as if it was homogenous. Howitt (1995) in relation to 11 offenders who used pornography, found that the use of commercial abuse images was rare, but that offenders created their own collections of materials. It appears likely that offenders who use pornography select material that is both available and which fits their own preferred sexual script.

A related area of research comes from social learning theory, which suggests that people may learn indirectly about their social world through observing others (modelling). The strength of this learning depends on the rewards and punishments (functional determinants) received by the model (Bandura, 1977) and the viewer's evaluation that they would obtain the same for performing a similar action. Such a theory would suggest that violent pornography can increase subsequent aggressive behaviour, because it portrays this behaviour as rewarding. Therefore the more the person identifies with what they are viewing, the more likely will they go on to engage in sexually aggressive behaviour. It is not such a leap from this level of theorising to more feminist approaches, where it is alleged that the sexualisation of physical, sexual and emotional harm enacted against women in pornography leads to the social subordination of women and their possible victimisation. Cowburn and Pringle (2000) talked of the exercise of power as central to pornography, not only in terms of the acts depicted but in the objectification central to the creation and use of pornography. Given this, there is then a fusion of abusive power with sexual gratification.

It is unclear as to whether pornography negatively alters both male and female perceptions of women and children, or whether sexual arousal towards aggression as depicted in pornography occurs alongside attitudes supportive of sexual aggression towards women and children. However, where depictions of sexual aggression suggest that the victim is correspondingly aroused, this appears to increase men's beliefs in 'rape myths', particularly in those who were inclined to be more aggressive towards women (Malamuth and Check, 1985). A useful review of the psychological literature pertaining to this area can be found in Seto et al. (2001).

Overall, there appears to be little support for the allegation of a direct causal link between viewing pornography and subsequent offending behaviour. A recent study by Langevin and Curnoe (2004) examined the use of pornographic materials by sex offenders during the commission of their crimes and in a sample of 561 people, only 17 per cent had used pornography at the time of their offences. Of concern was that pornography used in the commission of sexual crimes primarily involved child victims. One third of the offenders using pornography were taking pictures of children, and nine of these were for commercial exploitation. However, the majority of the studies in this area have been in the context of adult, rather than abuse images. There are also methodological and ethical difficulties in examining such relationships, particularly with adults who have a sexual interest in children. Laboratory studies for example that expose offenders to images and measure their level of physiological arousal can be particularly weak. They are likely to use comparatively short exposure times to picture material, whereas pornography users (particularly in the context of the Internet) are likely to view abuse images for extended periods. In addition, in laboratory studies the use of such sexual stimuli is rarely matched to the idiosyncrasies of preferred sexual images by individuals, and instead involves a category of stimuli presented to offenders as a group.

Seto et al. (2001: 46) argued that 'individuals who are already predisposed to sexually offend are the most likely to show an effect of pornography exposure and are the most likely to show the strongest effects'. It is also important to note that until recently, obtaining sexually explicit pornographic images of children was both difficult and dangerous, and therefore the use of such material as related to offending was possibly reduced by lack of opportunity. This necessarily limits the sample characteristics of offenders available for researchers to study.

The role of pornography

As we have noted in earlier chapters, there is a suggestion that there is not a single 'profile' of an offender in the context of pornography use. It may be that pornography exposure may influence, but not cause, the development of sexual offending in some men (Marshall, 2000). However, what is more likely is that having an appetite for pornography is just another manifestation of, and a way of meeting, sexual interest. Preferred content is likely to be dynamic, rather than static, reflecting both levels of habituation and the interaction of fantasy with real-life social settings. Leitenberg and Henning (1995) have also suggested that '. . . one needs to be concerned about these sorts of fantasies primarily in those individuals in whom the barrier between thought and action has been broken. Once this has occurred, sexual fantasies often become part of the chain of events leading to recurrent sexual crimes'.

We need also to give consideration to factors that allow people to engage in an array of highly disinhibited sexual behaviours on the Internet. These include accessibility, affordability and assumed anonymity, (Cooper, 1998). For example, in the context of on-line sexual relationships, there is an increased likelihood of superficial erotic contacts and ways of relating that can have very destructive results, such as accelerated, eroticised pseudo-intimacy. The availability of erotica (including abuse images) allows for the objectification of others, the ability to fragment one's own sexuality, and the possible emergence of otherwise dormant antisocial inclinations. On the Internet, people are more likely to allow themselves to behave in ways that are different from ordinary, everyday life and to express previously unexplored aspects of their personality. While in some ways this may be seen as liberating, in the context of abuse images it opens up the possibility of increasing the further abuse of children. It may be argued that the function of on-line resources such as abuse images is to heighten sexual arousal and disinhibition and to aid in the possible seduction of children through fantasy manipulation and masturbation.

Therapeutic issues

From a therapeutic standpoint, Middleton (2004: 106) has outlined how practitioners should assess the types of images most frequently viewed by the offender and the ways in which these are incorporated into fantasy and masturbatory behaviour. As part of this assessment, he suggested that it is important to identify the frequency and circumstances of engaging in such fantasies when off-line. This would again seem to emphasise a possible movement or blurring between on-line fantasy and sexual behaviour and engagement with the off-line world, 'Finally the therapist will seek to explore the incorporation into the abusive sexual fantasy of children to whom s/he has access or is in a position to commence a grooming relationship,

which may signal the beginning of the process of turning a fantasy into a 'hands-on' abusive sexual contact.'. Again, the focus here is on the possible relationship between sexual fantasy and the commission of a contact offence, rather than sexual fantasy and seeking new material.

Sullivan and Beech (2004), in the context of assessing Internet offenders, have suggested that it is important for practitioners to help clients differentiate between appropriate and inappropriate fantasies and their overlap between legal and illegal fantasies. This, in itself is fraught with difficulties, as while most of us would be able to differentiate between legal/illegal and appropriate/inappropriate acts, we tend to think of fantasies as being different, private events, and as we have already considered, many of us engage in such fantasies. Sullivan and Beech (2004) have further outlined how we might think of themes within fantasy and also what they have called 'the spectrum of control', which explored the notion of a continuum with at one end the offender imaging total control and at the other control lying in the realm of the other person. Implicit in this is an examination of the role of 'self' in the fantasy process. It would appear that central to this is a notion of willing engagement with the fantasy, and it's elaboration. The way that material is structured on the Internet is likely to facilitate this. For example, visual images of children are normally part of a sequence (maybe represented as a series of captures from a video sequence). Each picture will be identified as part of that sequence and may, for example, be a series of pictures depicting a child from a state of being dressed to undressed and engaged in some sexual activity. The very sequencing seeks to draw the viewer into the fantasies being portrayed.

Gee et al's (2004) descriptive model of the phenomena of sexual fantasy during the offence process (The Sexual Fantasy Content Model) comprised three level one and five level two categories. Level one categories were general sexual fantasy, non-specific offence fantasy and offence specific fantasy, while level two categories included demographic, behavioural, relational, situational and self-perceptual considerations. This analysis was not with regard to offences committed through the Internet, but is of interest to us because it suggested a dynamic process with types of offence fantasy being dependent on 'which phase of the offence process the individual was in at the time'. They suggested that, 'As an offender moved through the phases of the initial offence chain . . . general sexual fantasy themes gradually declined, while offence specific themes increased steadily. The initial offence brought the cessation of both general sexual fantasy and non-specific fantasy themes . . . Offence specific fantasy was the only fantasy content that was present at the time of the initial offence'. These authors suggested that if offenders can learn the importance of sexual fantasy across the offence process, it may put them in a better position to monitor their levels of risk.

As we considered in Chapter 2, fantasies have long been a target for treatment, particularly as studies such as that of Hanson and Bussière (1998) have indicated that deviant sexual preference is the biggest single predictor of sexual recidivism. In the past techniques such as aversion therapy, covert sensitisation and masturbatory reconditioning have all been used as a way of modifying fantasy and, as a consequence, sexual preference. However, as we have already noted, what we are ultimately interested in is reducing the likelihood of engaging in future behaviour that in some way victimises children rather than controlling or eliminating sexual fantasy *per se*. This may be through continuing to download images (and therefore providing a market for the production of further images), or through the commission of an actual contact offence against a child. Working with the offender requires not only an exploration of the fantasies and the person's engagement with the same, but an understanding of the function of the fantasy for the offender and it's relation to offending behaviour. This functional relationship is important if we are to facilitate the offender in acquiring self-control strategies that reduce the likelihood of future offending behaviour.

Points of concern

- Fantasy for most adults is a part of normal sexual behaviour. Such fantasy may extend to situations that if acted upon might be thought to be deviant.
- The relationship between fantasy, pornography and behaviour is unclear.
- There seems to be little empirical evidence of a direct link between viewing pornography and subsequent offending behaviour. It seems unlikely that there will prove to be a single factor linking pornography and offending behaviour and the most reasonable assumption

is that pornography may influence, but not cause, the development of sexual offending in some men.

- Most Internet offenders who have accessed abuse images agree that they are sexually aroused by the images they have accessed, often culminating in masturbation.
- Given the apparent extent of access to abuse images of children on the Internet, it might be hypothesised that many people are sexually aroused by such images.
- The availability of such large numbers of abuse images on the Internet may offer the opportunity for fantasy escalation leading to possible 'leakage' between on-line and off-line activities.
- Regardless of the relationship between individual offending and access to abuse images, the production of such images necessarily requires the sexual abuse of a child, and the demand for more images fuels more production, and therefore more abuse.

Working with the client

This chapter is aimed at clients whose collections or overt behaviour would indicate a progression through pornographies, or clients who possess a collection where recently acquired images are of younger or more extreme scenarios. In the Internet history, look for evidence of satiation or habituation to support this, reflected in moving between picture categories or age groups, or interest in progressively more extreme pictures.

Changing behaviour

The Internet offers unrivalled opportunity for individuals to access almost any kind of image and fantasy material. This is as much the case for the adult with a sexual interest in children as it is for people with other deviant or more usual sexual interests. We also know that for many if not most people, fantasy is an integral part of sexual behaviour, and for some people that fantasy *if expressed* might be termed deviant. It is not appropriate (nor possible) to seek to police fantasy; the issue relates to the likelihood for a given individual of the expression of fantasy in behaviour in some way, and the extent to which engagement with fantasy may itself fuel sexually inappropriate behaviour in its production.

In helping the client, one set of goals should relate to increasing awareness of the risk and reality of fantasy escalation for them through accessing pornographic material, the role of masturbation in reinforcing continuing, and perhaps escalating, engagement with pornography based fantasy, and the possibility of leakage between on-line and off-line behaviour. In helping the client make sense of the role of his own fantasy activity, it may be useful to introduce one or more of the models of fantasy use to help the client make sense of their own behaviour. A further set of goals relates to helping clients understand that fantasy generation through the use of abuse images is an element in increasing the demand for further images, and fuelling the process of abuse. Chapter 4, Images are Children, is also relevant to this.

Exercises

1. The first exercise attempts to get the offender to look at the diversity of their fantasies, and to identify the similarities and differences between fantasy usages across these contexts. A recording sheet is provided at the end of this chapter.
2. Looking at downloading behaviour, fantasy and masturbation. The client is asked to prepare a timeline of their downloading behaviour, looking at what images they started with and trying to create 'stage posts' that marked shifts in their downloading behaviour. Try and elicit the relationship between series of pictures, or categories of pictures, and masturbatory behaviour. What caused a shift (either an external shift, through for example discovering another Internet protocol, talking to others, or an internal shift, such as loss of arousal) to different kinds of images? A recording chart is provided at the end of the chapter.
3. Models of fantasy escalation. Demonstrate to the client using a pictorial representation of either Wolf's, Sullivan's or Brigg's model of fantasy escalation and behaviour. Ask the client to identify where the Internet fitted in relation to such fantasies (examples of these models are provided at the end of this chapter). For some clients, fantasy may be an end in itself as opposed to a pathway to the commission of a contact offence. This may further be explored using the diagram from Briggs (2003).
4. Detailed descriptions of fantasies. A lot of fantasy work may already have been completed as part of any SOTP. This exercise

is intended to reinforce the client looking critically at the role that the Internet may have played (and how) in the escalation of fantasy. The goal is to elicit as many fantasies as possible from the client and to put them into some sort of temporal relationship with each other. How did fantasies change, what facilitated that change, what role did pornography play, what was the role of others met through the Internet?

5. Creating alternative ways of responding. This reinforces the idea that we can experience feelings and thoughts without always having to act upon them in the same way. It builds on existing work on self-control techniques.

Completion criteria

By the end of this chapter the client should have:

1. Prepared a timeline of their downloading behaviour, looking at what images they started with and trying to create 'stage posts' that marked shifts in their downloading behaviour. Each shift should identify the critical factors that led to downloading more/different abusive images.
2. Used a model of fantasy escalation and identified in writing where the Internet led to an escalation in their sexual fantasies.
3. Described at least four sexual fantasies and placed them in a temporal relationship with each other, identifying how one fantasy led to another.
4. Looked at the relationship between fantasy and behaviour and generated alternative ways of coping with sexual thoughts and feelings.

1. Materials

1. Abuse images, fantasy and masturbation form. Complete for each of the following categories:
   - What **child abuse images** were downloaded?
   - What **thoughts or fantasies** accompanied these images?

2. Wolf's (1985) multifactorial model

1. Sexually deviant persons have a *disturbed developmental history* and this includes *'potentiators'* for future deviant attitudes and behaviours. For example:
   - Exposure to pornography as a child.
   - Sexual, emotional, physical abuse as a child.
   - Social isolation.

2. *Presence of 'disinhibitor's* i.e., situational factors which disrupt normal social controls against deviant behaviour. For example:
   - Use of drugs and/or alcohol.
   - Membership of a supportive culture.
   - Use of pornography.
   - Perceived opportunity.

3. *Deviant sexual fantasy.* Strong recurrent cognitions are associated with the deviant behaviour and these serve to reinforce positive associations between the sexual arousal and the behaviour. They also serve to desensitise the person's inhibitions against acting out. The three factors interact in a cyclic manner to develop and maintain the behaviour.
   - Membership of a supportive culture.
   - Use of pornography.
   - Perceived opportunity.
   - Masturbatory fantasy.
   - Justification or rationalsation for abuse.

Using the Wolf cycle with no-contact Internet clients

Identifying the 'potentiators'

- Before completing the Wolf cycle with a client, it is useful to first complete a full life history. This will enable you to gather useful clinical information. The client's family, social, intimate, and sexual relationships; as well as information about their education and employment history will help you gather information to inform your understanding of the 'potentiators' of abuse.

The stages of the cycle

Use a blank cycle without the prescribed stages – use as guide only.

- **'Low-self esteem and depression'** – do not assume that these particular factors were relevant to the client. It is more useful to ask open questions about moods and thoughts prior to the abuse.
- **'Expects rejection'** – as above concentrate on the thoughts, feelings and behaviours – individual and personally relevant to the client – what was his view of himself? What was his worldview? How did he cope with negative feelings?
- **'Social withdrawal'** – use of the Internet may fulfil an emotional need for closeness and intimacy not attained elsewhere. This may be because the client doesn't want intimacy, but may also be because they want it, but do not have the skills to achieve or maintain relationships with appropriate adults. Withdrawal into a 'virtual world' may have been an attempt to meet these unmet needs.
- **'Escape into sexual fantasy'** – ask the client about the nature and content of his fantasies/thoughts. How did these escalate and over what time scale? What was the function of fantasies/sexual thoughts for him – what needs were they meeting? Did these compensate for feelings of emotional loneliness and social isolation?
- **Identify the 'disinhibitors'** – what did the client do and say to himself to give him permission and justify his behaviour – these will be evident at all stages of the cycle. It is important not confuse post-arrest minimisation/excuses for permission givers – what we are trying to identify is the distorted attitudes which preceded abuse.
- **What situations/environments** are more likely to trigger abuse and what are the associated thoughts and feelings, which are linked to abusive behaviour or Internet misuse.
- **'Targeting'** – what particular sexual preferences did the client have – why were certain images selected or chosen and not others – identify what these were – what feelings, thoughts and behaviours were linked to the images.
- **'Grooming'** – although there is no direct victim with a no-contact offence – images are real – it may be useful to consider with the client how the child was groomed by others – and the part he played in creating and sustaining a demand and therefore the continuation of the abuse of real children.
- **'Grooming the environment and others'** – when was the computer purchased and for what purpose? When did his use of the Internet start and escalate? When did he start viewing/collecting child abuse images? How did he secure privacy to use the Internet? What security systems did he use? What did he say to family/partner/ friends to keep his misuse of the Internet secret? Where was the computer in the house?
- **'Post-abuse'** – identify feelings immediately following engagement with the Internet. The client may have experienced feelings of guilt and shame knowing his behaviour was wrong. He may have tried to stop. He may have

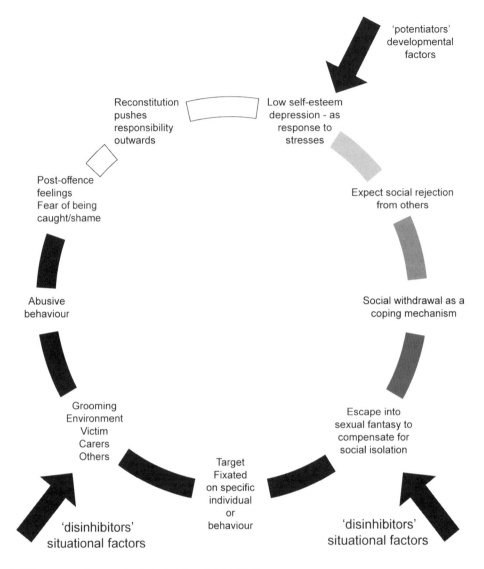

Figure 5.1 The sexual abuse cycle. Adapted from Wolf (1985)

deleted files – although this may have been more to do with fear of being caught than actually believing he was doing any harm.

- **'Reconstitution'** – How did he push away feelings of responsibility and repeat the behaviour? How quickly did he repeat the behaviour – identify patterns of engagement – did it escalate over time – were stages of the cycle 'skipped' as the speed of engagement increased?

3. The Spiral of Sexual Abuse (Sullivan, 2002)[1]

Sullivan has developed the concept of the spiral of sexual abuse as a result of clinical assessment and treatment work with several hundred sexual abuse perpetrators. Primarily, it has been used as a clinical tool to assist perpetrators to fully explore their pattern of sexual offending, however, it has also been useful in assisting professionals,

---

[1] This is an abbreviated version of Sullivan's (2002) paper, and produced with the author's permission.

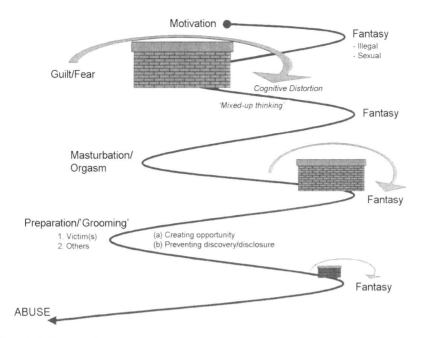

Figure 5.2 The spiral of sexual abuse

unfamiliar with the concepts, to better understand perpetrator behaviour. As indicated by Sullivan, one of the benefits of the conceptual framework of a spiral is that it lends itself to illustrating the developing and escalating nature of abuse. It moves from the initial motivation, through the internal struggle, to the decision to offend and follows the steps taken to facilitate the abuse and dealing with the aftermath. The spiral is an open ended conceptual framework which allows for the illustration of the evolutionary nature of a pattern of offending. Alternatively, as in the example given, it is possible to focus on a part or *phase* of the overall offending pattern. This may relate to one incident or a series of offences against one victim.

Figure 5.2 shows the spiral, which depicts the evolution of a sexual offence, from motivation to sexually offend to a sexual offence. From this point the spiral will develop in any number of ways depending on the behaviour of the perpetrator, the victim and others who might protect the victim. There is also scope for including other stages such as 'targeting' and 're-grooming' and repeating stages, placing them in the order which best fits each individual perpetrator's specific pattern.

Clinical experience suggests that typically, offenders are aware of their sexual arousal to younger children in their late childhood or adolescence and many will have sexually abused in a variety of different contexts prior to the current conviction or offence. Practitioners can work with perpetrators on phases of their spiral which may relate to a specific victim and/or set of offences and later combine these with other phases of their offending pattern to produce a complete spiral which can be as long as necessary to illustrated all the different phases of offending in a perpetrator's life.

It should be noted that this model is a blueprint to assist understanding of the typical phases of a spiral from which offenders can start to explore and establish their own, offending, component elements and sequence of events. It is critical for perpetrators engaged in the cognitive behavioural therapeutic process to understanding the stages of their spiral. These are discussed in detail by Sullivan (2002) and practitioners are recommended to read the full text of this paper.

4. Sexual fantasies and self-control

Few of us would like to think that we are controlled by our fantasies. Yet many people say that it is hard to ignore powerful images or thoughts, but masturbating to these is, in a way, acting on them.

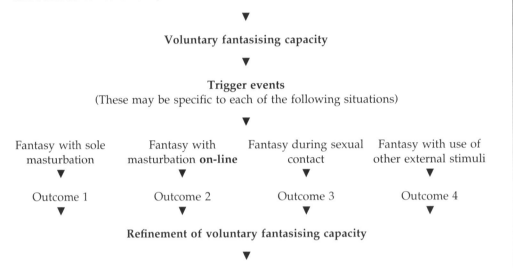

Fantasy model (Briggs, 2003)[2]

1. **What are the distal setting events to the use of sexual fantasy?** (These may include pre-adolescent sexualizing experiences; attachment based cognitive scripts and schema relating to acceptance of intimacy; models of sexual expression; technical sophistication, including the wherewithal to explore and elaborate on-line sexual activity.)

▼

2. **What were the offender's idiosyncratic masturbatory practices in adolescence and beyond?** (This should include the duration and frequency of masturbatory fantasising via paraphilias and overt sexual behaviour.)

▼

Voluntary fantasising capacity

▼

Trigger events
(These may be specific to each of the following situations)

▼

Fantasy with sole masturbation	Fantasy with masturbation **on-line**	Fantasy during sexual contact	Fantasy with use of other external stimuli
▼	▼	▼	▼
Outcome 1	Outcome 2	Outcome 3	Outcome 4
▼	▼	▼	▼

Refinement of voluntary fantasising capacity

▼

(Repeat of above)

[2] Briggs (2003). Personal communication from David Briggs Associates. Produced with kind permission of the author.

We are giving them all our attention, and when masturbation is accompanied by ejaculation we increase the chance that the next time we think/see something or somebody that reminds us of those thoughts we will want to do the same again.

Sometimes we feel that it is too hard to control these fantasies, but we need to make a choice as to 'who is driving the bus' – you or your demanding thoughts and feelings. It's important to realise that you are more than your thoughts and feelings and that you can make a choice as to how much attention you choose to give to them. If you always attend to your fantasies by acting on them, then you are giving up control of the bus – they are doing the driving instead of you.

Lots of techniques have been developed to deal with fantasies, to ensure that they don't 'drive the bus' and take over from you. Here are some of the most common. It is important that you explore what might work for you.

5. Techniques for dealing with abusive fantasies

1. **Thought stopping and challenging**: What are the consequences of paying attention to and acting on this fantasy?
2. **Channel hopping/channel changing**: We can make decisions as to whether we engage with a thought or whether we stand back from it.
3. **Fantasy blockers**: Associating a bad ending with the fantasy (getting caught by someone important to you).
4. **Fantasy replacement**: Trying out exciting but non-abusive fantasies and praising yourself for doing so.

5. **Urge surfing**: Imagine the abusive fantasy as being like a giant wave that builds to a peak and then declines in intensity. You surf the fantasy in the same way that we might surf frightening thoughts.
6. **Escape route**: Sometimes we need to remove ourselves from the situation in which we are fantasising. This might mean breaking the on-line connection, turning off the computer or making some coffee.
7. **Distraction**: Again take the focus off the fantasy. Call a friend, go for a walk, read a magazine.

Abuse images, fantasy and masturbation form

1. What images downloaded? List category (such as 'girl oral' or series name). Where from? Give approximate time frame.

2. What fantasies accompanied these images?

Abuse images, fantasy and masturbation form *continued*

3. What level of arousal was experienced? How intense (0-100)? How often resulting in masturbation?

Chapter Six

Emotional Avoidance

The aims of this chapter are to:

- Provide a review of the literature that relates to the importance of emotions in offending behaviour and the relevance of this to the Internet.
- Give a summary of areas of concern relating to this.
- Suggest ways of assessing how client's values might be a vehicle for accepting distressing thoughts and feelings, without acting on them.
- Help clients recognise in their own behaviour how they have engaged in emotional avoidance and provide strategies for committing to behavioural change.

Background

The role of emotions in sex offending has been a neglected area of research and whilst traditional intervention strategies have focused on changing emotional states, there is little evidence to suggest that these have been effective. This chapter reviews some of the existing literature highlighting the increasing emphasis on the importance of values in giving both direction and dignity to treatment models (Quayle et al., in press). We then go on to explore how strategies that focus on the acceptance of emotional states, along with commitment to behavioural change, might provide an alternative evidence based approach to therapeutic change. It is suggested that offenders, in the context of making explicit their personal values and goals, might be helped to accept the negative emotions that are part of their life and commit themselves to generating behavioural goals that will move them towards what they personally value.

Internet addiction

As previously discussed in Chapter 3, there is increasing reference in the literature to 'Internet Addiction', reflecting a use of the Internet that is problematic. Earlier research by Kandell (1998) defined Internet addiction as:

- *An increasing investment of resources on Internet-related activities.*
- *Unpleasant feelings (e.g. anxiety, depression, emptiness) when offline.*

- *An increasing tolerance to the effects of being online and denial of the problematic behaviours.*

This approach characterises Internet addiction as primarily behavioural and similar in character to other impulse control disorders. Those who meet the criteria are thought to experience social, psychological and occupational impairment. In much the same way that sexually abusive behaviour was initially characterised as 'addictive' in the early literature with the limitations of this framework later becoming apparent, so there are concerns about this description of problematic Internet use. Research by Caplan (2002) has suggested that the addiction framework when applied to Internet related behaviour suffers from three major limitations in this context: it lacks conceptual or theoretical specificity; there is a paucity of empirical research within the addiction paradigm and it fails to account for what people are actually doing online.

Beard and Wolf (2001: 378-81) were also critical of use of the term addiction, '. . . this term does not accurately reflect the phenomenon of excessive Internet use. While there are commonalties between excessive Internet use and an addiction, excessive Internet use does not result in all of the symptoms or behaviours associated with a chemical addiction, such as physical withdrawal'. This also raises the question as to what it actually is that people are addicted to, 'Is it the computer? Is it the typing? Is it the information gained? Is it the anonymity? Is it the types of activity in which the individual is engaged? All of these factors may play a role in making the Internet reinforcing'. Song et al. (2004) have further examined the relationship between what they have termed 'Internet gratifications' and addiction. Gratifications can be conceptualised as seeking a desired outcome, which may also include diversionary activities such as seeking entertainment or relieving boredom. These authors argued that such gratifications reflect the pursuit of self-reactive incentives. These are goal oriented efforts to adjust our own internal psychological states, which may be achieved inside the Internet media system (process), or through the Internet media system (content). An example of process might be diversion, whilst content may relate to finding a bargain flight online.

It would therefore seem important to address issues that relate not only to content of the material (Internet child abuse images) but also to the function that the Internet may be playing in the client's life.

Obsessive-compulsive behaviours

One other clinical presentation, which may be of relevance to the issue of compulsive or problematic Internet use, is that of obsessive-compulsive disorder (OCD). OCD is thought to be maintained by the escape from and avoidance of anxiety, which is accomplished by typically overt, and occasionally covert, compulsions. Overt compulsions may include activities such as checking or hand washing, whereas covert compulsions may take the form of saying certain words in one's head a given number of times. Encouraging the person to gradually tolerate more intense levels of anxiety by preventing the completion or initiation of compulsions and allowing the individual to observe that anxiety habituates both within and between exposures has been at the centre of most behavioural treatments (Whittal et al., 2002). Within this framework, a study by de Silva et al. (2002) used an exposure model to reduce covert compulsions. Such compulsions were provoked by the clinician, followed by a period of response prevention, when the client was not allowed to follow through on the normal neutralising thoughts that would reduce their feelings of anxiety. These authors found that there was a rapid and spontaneous decay of both urges and compulsions within 15 minutes of provocation, which led them to suggest that 'The challenge for the therapist . . . is to establish, with the patient, a strategy that will enable the latter to desist from carrying out the compulsion for a relatively short period'.

Intuitively, it would seem appropriate to try and reduce the compulsive element of problematic Internet use by using a similar response prevention model. But as LoPiccolo (1994) has indicated, 'The emotional valence of the emotions and behaviours involved in a paraphilia is quite the opposite of what the patient experiences in an anxiety or depressive disorder. Sexual desire is a pleasurable emotion,

and the approach behaviours motivated by it result in sexual arousal and orgasm, which are intrinsically rewarding . . . For many paraphilic patients, their deviation is ego syntonic, and it is only the societal consequences of their behaviour which causes them distress'. This comment was not made with respect to the Internet, and while it highlights the problematic nature of this population, it does not address the fact that offending may also function as a way of avoiding or changing unpleasant emotional states, rather than only being a means to sexual arousal. Unintentionally, the Internet may be an apparently perfect vehicle for this. Unlike contact offences, access to the Internet and preferred content is easily available, can be immediate, and can easily be within the user's control. Most Internet users will have their computer in an area that provides privacy, security and potentially sustained access. The offender can stay online as long as it takes for them to feel better and to secure preferred material or communication.

Emotions and sex offending

The literature pertaining to the relationship between affect, emotions and sex offending has been recently reviewed by Howells et al. (2004: 180). They have suggested that 'An emerging issue in the field of sex offender theory and treatment is whether emotional and other affective states in perpetrators are functionally important, particularly as antecedents, for offences. In rehabilitation terms, are affective states criminogenic needs?' They noted that there are problems with definition, in that negative affect is used to describe emotions, moods and feelings, and they questioned whether states such as boredom or excitement might be genuinely construed as moods. Substantial empirical support is provided for the relationship between affect and offending in relation to studies on anger and sexual arousal, offence pathways studies, and sexual fantasy studies, and concluded that the most convincing evidence for the role of affect as a causal factor in sex offending comes from the offence-process or offence chain studies. In this context, earlier work by Hudson et al. (1999) had described positive and negative affect routes to sexual offending. In their sample of offenders, 37 per cent had evidenced a positive affect chain and 44 per cent a negative affect chain. Negative affect at the onset of the offence chain was typically evidenced as depression, feeling down or lonely for child molesters and angry for rapists.

However, while Howells et al. (2004) have suggested that it is relatively easy to explain why some emotions such as anger may result in sexual aggression, it is less clear why emotions such as anxiety and sadness should elicit deviant sexual behaviour. One explanation comes from the work of Marshall and Marshall (2000) which looked at affective states and coping behaviour. These authors proposed that when in a state of negative affect, sex offenders are more likely to use sexual behaviours as a means of coping than are non-offenders. Sex becomes a way of resolving non-sexual problems which Howells et al. (2004) have suggested is reinforced and learned precisely because it is effective in reducing a state of negative affect. Linked to this is the idea that some states of emotional arousal, such as anger, anxiety and loneliness, may produce situational suppression of empathic responses and affect subsequent decision making processes. In the context of Internet related offences, a qualitative study by Quayle and Taylor (2002) found that offenders reported increased risk taking during such states and were more likely to tell themselves that the images that they were looking at were unrelated to the abuse of actual children.

A recent study by Middleton et al. (2005), examining the psychological profiles of Internet child abuse image users, based their analysis on Ward and Siegert's (2002) pathways model of child sexual abuse. This model suggests several pathways to offending including intimacy deficits, distorted sexual scripts, emotional dysregulation, antisocial cognitions and multiple dysfunctional mechanisms. Within Middleton et al.'s (2005) sample, of the 43 subjects convicted of Internet related offences, 38 per cent fell within the intimacy deficit pathway and 35 per cent within emotional dysregulation. The latter group all reported high levels of problems in dealing with negative emotions and both of these groups appeared to use sex as a coping mechanism. These authors felt that the implications of their study with regard to treatment included the importance of a functional analysis of the individual's offending behaviour; a focus within therapy on overcoming intimacy deficits or the acquisition of skills to deal with negative affect; and a focus on increasing victim awareness and empathic responses.

Implications for treatment

The possible relationship between affect and offending clearly has important implications for treatment. Howells et al. (2004) differentiated between treatment approaches that are based on antecedent-focused emotion regulation and response-focused emotion regulation. Cognitive Behaviour Therapy (CBT) might be seen as an example of the former, where offenders are helped to examine the thoughts and contexts that are associated with negative emotions and to generate alternative ways of thinking. However, Marx et al. (1999) have suggested that sexually aggressive individuals may also be reinforced through the reduction or removal of aversive stimuli, such as feelings of inadequacy or frustration resulting from life stress, rejection from another individual, lack of control, boredom or avoidance of failed relationships. In this context, relieving tension or other aversive emotional states may function as a negative reinforcer. CBT, which emphasises changing the content of cognitions, emotions and physiological states, may in fact result in further distress as thoughts and feelings are perceived by the individual as being more threatening than otherwise would be the case. In contrast to traditional CBT approaches, however, Hayes (1994) has suggested that people do not do harm to themselves by being open to their psychological experiences, but do themselves harm when they try not to think, feel and remember. Psychological acceptance, as this process may be termed, is focused on harnessing the person's capacity for deliberate change to the domains in which this effort is useful, rather than tying them to areas in which it is not. In a similar vein, Polaschek et al. (1997) proposed that increasing efforts toward emotional awareness and psychological acceptance may be a valuable addition to current treatment approaches.

Until recently, acceptance based approaches to sexual offenders have been seen as antithetical to current CBT procedures (aimed at controlling or suppressing deviant thoughts). LoPiccolo (1994) lists several factors that may have inhibited the development of acceptance-based procedures:

1. Paraphilia is a pleasurable disorder, rather than being aversive, as is the case with anxiety or depression.
2. Paraphilia is ego-syntonic for many patients.

3. Our innate sex drive implies that deviant thoughts come with a biological imperative to action that cannot be ignored, so deviant thoughts must be suppressed and not accepted.
4. There is confusion around the issue that 'acceptance' implies acceptance of deviant behaviour, with attendant harm to innocent victims.

However, as we have already considered, sexual deviation can also be a form of self-medication, to ward off anxious, lonely or depressed feelings. It can result from sexual anxiety and a means to reduce stress. Importantly from our perspective, LoPiccolo (1994) asserted, 'In all such cases, the patient typically is not allowing himself to accept the reality of his life situation and his emotional reaction to it. Instead he is displacing his emotional distress onto sexually deviant acting out'. An integration of acceptance procedures with relapse prevention would have the client accept both dysphoric emotions which previously elicited deviant behaviour, and also accept the inevitability of deviant thoughts and urges, without having to escape or avoid either types of thoughts or feelings. For many practitioners, such a therapeutic approach might seem problematic, as rather than challenging the thoughts that are meant to be inextricably linked to dangerous behaviour we are asking offenders to accept the thoughts-as-thoughts, rather than thoughts-as-actions. Our culture embraces the notion that positive emotions, cognitions, and bodily states cause good behaviour and negative emotions, cognitions and bodily states cause bad behaviour (Wilson and Roberts, 2002). Practitioners have therefore tended to focus treatment on the elimination or reduction of problematic private events, such as thoughts and feelings. However, attempts to suppress or avoid negative private events may work to reduce those negative states over the short term, but may actually worsen outcomes in the long-term. Fennell (2004: 1054) has suggested that '. . . rather than seeking to alter the content of cognitions (the intervention that constitutes the meat and drink of classical cognitive therapy), we should seek to reduce their unhelpful impact by changing the nature of the patient's relationship with them'. Acceptance based treatments for experiential avoidance seek to ameliorate avoidance in the sense of increasing the client's capacity to engage in a rich and meaningful life. The focus then is changing behaviour rather than doing battle with private events.

The theoretical background to such acceptance procedures is different to that underpinning simple response prevention, and while it is beyond the scope of this chapter to examine the relevant literature of this area in detail, a brief overview of the development of this subject is presented here. Clinical behaviour analysis is a relatively recent and rapidly growing branch of applied behaviour analysis (which focuses on the use of contingency management procedures to treat severely impaired populations such as autism) and emphasises the use of verbally based interventions to treat verbally competent clients who seek treatment for problems such as anxiety, depression, personality disorders, substance abuse, stress disorders and relationship difficulties.

The origins of clinical behaviour analysis are in the work of Skinner (1953; 1957; 1974), Ferster (1972a; 1972b), Goldiamond (1974) and Hawkins (1986). Two sets of events have been particularly important to the development of the field. The first is the relatively recent and rapid increase in basic research on verbal behaviour. The second set of events that has significantly affected the growth and direction of clinical behaviour analysis was the development of Kohlenberg and Tsai's Functional Analytic Psychotherapy (FAP), (Kohlenberg and Tsai, 1991) and Hayes' Acceptance and Commitment Therapy (ACT) (Hayes and Wilson, 1994; Hayes, Strosahl and Wilson, 1999). To a large extent, FAP relies on direct contingency shaping of client related behaviours. However, it incorporates a basic premise of psychodynamic therapies, that the best place to observe and modify these behaviours is within the therapeutic session. ACT, on the other hand, stems directly from a radical behavioural perspective on private experience (i.e., thoughts, emotions and bodily sensations) and recent research on derived stimulus relations. Its aim is to help clients to openly experience both private and public events as they are and without distortion. While ACT may broadly be identified as a cognitive behavioural therapy, perhaps surprisingly, its objectives and some of its techniques are similar to those advocated by Eastern psychology, Gestalt therapies and existential therapies.

Hayes and Wilson (1994) state that though acceptance is often non-technically defined as a willingness to experience events fully and without defence, its technical definition refers to a willingness to make contact with the automatic and direct stimulus functions of events without acting to control, reduce, eliminate, or otherwise reduce the frequency, occurrence, or impact of such events. In contrast, 'Experiential avoidance is the phenomenon that occurs when a person is unwilling to remain in contact with private experiences (e.g. bodily sensations, emotions, thoughts, memories, behavioural predispositions) and takes steps to alter the form or frequency of these events and the contexts that occasion them, even when doing so creates life harm' (Hayes and Wilson, 2003: 162). Arising out of this radical behavioural perspective, acceptance is seen as a stated goal and refers to the client's willingness to experience a full range of emotions, thoughts, memories, bodily states and behavioural predispositions without having to change, escape from or avoid them.

Kohlenberg et al. (1993) have suggested that when private behaviours need not be changed, their controlling effects over overt behaviour might be reduced considerably, and concern could shift from emotional or cognitive manipulation to overt action. Within the context of concern here, this is an important point. Paul et al. (1999) used such an acceptance-based therapy in the successful treatment of a client displaying exhibitionistic behaviour. The therapeutic approach was that of Acceptance and Commitment Therapy, the main goals of which were to give the client a counterintuitive method of accepting rather than eliminating troublesome internal events and to focus on long-term adaptive behaviour. These authors give an overview of the therapeutic stages involved:

1. To understand that previous struggles to control their inner experiences have been unsuccessful (also termed 'creative hopelessness).
2. To see that previous struggles may have made matters worse (with control as a problem).
3. To help clients delineate between their personal self and their cognitive, emotional and physiological experiences.
4. To willingly experience the aversive private events that they had previously avoided to accomplish their previously unreachable goals.
5. The client committing to making change.

In the context of substance abuse (which possibly shares some of the characteristics of problematic Internet use at least in its relation to poor impulse control) Forsyth et al. (2002) suggest that the efficacy of treatment strategies may improve where there is an attempt to increase patients' sense of control over their own responses and the environment, and where intervention decreases attempts to avoid unpleasant emotions. Inevitably, however, impulsive behaviour is also related to problems of self-control, conceptualised by Gifford (2002: 126–7) as a conflict between present and future gratification. Gifford suggested that since humans are a highly visual species, delay of gratification tasks are particularly taxing on self-control when the reward or other consequence may be visible for the individual during the delay period. For the Internet offender, the presence of the computer may elicit a pre-potent response, while alternatives that are more abstract, or are not present, are weighed less highly. They argue that 'When contemplating this choice problem in abstract, those with self-control problems understand their difficulties, but when faced with a real choice they cannot muster enough inhibition to deliberate – they simply grab the pre-potent option'. However, these authors suggested that people with better initial self-control are able to employ 'rule-following' behaviour, involving internal speech, which further facilitates self-control. 'Use of internal speech shifts the deliberation process to the symbolic level and reduces the saliency of pre-potent stimuli'. However, the problem of self-control may also be resolved by making contact with the harmful long-term effects of immediately reinforced acts (Kudadjie and Rachlin, 2002).

Values

How do we convince clients that it is worth engaging with their emotional distress without using the Internet as a means of avoidance? In addition, we are also asking them to forego the immediate pleasure and gratification that comes from accessing and using child abuse images. One potentially powerful strategy, that lies at the heart of all acceptance based treatments, is getting the client to explicitly state their values and to look at how immediate gratification may inhibit their ability to fulfil those values. Ward (2002: 514–5) has argued that such a strategy implicitly lies at the heart of all sex offender treatment programmes, which conceptualise possible good lives for offenders and the necessary internal and external conditions for living such lives. He says, '. . . individuals are unlikely to refrain from offending if their lives are characterised by an absence of valued outcomes . . . one of the reasons individuals commit crimes is that they are perceived to be rewarding in some ways, a criminal lifestyle represents one way of achieving personal goods . . . offenders need to make their own choices and this is guided by a conception of good lives and the belief that it is possible to achieve different ways of living in the world'.

Ward goes on to discuss the fact that while the role of values in the rehabilitation of offenders has often been acknowledged, there has been little discussion of the explicit ways in which this should occur. He suggests that '. . . it is necessary for individuals working to rehabilitate offenders to explicitly construct conceptions of good lives for different offenders and to use these conceptions to shape the behaviour change process'. Ward used a study by Maruna (2001:524–6) who interviewed offenders desisting from and persisting with lives of crime to illustrate his argument. The major tasks for offenders attempting to live a crime-free life was to 'make good' by working out a different way to live based on a clear set of personal values and a consistent self-narrative. Ward suggests that, 'This means that therapists attempting to rehabilitate offenders ought to be guided by an awareness of the role that values and primary human goods play in facilitating well-being'. However, values cannot be pre-packaged, and what is relevant to one offender may not be for another, 'The reliance on manual-based interventions in the treatment of offenders can add to this problem. Because therapists tend to follow standardised procedures, they may fail to consider the appropriate form of life for a given individual'. Ward and Marshall (2004: 155) have argued that the focus of treatment models on risk management has led to a lack of attention to personal identity and human needs and, 'the perception of offenders as bundles of risk factors rather than integrated, complex beings who are seeking to give value and meaning to their lives'.

In contrast, acceptance based therapies such as ACT are values oriented interventions, which focus on valuing as an activity. Quite literally the client is being asked to 'value with their feet', and to begin to experience their life as chosen rather than imposed. ACT is not aimed at making people feel better feelings and think better thoughts, but at helping people live better lives, where 'better' is 'always gauged by the extent to which people are living lives that are consistent with their values' (Wilson et al., 2000: 227). An active part of this approach is the assessment of client values, where the practitioner's role is to clarify the direction inherent in what might be fairly concrete valued ends. The practitioner also assesses variables controlling the client's statements about valued ends, and should attempt to intervene when the responses are based on 'pliance' (these might be statements controlled by the presence of the practitioner, or by the emotional proximity of others such as parents, or that may be culturally desirable values). The assessment of values is followed by the generation of goals and actions that are relevant to those values, and the examination of private events that act as barriers to moving forward in their life in these areas. Underlying this is the assumption that emotional acceptance is a means to an end, and putting values into action is that end. Although coming from a very different perspective, such individual operationalisation of values and goals in the context of emotional acceptance would seem to have relevance to Ward's (2002) critique of current Sex Offender Treatment Programmes. With Internet offenders it would allow an exploration of the function of the Internet in terms of individual needs, and how far immediate emotional avoidance and gratification reduced the likelihood of the offender realising his personal values.

ACT

Traditionally therapeutic strategies in this area have focused on control skills (for example distraction techniques). Ward and Brown (2004: 245) have argued that this places an emphasis on negative, or avoidant treatment goals and suggested that, 'The focus is on the *reduction* of maladaptive behaviours, the *elimination* of distorted beliefs, the *removal* of problematic desires, and the *modification* of offence supportive emotions and attitudes'. The concern is with 'eradicating factors rather than promoting pro-social and personally more satisfying goals'. In the context of exploring personal values, acceptance skills focus instead on encouraging the client to experience private events (emotions, thoughts, bodily sensations) without trying to change them. One of the most important acceptance skills is mindfulness, which consists of six specific skills:

1. Observing.
2. Describing.
3. Participating spontaneously.
4. Being non-judgmental.
5. Being mindful or focusing attention completely and only on one thing at a time.
6. Focusing on what is effective in a given situation.

Mindfulness is not unique to ACT and historically has been associated with Buddhist teachings. Hayes and Wilson (2003: 161) have been critical of the ways that mindfulness has been treated '. . . sometimes as a technique, sometimes as a more general method or collection of techniques, sometimes as a physiological process that can produce outcomes, and sometimes as an outcome in and of itself'. For practitioners this can be confusing as the actual principles that unite all of these levels typically remain unspecified. In the context of ACT, the goal of mindfulness is to develop a life style of participating with awareness. Participating without awareness it is assumed, is a characteristic of impulsive and mood dependent behaviours. Self-conscious observing and describing of one's own behaviour is usually only necessary when a new behaviour is being learned or change is necessary. For example, beginner drivers pay close attention to the location of their hands and feet and might mentally check off or rehearse verbally aloud what they are doing, what other cars are doing, and what instructions they should follow as they drive. As skills improve, however, such observing and describing drop out. But if an habitual mistake is made after learning to drive, the driver may have to revert back to observing and describing until a new pattern has been learned.

A part of mindfulness is learning to observe internal and external events without necessarily trying to terminate them when painful, or prolong them when pleasant. Rather than leaving the situation or trying to inhibit the emotion, the individual attends to experience no matter how distressing that attention may be. This focus is based on Eastern psychological approaches to reducing suffering as well as on Western theories of non-reinforced exposure (similar to that used with OCD) as a method of extinguishing automatic avoidance and fear responses. Marcks and Woods (2004) reported a comparison of

thought suppression to an acceptance based technique in the management of personal intrusive thoughts. Their results suggested that those who tended to be more accepting of their target intrusive thoughts experienced lower levels of depression, obsessionality and anxiety. Observation of and acceptance of thoughts was also, paradoxically, associated with a lower level of intrusive thoughts and less discomfort when they did occur. This may be because an 'accept-and-move-on strategy' provides an opportunity for the intrusion to remain a *fleeting* thought (Kavanagh et al., 2004). A second mindfulness skill is that of verbally describing events and personal responses. Here, the focus is on learning how to differentiate literal events from thoughts and feelings about those events. Describing requires one to be able to 'step back' from events, so to speak. This strategy is very similar to the treatment strategies described in ACT therapy.

Non-judgmental stance

A third skill is participating. In the context of mindfulness skills, this is entering completely into the activities of the current moment, without separating one's self from ongoing events and interactions. Most of us are ordinarily largely unaware of our moment-to-moment experience, and often operate on an 'automatic pilot mode' (Grossman et al., 2004). A good example of mindful participating is the skillful athlete who responds flexibly but smoothly to the demands of the task with alertness and awareness but not with self-consciousness. Non-judgmental stance requires the individual to take a non-evaluative approach, judging something as neither good nor bad. It does not mean going from a negative judgment to a positive judgment. The position here is not that clients should be more balanced in their judgments but rather that judging should, in most instances be dropped altogether. For example, saying that 'every day is a good day' would be the same as saying, 'every day is a bad day'. The point may be subtle but it is, nonetheless, a very important one. The idea is that if one can be worthwhile, one can always in the next moment, become worthless. From a non-judgmental stance, a focus on the consequences of behaviour and events replaces evaluations of good and bad. A non-judgmental approach observes painful or destructive events and consequences of events, and might suggest changing behaviour or events, but would not necessarily add a label of bad to the behaviour and events. Singh et al. (2004: 281), in the context of mindfulness-based treatment for obsessive-compulsive disorder, have suggested that enhanced mindfulness '. . . brings the person's consciousness into the present moment and allows the person to be fully engaged with her environment, calmly paying attention moment by moment. This allows the person to make conscious choices in terms of how to act, based on her awareness of her thoughts, feelings, and emotions. Furthermore, the individual has a choice of either acting in the physical sense or simply being aware of her thoughts, feelings and emotions and letting them go without judging or engaging them or trying to remove them in a mental or physical sense'.

One-mindfulness

Doing one thing at a time refers to focusing the mind and awareness in the current moment's activity rather than splitting attention between several activities or between a current activity and thinking about something else. Such one-mindfulness requires control of attention. Like participation described above, one-mindfulness requires for its practice acceptance of the moment since a focus on change, i.e., on a different but changed moment, of necessity interferes with staying in the current moment. Focusing one's attention in a non-judgmental or accepting way on the experience within the present moment can be contrasted with states of mind in which attention is focused elsewhere, including preoccupation with memories, fantasies, plans or worries, and behaving automatically without awareness of one's actions (Baer et al., 2004). Often clients in therapy are distracted by thoughts and images of the past, worries about the future, ruminative thoughts about troubles, or current negative moods. They are sometimes unable to put their troubles away to focus attention on the task at hand. The desire to get out of the current moment or to repair the past is so great that staying in the present is nearly impossible. The focus of one-mindfulness practice is to teach the client how to focus attention on one task or activity at a time, engaging in it with alertness and awareness. Clients are encouraged to bring an attitude of friendly curiosity, interest and acceptance to all observed phenomena while refraining from

evaluation, self-criticism, or attempts to eliminate or change the events they observe. Cognitions and emotions are simply noted and observed as they come and go. Baer et al. (2004) have suggested that when thoughts are seen as just thoughts, numerous, transient and not necessitating specific behaviours, this may result in improved observation skills, which may lead to better recognition of sensations, cognitions and emotional states and an improved ability to respond skillfully to these phenomena as they arise.

Effectiveness refers to 'Doing what works', and the focus on effectiveness within mindfulness is directed at balancing the tendency to focus on what is 'right' with a corresponding emphasis on doing what is needed to be effective in a particular situation. A central issue for many clients is whether they can indeed trust their own perceptions, judgments and decisions; can they expect their own actions to be correct or 'right'. Taken to an extreme, an emphasis on principle over outcome can lead to disappointment and alienation of others. Clients often find it much easier to give up being right for being effective when it is viewed as a skillful response rather than as giving up or giving in.

Distress tolerance skills

Representing a natural progression from mindfulness skills, distress tolerance skills represent the ability to experience and observe one's thoughts, emotions and bodily states without evaluation and without attempting to change or control them (Lenihan, 1993: 1994). Distress tolerance skills focus on both tolerating and radically accepting reality just as it is in the moment. Such acceptance does not include resigning oneself to all experiences of suffering, but does include facing and tolerating some suffering so that an ultimately healthy course of action can be followed. McCracken et al. (2004: 6), in the context of chronic physical pain, have suggested that 'acceptance is not a global act of resignation or quitting. It is acknowledging reality and quitting efforts that are not working so that workable efforts can be pursued and meaningful goals achieved'. The focus in most standard behaviour and cognitive therapies on ameliorating distressing emotions and events is balanced by a corresponding emphasis on learning to bear pain skillfully. The automatic inhibition or avoidance of painful emotions, situations, thoughts, etc. is viewed as an important component in psychological dysfunction and the prolongation of the very pain one is seeking to avoid. Tolerating distress does not imply giving up or necessarily approving of the situation, but it allows one to cope with pain in the moment to reduce long-term suffering. Indeed, the premise is that tolerance and acceptance of a situation as it is in the moment are prerequisites of any coherent and effective change strategy. Distress tolerance skills are aimed at tolerating distress – rather than impulsively acting to remove the pain without thought of whether the act would lead to more distress in the long run. Four sets of distress tolerance are taught:

1. Distraction skills, which focus on occupying the mind or the body with other sensations, perceptions, thoughts, activities, etc.
2. Self-soothing skills, which focus on comforting and encouraging one's self until the painful event is lessened or over.
3. Improving the moment, which includes imaginal and cognitive-verbal strategies for changing the meaning of an event until the stress is relieved.
4. Pros and cons, which require one to review the pros of tolerating versus the cons of not tolerating. The skills are taught as 'crisis survival skills' and the task is presented much like the task of the individual in prison: if you have to stay in prison for a number of years, it is more adaptive to find a way to tolerate it while there rather than only fight to get out.

Values and goals

A key aspect of this approach is to help clients to recognise in their own lives behavioural goals related to what they *value* and to help them to commit themselves to these goals. Valuing as described by Hayes et al. (1999) is action of a special kind; it is the kind that cannot be evaluated by the person engaging in it. Values can motivate behaviour even in the face of tremendous personal adversity. Valuing is seen as a choice, not a judgment. Acceptance of negative thoughts, memories, and emotions is legitimate and honorable only to the extent that it serves ends that are valued by the client.

Several distinctions need to be made when discussing the issue of values. Among the most important is distinguishing valuing as a feeling versus valuing as an action. These two aspects are

often thoroughly confused for the client. The example of valuing a loving relationship is instructive. One's feelings of love may come and go across time and situations. To behave lovingly, (e.g., respectfully, thoughtfully, etc.) only when one has feelings of love, and to behave in opposite ways when the opposite feelings emerge, would be very likely to have problematic effects on the relationship. Yet, this is precisely the problem we are in when values are confused with feelings, because feelings are not fully under voluntary control and tend to come and go. The cultural context that supports the association between feelings of love and acts of love is the same cultural context that supports the client with agoraphobia staying at home in the presence of high anxiety and the client downloading child abuse images in the presence of strong urges. If the client bases living entirely on the absence of emotional or cognitive obstacles, then valued directions cannot be pursued in a committed fashion, because sooner or later the obstacle (e.g. a sexual urge) will be encountered. Valuing as a behaviour is always occurring in the client's life. It cannot be avoided, no matter how shut down and benumbed the client is. Why might this be the case? Because most behaviour is purposeful, whether there is an experienced sense of direction or not.

The values assessment process serves a variety of assessment and intervention purposes. First, the client may become aware of long suppressed values. This process is motivational in the sense that the client may find major discrepancies between valued versus current behaviour. Second, the process of values assessment can help to highlight a place in the client's life in which things are 'better'. A person's values may not be what someone else thinks they should be, but are always complete within themselves. The assessment of values, goals, actions and barriers can be effected through the completion of a series of structured exercises, using materials developed by Hayes et al. (1999) and Luciano and Wilson (2002). The values assessment work sheets are reviewed by the practitioner and client and then modified in a collaborative fashion. The practitioner's task is to attempt to clarify the direction inherent in what might be fairly concrete valued ends. The practitioner should also attempt to assess for other factors that may be influencing the client's statements about valued ends: the presence of the practitioner; cultural factors; immediate family members.

It would be difficult to imagine a client who would have values that were not controlled in part by all of the aforementioned variables. The key is whether the removal of an influence would significantly affect the potency of the value as a source of life direction. This task cannot be completed in one discussion. The issue of 'ownership' of a value is likely to resurface time and again. Some of these issues may be addressed by asking the client to talk about the value while imagining the absence of a relevant social consequence. To illustrate, consider a client who forwards the value of being well educated. The practitioner may ask if the level of valuing (or the value itself) would change if it had to be enacted anonymously: 'Imagine that you had the opportunity to further education, but you could not tell anyone about the degree you achieve. Would you still devote yourself to achieving it?'

The client is asked to generate responses in various life domains. Clients may leave domains empty or generate very superficial answers. Here, the practitioner needs to patiently and in a non-confrontational way, discuss each domain. It often helps to go back earlier in the client's life and look for examples of wishes and hopes that have disappeared because of negative life events. At other times the practitioner may have to assist the client either in generating the directions inherent in specific life goals or, conversely, in generating specific goals from more global directions. The client may also list ends that are not possible. For example, a man may say that he wants to gain custody of children that he has not seen for 10 years. In such instances, the practitioner tries to find the underlying value and goals that might be achievable if one were moving in that direction.

The assessment requires the client to focus on developing goals and specifying the actions to be taken to achieve those goals. This is the most applied part of the assessment and the most critical, because it directs the therapy. The work on goals, actions and barriers stands on the foundation of the client's values. Given the direction specified in each life domain, the client is asked to generate specific goals. A goal is defined as a specific achievement, accomplished in the service of a specific value. The client defines the actions that would be likely to achieve the goal. The practitioner and client try to generate acts that can take the form of homework. In some cases they may involve single instances.

At other times they may involve a commitment to repeated and regular acts.

Effective behavioural goal setting requires a candid analysis of the barriers the client is likely to encounter that may forestall action. Barriers may involve negative psychological reactions or pressure from outside sources. Negative anticipatory emotions such as fear, anxiety or shame may also appear. If previous therapy has been successful, the client may be ready to recognise the barriers for what they are, not for what they advertise themselves to be. Part of the values clarification process helps the client identify the barriers to valued action in each domain. As these barriers are discussed the practitioner helps the client to examine several issues: what type of barrier is this (is it negative or private events or an external consequence that conflicts with another value?); if this barrier did indeed present itself, is it something that the client is willing to experience? what aspect of the barrier is most capable of reducing the client's willingness to experience it?; are any of these barriers another form of emotional control or emotional avoidance?

A common problem that may occur at this point is the practitioner's inability to detect goals that are presented as values by the client. For example, the client may say, 'I want to be happy'. This sounds like a value, but it is not. Being happy is something you can have or not have, like an object. A value is a direction – a quality of action. By definition, values cannot be achieved and maintained in a static state, they must be lived out. When goals are mistakenly taken as values, the inability to achieve a goal seemingly cancels out the value. A practical way to avoid this confusion is to place any goal or value statement produced by the client, under the following microscope: 'What is this in the service of?' or 'What would you be able to do if that was accomplished?' Very often this exercise may highlight the hidden value that has not been stated. Some values are really means to an end, in which case they are not values at all. Experiential avoidance is a good example of this.

Marx et al. (1999: 887) have suggested that this approach might be used in the context of a different group of sexual offenders, rapists, suggesting that 'instead of an emphasis on changing or controlling psychological events, the emphasis should be on changing the context in which the rapist experiences his deviant thoughts, feelings or sensations'. Thoughts, feelings and emotional arousal therefore need not be seen as a reason for behaving in a particular way, and moves the offender away from thinking of such experiences as behavioural imperatives. In the context of making values explicit, the offender is being given the opportunity to learn to tolerate levels of emotional distress without having to escape or avoid them (for example, through downloading and masturbating to child abuse images) in order to be able to work towards a 'good life' which has personal, rather than imposed, relevance. As yet there is little empirical evidence on which to judge the effectiveness of acceptance-based therapies with sex offenders who have downloaded abusive images from the Internet. There is, however, a body of both research and intervention with other clinical populations who engage in emotional avoidance (Jacobson et al., 2000; Wilson et al., 2000; Wilson and Roberts, 2002; McCracken et al., 2004; Grossman et al., 2004), and this approach may offer a particularly attractive alternative to existing CBT approaches.

Howells et al. (2004) concluded 'Improving our understanding of the affective dimensions of sex offending is an important task for the future'. In the context of the heterogeneous Internet offender population, such understanding is likely to be furthered by a framework that helps us examine the function of the behaviours for the individual. This will help us move away from a generic model of treatment that exists in many current sex offender treatment programmes to help us focus on what might work for the individual. Middleton (2004: 110), in his review of current treatments for sex offenders stated that 'At the very least the treatment needs to be based on a specific assessment of the individual including the context in which the behaviour was developed and sustained. Most human behaviour can be understood as meeting needs for the individual and, in order to be effective, treatment will help the individual to meet these needs in a more appropriate manner.' This does not require us to abandon the substantial body of work that exists in relation to the treatment of sex offenders, but rather return to a model that places an emphasis on the individual and acknowledges that people may behave in ways that are topographically alike but which function in very different ways across individuals. Clearly for some offenders, but not all, accessing child abuse images on the Internet may function as a way of avoiding or dealing with difficult emotional states

and we need to at least see this as worthy of assessment in the context of providing effective treatment. Hayes and Wilson (2003) concluded 'The problem is not the presence of particular thoughts, emotions, sensations or urges: It is the constriction of a human life. The solution is not removal of difficult private events: It is living a valued life' (p 165). This would seem to have a resonance for this offender group.

Areas of concern

- Sexual activities may be used as a way of avoiding aversive emotional states as well as a means of satisfying sexual urges.
- For some clients there is a compulsive quality to this that they may label as 'addictive'.
- Internet use may be associated with other obsessional activities, or may be related to anxiety or depressive states.
- Acceptance based approaches may be associated with an initial increase in distress and should only be negotiated with respect for the client and an exploration of valued directions that they wish to pursue in their lives.

Working with the client

Values clarification and assessment of values, goals, actions and barriers

The values assessment process is an important part of intervention. It enables the client to gain insight into values that may have been suppressed and motivates the client to examine the discrepancies between what they value and their current behaviour. For example, we may all say that we value living a healthy life, but if we look at our current lifestyles we may see that what we value bears little or no relationship to what we do. Secondly, the process of values assessment might help identify a better life. This is similar to the emphasis placed on treatment by Ward and Marshall (2004). Our values may not always fit with what others think they should be, but in the context of therapy they are seen as complete in themselves.

1. The values assessment process consists of the following steps:

- The practitioner describes the Values Assessment Exercise to the client (see end of this chapter).

- The client completes the Values Assessment Exercise.
- The practitioner and the client discuss values in each domain and generate brief values narratives that simplify, focus and encapsulate the free-form values statements from the exercise. Typically, the main task is to help the client distinguish goals from values and to state their values in terms of directions, not merely concrete ends (see the Values Narrative Form).
- The practitioner distributes the Valued Living Questionnaire which is rated by client.
- The practitioner and the client collaborate to generate Goals, Actions and Barriers related to the client's stated values (see Goals, Actions and Barriers Form).

The values assessment, as with other CBT approaches, is collaborative. At this stage, the role of the therapist is to try and discover the direction of the value, rather than the more concrete goals that may be seen as the end achievements of the value.

2. Assessing goals and actions

This part of the assessment is central because it will give a direction to the therapy. The work on goals, actions and barriers is intrinsically based on the client's values. The value assessment focuses on different life domains, and the client is asked to specify goals in each of these. Goals are the specific achievements linked to, and in the service of, a specific value. The client is helped to identify the steps that they might take to achieve that specific goal. This will inevitably involve work outside the therapeutic session and may take the form of 'homework' tasks. As with problem solving, sometimes there may be only one step needed to accomplish a goal, and on other occasions there may be many.

3. Identifying and undermining barriers

To be effective in setting goals, the client needs to be helped to identify the barriers that they anticipate will slow down or get in the way of effective action. Such barriers may include negative private events, such as unpleasant emotions or thoughts, or events that are external to the client. Sometimes when a client has already experienced therapy, they can see these barriers as what they are, rather than what they might appear to be. The therapist needs to help the client identify barriers across all the domains.

This process may help the client examine several issues:

- What type of barrier is this? Is it negative or private events or an external consequence that conflicts with another value?
- If this barrier did indeed present itself, is it something that the client is willing to experience?
- What aspect of the barrier is most capable of reducing the client's willingness to experience it?
- Are any of these barriers another form of emotional control or emotional avoidance?

4. Confusing values and goals

A common problem that the practitioner needs to be aware of is that the client may identify values which are really goals. As previously mentioned, values are a direction – a quality of an action. They are dynamic rather than static, aspirational rather than concrete ends. This is important because during therapy we may have to evaluate our ability to achieve certain goals. If this is confused with values, then clients may feel that a value is pointless because it has not been achieved.

There may also be a cultural aspect to this in terms of a focus on object-like outcomes (e.g. goals that are attained). In most cases, the first time the client completes the values exercise it will be an exercise in goal definition, not in values clarification. The practitioner can attempt to detect this confusion of process and outcome and help the client connect specific behavioural goals to values.

Conclusion of this phase is marked by the completion of the values, goals, actions and barriers exercise, and when the identified barriers have been reduced to the 'critical few'. Another indicator that this phase is over may be the client's emerging readiness to engage in action. The client may still report anxiety or uncertainty about handling the 'fallout' from engaging in committed action. At the same time the client may have connected to values and have focused on goals and actions that promise to make life better if they are put into motion.

Changing behaviour

Some of the following may be new to practitioners and is therefore outlined in more detail than in other chapters.

Exercises

1. Learning acceptance skills

Traditionally therapeutic strategies in this area have focused on control skills (for example distraction techniques). Acceptance skills focus instead on encouraging the client to experience private events (emotions, thoughts, bodily sensations) without trying to change them.

2. Mindfulness

Mindfulness skills

Emotion mind and *reasonable mind* are defined as states of being where thoughts, actions and feelings are under the primary influence of concurrent high emotional arousal (emotion mind) or of non aroused intellectual and or rational thought (reasonable mind). *Wise mind* is a functioning which reflects a synthesis of contextual influence with balanced awareness of both events that are currently happening as well as of emotional responses to these events.

Mindfulness skills are presented as the vehicles for balancing emotion mind and reasonable mind to achieve wise mind. Accessing wise mind is presented as a conscious effort to take in the entire context that is relevant to a particular problem or moment as well as to become aware of one's immediate and primary response to that context. In contrast to some approaches to treatment, which put very high value on rational thought, intuitive thought and responses are presented as equally valuable and trustworthy.

States of mind

- *Reasonable mind*

Reasonable mind can be very beneficial. Without it, people could not build homes, roads, or cities; they could not follow instructions; they could not solve logical problems, or run meetings. Reasonable mind is easier when people feel good, and much harder when they don't. When other people say that 'if you could just think straight you would be all right,' they mean that 'if you could be in reasonable mind you would do okay'. Elicit from clients times other people have said or implied that if they would just not distort, exaggerate, or misperceive things, they would have far fewer problems. How many times have clients said the same thing to themselves? Is there any truth to these positions?

- *Emotion mind*

Explain that 'you are in your emotion mind when your emotions are in control – when they influence and control your thinking and your behaviour'. Emotion mind can be very beneficial. Intense love (or intense hate) has fuelled wars. Intense devotion can motivate staying with very hard tasks. A certain amount of emotion mind is desirable. People high in emotion mind are often passionate about people, causes, beliefs, etc. Problems with emotion mind occur when the results are positive in the short term but negative in the long term, or when the experience itself is very painful, or leads to painful states and events (e.g., anxiety and depression can be painful in themselves). Emotion mind is exacerbated by illness; sleep deprivation; tiredness; drugs; alcohol; hunger; overeating; poor nutrition; environmental distress (too many demands); and environmental threats. Elicit other factors from clients.

- *Reasonable mind and Emotion mind*

Discuss pros and cons of both types of mind. Draw from clients their experience of *reasonable mind* and *emotion mind*.

- *Wise mind*

Explain: 'wise mind is the integration of emotion mind and reasonable mind. You cannot overcome emotion mind with reasonable mind. Nor can you create emotions with reasonableness. You must go within and integrate the two'. Wise mind is that part of each person that can know and experience truth. It is where the person knows something to be true or valid. It is almost always quiet; it has a certain peace. Wisdom, or wise mind depends on the integration of all ways of knowing something: knowing by observing, knowing by analysing logically, knowing by what we experience in our bodies, knowing by what we do and knowing by intuition. Everyone has a wise mind; some simply have never experienced it. Also, no one is in wise mind all the time. Get feedback from clients on their own experiences of wise mind. Clients will sometimes say that they don't have wise mind. Believe in the clients' abilities to find wise mind. Wise mind is like having a heart; everyone has one, whether they experience it or not. The 'Well' analogy may be useful to describe the concept of wise mind to the client. Explain:

Wise mind is like a deep well in the ground. The water at the bottom of the well, the entire underground ocean is wise mind. But on the way down there are often trapdoors that impede progress. Sometimes the trapdoors are so cleverly built that you actually believe that there is no water at the bottom of the well. Perhaps it is locked and you need a key. Perhaps it is nailed shut and you need a hammer.

Elicit an example from the client. Wise mind is sometimes experienced in the centre of the body (the belly) or in the centre of the head, or between the eyes. Sometimes the person can find it by following the breath in and out. Have clients attend to their breath coming in and out as they breathe naturally and deeply, and after some time try to let their attention settle into their centre, at the bottom of their inhalation. Elicit the client's experience.

- *Emotion mind versus wise mind:* how to know the difference

Emotion mind and wise mind both have a quality of 'feeling' something to be the case. The intensity of emotions can generate experiences of certainty that mimic the stable certainty of wisdom. Continue the analogy above: 'After heavy rain, water can collect on a trap door within the well. You may then confuse the still water on the trap door with the deep ocean at the bottom of the well'. There is no simple solution here. Suggest: 'If intense emotion is obvious, suspect emotion mind. Give it time; if certainty remains, especially when you are feeling calm and secure, suspect wise mind'. Ask clients for other ideas on how to tell the difference.

As previously discussed, the formal mindfulness skills practice consists of six specific skills:

1. Observing.
2. Describing.
3. Participating spontaneously.
4. Being non-judgmental.
5. Being mindful or focusing attention completely and only on one thing at a time.
6. Focusing on what is effective in a given situation.

- **Observing:** If we participate in living our lives without awareness, then we are more likely to engage in impulsive or mood dependent behaviours. For the most part we do not need to self-consciously observe or describe our behaviour. This sometimes happens when the behaviour is new to us, or where we have to make changes to our behaviour. For example, many complicated tasks follow a sequence, and when we are learning the sequence we might verbally rehearse each step. As we are successful in the task, we no longer observe and describe, but simply 'get on with it'. However, if the task changes in some way, we might have to revert back to our earlier behaviour.

As part of mindfulness, we have to learn to observe both internal and external events without having to change them. We do not need to try and prolong feelings that are pleasant or end those that are painful or uncomfortable. Rather than escaping from the situation or trying to block or inhibit the feelings, the goal is to experience and be present to how we feel, no matter how distressing that may be.

- **Describing:** The second mindfulness skill is being able to describe both events and our responses to them. We are very much focusing on being able to distinguish actual events from the way that we think and feel about them. Many clients find this difficult, as they are being asked to step back from the events themselves.
- **Participating spontaneously:** Often we struggle to distance ourselves from our experiences. Here participating is about entering completely into what we are experiencing in the current moment.
- **Being non-judgmental:** For much of the time we make judgments about events and our experiences of them. We see some feelings (such as anxiety or depression) as bad. A non-judgmental stance requires the client not to evaluate but to let go of judging. This allows us to observe and make changes to our behaviour or events, but without giving them a label of bad or dangerous.
- **Being mindful or focusing attention completely and only on one thing at a time:** This refers to focusing our attention on the current moment's activity, rather than trying to move between several activities or between one activity while thinking about something else. Most of us would have had the experience of something as simple as eating a bar of chocolate while using the computer. Only when we see the empty wrapper do we realise that the chocolate has been eaten. Instead we are asking the client to control their attention and stay in the moment. Often we are

distracted by thoughts about the past, or worries that we may have about the future. It can be difficult to put these thoughts to one side and focus on the task in hand. Indeed, very often we give these thoughts such importance that the imperative is to stay there and try to repair or dilute what is troubling us. This means that staying in the present moment becomes almost impossible. The focus of one-mindfulness practice is to teach the client how to focus attention on one task or activity at a time, engaging in it with alertness and awareness.

- **Focusing on what is effective in a given situation:** This is not the same as 'doing what we want to do', but rather is an attempt to balance what we think is 'right' with an equal emphasis on what we need to do to be effective in a particular situation.

Explain the focus of mindfulness skills

'Learning to be in control of your own mind, instead of letting your mind be in control of you'. To a certain extent, being in control of ones mind is actually learning to be in control of attention processes – that is one pays attention to how long one pays attention to it. Draw from clients' examples of how their inability to control their attention creates problems. Examples may include inability to stop thinking about things, (e.g. an image of a child); inability to concentrate on a task when it is important to do so; inability to focus on another person or to stay on a task because of distraction (e.g. thoughts of going on-line while with others or at work).

Mindfulness skills require continual practice

Discuss with client the crucial importance of behavioural practice in learning any new skill. Behavioural practice includes practicing control of one's mind, attention, overt behaviour, body, and emotions. Draw from clients their beliefs about the necessity of practice in learning: 'can you learn without practice?' See the end of the chapter for guidelines on mindfulness skills.

Exercises for types of mindfulness skills

Describe two types of mindfulness skills:

1. 'What' skills (i.e. what to do).
2. 'How' skills (i.e. how to do it).

With respect to 'What' skills, it is very important to point out that a person can only do one thing at a time – observe, or describe, or participate, but not all three at once. In contrast, the 'How' skills can be applied all at once.

1. 'What' skills

- **Observing.** Explain: Observing is sensing or experiencing without describing or labelling the experience. It is noticing or attending to something. Have clients try some of the following.
  1. Experience your hand on a cool surface (e.g. a table or chair) or a warm surface (e.g. your other hand).
  2. Attend to and try to sense your stomach, your shoulders.
  3. Watch in your mind the first two thoughts that come in.
  4. If you find yourself distracted, observe that; observe yourself as you become aware that you were distracted.
  It is essential to help clients observe in a non-attached way. Thus, whatever happens in their minds is 'grist for the mill,' so to speak. Get feedback. Work with clients until they get the idea of observing. Check how long each person can observe. It is common to have to start and restart many times in the course of one or two minutes.

- **Describing.** Explain: Describing is using words to represent what you observe. Describing is a reaction to observing; it is labelling what is observed. Discuss how describing a thought as a thought requires one to notice that it is a thought instead of a fact. Give examples of the differences between thinking 'I am stupid' and being 'stupid'. Get feedback. Elicit examples. Have clients practice observing thoughts and labelling them as thoughts. Suggest labelling them into categories (e.g. thoughts about myself, thoughts about children, thoughts about child abuse images).

- **Participating.** Explain: Participating is entering wholly into an activity. It is throwing yourself into something. Note that participating is the ultimate goal. The only reason we observe and describe is to understand and improve things. Elicit examples of participating (e.g. driving a car). If we go to a country where they drive on a different side of the road we suddenly need to stop and observe and describe. Gather other examples from clients.

2. 'How' skills

- **Non-judgmentally.** The goal here is to take a non-judgmental stance when observing, describing and participating. Judging is any labelling or evaluating of something as good or bad, as valuable or not, as worthwhile or worthless. An important mindfulness skill is not judging things in this manner. Get examples of the difference between judging and noticing consequences. Point out how judging is sometimes a shorthand way of comparing things to a standard; in this case, judging gives information. For example, saying that a tomato is 'bad' may mean that it is not a fresh tomato. Or judging may be a shorthand way of stating a preference. Saying that the room looks 'bad' or a book was 'terrible' is based on a personal preference in decorating or in reading material. The problem is that over time, people forget that judging is shorthand and begin to take it literally as a statement of fact. Get other examples.
- **One mindfully.** Doing one thing at a time. Explain the process of doing one thing at a time with awareness. Emphasise focusing attention on only one activity or thing at a time, bringing the whole person to bear on a task or activity. This is the opposite of how people usually like to operate. Explain: 'Most of us think that if we do several things at once we will accomplish more; this is not true. However, this does not mean that you cannot switch from one thing to another and back. The trick is to have your mind completely on what you are doing at the moment. This refers to both mental and physical activities'.
- **Effectively.** The aim here is to focus on being effective – to focus on what works, rather than what is right versus wrong or fair versus unfair. Doing what works requires knowing what one's goal or objective is. For instance, a person may want to get a raise at work, but they may also think that the supervisor should know without being told that they deserve one, so they refuse to ask for it. In this case the person is putting being right over achieving their goal. Being effective requires knowing the actual situation and reacting to it, not to what one thinks should be the situation. For example, when driving on the motorway, people who drive more slowly are instructed by signs to drive on the inner lane. People who tailgate slower drivers in the inner lane

(instead of just passing) are acting as if all are prepared to follow the directions.

Discuss with your client which 'how' skill (taking a non-judgmental stance, focusing on one thing in the moment, being effective) is their strength and which is their weakness. The one they have most difficulty with is the one to practice the most.

3. Distress tolerance skills

These skills are ones that help people get through life when they can't make changes for the better in their situation and when, for any number of reasons, they can't sort out their feelings well enough to make changes in how they feel. Basically, the skills are ways of surviving and doing well in terrible situations without resorting to behaviours that will make the situations worse. Everyone has to tolerate some amount of pain and distress in life. Always trying to avoid pain leads to more problems than it solves. Get examples from clients of this point. For example, Post-traumatic stress disorder is primarily a result of trying to avoid all contact with cues that cause discomfort. Trying to suppress emotional pain or avoid contact with pain related cues leads to ruminating about the painful events; paradoxically, trying to get rid of painful thoughts creates painful thoughts. Experiencing and accepting emotional pain are ways to reducing pain.

- **Distraction skills.** But there are times for people to distract themselves from pain also. Painful situations cannot always be immediately processed. It is often not an appropriate time for working on painful emotions or situations. At work, or at meetings, people may feel emotional pain or be upset. However, they may simply have to tolerate the feeling. Elicit from clients' crisis situations they need to tolerate. Surviving crisis situations is part of being effective, 'doing what works'.

    Distracting methods have to do with reducing contact with emotional stimuli (events that set off emotions). Or, in some cases, they work to change parts of an emotional response. There are seven distracting skills. A useful way to remember these skills is the phrase 'Wise Mind ACCEPTS': **A**ctivities; **C**ontributing; **C**omparisons; **E**motions; **P**ushing-away; **T**houghts; **S**ensations. Elicit from clients' examples of each of these skills.
- **Self-soothing skills.** Self-soothing has to do with comforting, and being gentle and kind to

oneself. A way to remember these skills is to think of soothing each of the five senses: vision; hearing; smell; taste; touch. The meaning and intent of these are reasonably self evident, so it may only be necessary to review a few in session. Some individuals believe that they don't deserve soothing, kindness, and gentleness; they may feel guilty and ashamed when they self-soothe. Others may believe that they should get soothing from others; they don't self-soothe as a matter of principle. Elicit examples from clients.

- **Improving the moment.** This works by replacing immediate negative events with more positive ones. Some strategies for improving the moment are cognitive techniques having to do with changing appraisals of oneself (encouragement) or the situation (positive thinking, meaning, imaging). Some involve changing body responses to events (relaxing). Elicit examples from clients.
- **Thinking of pros and cons.** This skill consists of thinking about the positive and negative aspects of tolerating distress and the positive and negative aspects of not tolerating it. The eventual goal here is for the person to face the fact that accepting reality and tolerating distress lead to better outcomes than do rejecting reality and refusing to tolerate distress. Get clients to generate pros and cons of tolerating a crisis without doing something harmful or impulsive (i.e. downloading and masturbating to images of child abuse images or harming a child). Try to focus on the short-term and long-term pros and cons. Compare the two sets.

Completion criteria

By the end of this chapter, the client should have:

1. Completed the following exercises:
   - Values Assessment Exercise.
   - Values Narrative Form.
   - Valued Living Questionnaire.
   - Goals, Actions and Barriers Form.
2. An understanding of the six formal mindfulness skills:
   - Observing.
   - Describing.
   - Participating spontaneously.
   - Being non-judgmental.
   - Being mindful or focusing attention completely on one thing.
   - Focusing on what is effective in a given situation.

3. An understanding of distress tolerance skills:
   - Distraction skills.
   - Self-soothing skills.
   - Improving the present moment.
   - Pros and cons.

An understanding of their values, their goals, actions to achieving their goals and possible barriers to achieving their goals.

Value guidelines

The practitioner should also attempt to assess other factors that may be influencing the client's statements about valued ends:

- Values statements controlled by the presence of the practitioner, in conjunction with the client's assumption about what would please the practitioner. Relevant consequences are signs of the practitioner approval or the absence of practitioner disapproval.
- Values statements controlled by the presence of the culture more generally. Relevant consequences include the absence of cultural sanctions, broad social approval, or prestige.
- Values statements controlled by the stated or assumed values of the clients parents. Relevant consequences are parental approval – actually occurring or verbally constructed.

For most of us, values are controlled in part by all of the above. What is important is whether removing an influence is going to effect the strength of the value and the direction it might give. Again, it may be useful to address this by talking about the value in the absence of a social consequence.

As noted on the values forms, the client is asked to generate responses in various life domains. Many clients may find it hard to generate values for some of the domains. Others will give very superficial answers. The role of the practitioner is to patiently explore each of the domains, using stories from the client's life to generate examples of what they hoped or wished for that may have disappeared due to other life circumstances. On other occasions, we may have to use goals where the client has to look at the underlying values. It also happens that clients aspire to things that may not be possible. For example, re-establishing a relationship when their partner has found someone else. In such instances, the practitioner tries to find the underlying value and goals that might be achievable if one were moving in that direction.

Values Assessment Exercise

The following are areas of life that are valued by some people. Not every person has the same values and this work sheet is not a test to see whether you have the 'correct' values. Describe your values as if no one will ever read this work sheet. As you work, think about each area in terms of the concrete goals you may have and in terms of more general life directions. For instance you may value getting married as a concrete goal and being a loving spouse as a valued direction. The first example, getting married, is something that could be completed. The second example, being a loving partner does not have an end. You could always be more loving, no matter how loving you already were. Work through each of the life domains. Some of the domains overlap. You may have trouble keeping family separate from marriage or intimate relations. Do your best to keep them separate. Your therapist will provide assistance when you discuss these goals and values assessment. You may not have any valued goals in certain areas; you can skip those areas and discuss them directly with your therapist. It is also important that you write down what you would value if there were nothing in your way. We are not asking what you think you could realistically get, or what you or others think you deserve. We want to know what you care about, what you would want to work toward, in the best of all situations. Please use additional sheets if necessary.

Family (other than marriage or parenting)

In this section, describe the type of brother/sister, son/daughter, father/mother you want to be. Describe the qualities you would want to have in those relationships. Describe how you would treat the other people if you were the ideal in these various relationships.

Marriage/couples/intimate relations

In this section, write down a description of the person you would like to be in an intimate relationship. Write down the type of relationship you would want to have. Try to focus on your role in that relationship.

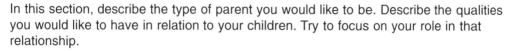

Values Assessment Exercise *continued*

Parenting

In this section, describe the type of parent you would like to be. Describe the qualities you would like to have in relation to your children. Try to focus on your role in that relationship.

Friends/social life

In this section, write down what it means to you to be a good friend. If you were able to be the best friend possible, how would you behave towards your friends? Try to describe an ideal friendship.

Values Assessment Exercise *continued*

Work

In this section, describe what type of work you would like to do. This can be very specific or very general. Discuss what type of worker you would like to be. What would you want your work relations to be like?

Education/training

If you would like to pursue an education, formally or informally, or to pursue some specialised training, write about that. Write about why this sort of training or education appeals to you.

Values Assessment Exercise *continued*

Recreation/fun

Discuss the type of recreational life you would like to have, including hobbies, sports and leisure activities.

Spirituality

We are not necessarily referring to organised religion in this section. What we mean by spirituality is whatever that means to you. This may be as simple as being close to nature, or as formal as participating in an organised religious group. If this is an important area of life, write about what you would want it to be.

Values Assessment Exercise *continued*

Citizenship/community life

For some people, participating in community affairs is an important part of life. If community oriented activities are important to you, write about what appeals to you in this area.

Physical self-care (diet, exercise, sleep)

In this section, include your values related to maintaining your physical well-being. Write about what you would like your physical health to be like.

Values Narrative Form (Adapted from Hayes et al. 1999)

Generate a brief narrative for each domain, based on discussion of the client's values assessment. If none is applicable, put 'none.' After generating all narratives, read each to the client and refine. Continue this process, simultaneously watching for compliance type answers, until you and the client arrive at a brief statement that the client agrees is consistent with their values in a given domain.

Domain	Valued direction narrative
Family (other than marriage or parenting)	_____
Marriage/couples/ intimate relations	_____
Parenting	_____
Friends/social life	_____

Values Narrative Form (Adapted from Hayes et al. 1999) *continued*

Work

_____

_____

_____

Education/training

_____

_____

_____

Recreation/fun

_____

_____

_____

Spirituality

_____

_____

_____

Citizenship/
community Life

_____

_____

_____

Physical self-care
(diet, exercise,
sleep)

_____

_____

_____

Valued Living Questionnaire (Part 1)

Below are areas of life that are valued by some people. We are concerned with your quality of life in each of these areas. One aspect of quality of life involves the importance one puts on different areas of living. Rate the importance of each area (by circling a number) on a scale of 1–10. 1 means that area is not at all important. 10 means that area is very important. Not everyone will value all of these areas, or value all areas the same. Rate each area according to **your own personal sense of importance**.

Area	Not at all important								Extremely important
1. Family (other than marriage or parenting)	1 2 3 4 5 6 7 8 9 10								
2. Marriage/couples/intimate relations	1 2 3 4 5 6 7 8 9 10								
3. Parenting	1 2 3 4 5 6 7 8 9 10								
4. Friends/social life	1 2 3 4 5 6 7 8 9 10								
5. Work	1 2 3 4 5 6 7 8 9 10								
6. Education/training	1 2 3 4 5 6 7 8 9 10								
7. Recreation/fun	1 2 3 4 5 6 7 8 9 10								
8. Spirituality	1 2 3 4 5 6 7 8 9 10								
9. Citizenship/Community Life	1 2 3 4 5 6 7 8 9 10								
10. Physical self-care (diet, exercise, sleep)	1 2 3 4 5 6 7 8 9 10								

Valued Living Questionnaire (Part 2)

In this section, we would like you to give a rating of how **consistent** your actions have been with each of your values. We are **not** asking about your ideal in each area. We are also not asking what others think of you. Everyone does better in some areas than others. People also do better at some times than at others. **We want to know how you think you have been doing during the past week**. Rate each area (by circling a number) on a scale of 1–10. 1 means that your actions have been completely inconsistent with your value. 10 means that your actions have been completely consistent with your value.

During the past week

Area	Not at all consistent with my value									Completely consistent with my value
1. Family (other than marriage or parenting)	1	2	3	4	5	6	7	8	9	10
2. Marriage/couples/intimate relations	1	2	3	4	5	6	7	8	9	10
3. Parenting	1	2	3	4	5	6	7	8	9	10
4. Friends/social life	1	2	3	4	5	6	7	8	9	10
5. Work	1	2	3	4	5	6	7	8	9	10
6. Education/training	1	2	3	4	5	6	7	8	9	10
7. Recreation/fun	1	2	3	4	5	6	7	8	9	10
8. Spirituality	1	2	3	4	5	6	7	8	9	10
9. Citizenship/Community Life	1	2	3	4	5	6	7	8	9	10
10. Physical self-care (diet, exercise, sleep)	1	2	3	4	5	6	7	8	9	10

Scoring Template for Valued Living Questionnaire

Domain	Importance Score	Consistency Score	Discrepancy Score

1. Family (other than marriage or parenting)   _____ minus _____ = _____

2. Marriage/couples/intimate relations   _____ minus _____ = _____

3. Parenting   _____ minus _____ = _____

4. Friends/social life   _____ minus _____ = _____

5. Work   _____ minus _____ = _____

6. Education/training   _____ minus _____ = _____

7. Recreation/fun   _____ minus _____ = _____

8. Spirituality   _____ minus _____ = _____

9. Citizenship/community Life   _____ minus _____ = _____

10. Physical self-care (diet, exercise, sleep)   _____ minus _____ = _____

Total Discrepancy Score   _____

Total Importance Score   _____

Total Consistency Score   _____

Scoring

Discrepancy scores can range from 0 to 90. A score of 0 means no discrepancy between efficacy and importance. A score of 90 is the highest discrepancy between stated values and consistent action.

If importance > consistency subtract consistency from importance. If consistency is greater than importance, enter zero.

Goals, Actions and Barriers Form

Given the valued directions listed, work with the client to generate goals (obtainable events) and actions (concrete steps the client can take) that would manifest these values. Using interviews and exercises, identify the psychological events that stand between the client moving forward in these areas (taking these actions, working towards these goals). If the client presents public events as barriers, reformulate them in terms of goals and place them within their relevant value (the domain may differ from that which originally raised this issue). Then look again at actions and barriers relevant to these goals as well.

Domain	Valued Direction	Goals	Actions	Barriers
Family (other than marriage or parenting)	_____	_____	_____	_____
Marriage/couples/intimate relations	_____	_____	_____	_____
Parenting	_____	_____	_____	_____
Friends/social life	_____	_____	_____	_____

Goals, Actions and Barriers Form *continued*

Domain	Valued Direction	Goals	Actions	Barriers
Work	_____	_____	_____	_____
Education/training	_____	_____	_____	_____
Recreation/fun	_____	_____	_____	_____
Spirituality	_____	_____	_____	_____
Citizenship/community life	_____	_____	_____	_____
Physical self-care (diet, exercise, sleep)	_____	_____	_____	_____

(Adapted from Hayes et al. 1999)

Chapter Seven

Social Activity and Internet Images

The aims of this chapter are to provide:

- A review of the literature that relates to ideas of community and the Internet.
- A summary of why this might be relevant for some people with a sexual interest in children who commit offences through the Internet.
- Ways of assessing the extent of their problem.
- Strategies for changing offending behaviour.

Background

In a very obvious way, anyone who engages with the Internet participates in that community. Indeed, it might be argued that one of the most critical aspects of our growing use of the Internet is how it has been embraced as a community-forming device, 'a space where they may meet and interact with one another and, in many cases, develop what has become commonly referred to as a virtual community' (Fox, 2004: 48). But engagement in the community of the Internet can occur at multiple levels, from using the Internet as a source of information to membership of virtual groups whose social relationships assume the same importance as those in the off-line world.

In the context of abuse images on the Internet, a limited off-line social network has undergone a radical transformation. What was a small and largely hidden world has now expanded and become readily available to all who care to look. It is now possible for people who share a similar set of interests, no matter how previously hidden or unusual, to form alliances in cyberspace. For many people such alliances are positive and allow the building of a sense of belonging and commonality that was unavailable because of geographic separation. Mitra (2001) has discussed this in the context of immigrant groups where renegotiating an identity has been crucial for marginalised groups and where the Internet has been used to 'voice unspeakable stories and eventually construct powerful connections that can be labelled as 'cyber communities' '. Such marginalised communities can use this new found voice to seek acknowledgement. The same might also be said for communities who have as their focus the sexualisation of children.

The functions of such communities are complex. At their simplest level they provide information and materials that support the realisation that the individual is part of a larger group. Where people communicate with each other, they can provide a supportive community that gives access not only to information about an area of interest, such as abuse images, but also to information about children and issues that relate to security. Such communication can also provide friendship, the catalyst for which is illegal or sexual images of children. On the Internet, such friendships may well seem every bit as real as in the off-line world, but it is important to note that such communities also have qualities that are peculiar to the Internet.

The growing realisation that the Internet may have distinctive qualities has been paralleled by an interest in how it is used by people. The interaction between the individual and technology allows us to see the effect of the Internet on the user as something potentially greater than a passive means of quickly and cheaply transmitting information between points. Communication on the Internet appears to also include social and emotional factors that we more usually associate with real life communication. At present, communication between individuals on the Internet is largely text based, and appears more limited than face-to-face communication. But there is a sense in which the exchange of information can generate a sense of group membership, develop social networks, and create a sense of community. For authors such as McLaughlin et al. (1995) community is located in the emergence of standards of conduct, and this is particularly applicable to electronic communication and is geared towards the preservation of the group. Strategies for the management of virtual spaces with respect to issues of power and control, authority, dominance and submission have evolved as well. In this context human and non-human agents (moderators and Webmasters, listservers and cancelbots) serve as gatekeepers, adjudicators and imposers of sanctions for misconduct (McLaughlin et al., 1998).

Ideas about community

In the following, the notion of community is explored and examined in terms of its importance to on-line offending activity. Although much of this may not immediately relate to 'paedophile' communities, and may seem at first sight somewhat tangential to the main issue, it does provide an essential context to understanding the sense in which community on the Internet can facilitate engagement with activities related to adult sexual interest in children. Whilst not all abuse images offenders are socially engaged with the Internet at all in the sense used here, social contact generally implies trading of abuse images and there are some grounds for believing that those that have extensive social engagement may constitute a more significant risk for contact offending or Internet seduction.

Authors such as Rheingold (1993: 5) have used the term 'virtual' to refer to network-based communication, and related consequent communities. His definition of a virtual community was that: 'Virtual communities are social aggregations that emerge from the Net when enough people carry on public discourses long enough, with sufficient human feeling, to form webs of personal relationships in cyberspace'. One of the difficulties with the term 'virtual' is that it is often used in a way to imply something less than real. Authors such as Joinson and Dietz-Uhler (2002) have argued that an early complaint was that virtual communities, although they resembled real communities, were in fact pseudo-communities, with a lack of sincerity or genuineness and a pattern of relating which, although looking like highly interpersonal interaction, is essentially impersonal. Therefore, in the context of community, virtual may imply something 'like a community', but not really a community. This can be a misleading comparison, however, for in the sense used in respect of networked communication, virtual has a rather different meaning (Lévy, 1998).

Lévy discussed this idea in the context of a virtual company. A conventional organisation brings its employees together into a location, (usually a building) and gives each employee a location in that space where they can work. Such an organisation brings its employees together into a geographical location so that they can work co-operatively together. A virtual company, on the other hand, locates individual workers on an electronic communications network, and software resources of various kinds promote and enable co-operation. Any one individual participates in the virtual organisation by joining the network, and their physical location is largely irrelevant. This also implies a possible change in temporal relationships, as work may be done at any time so long as it functions in relation to the larger network. For most of us, our engagement with communities extends beyond that of work of course, to include recreational groups, activity groups, interest groups, and school groups of all kinds. Not all of these groups would readily translate into 'virtual'. A squash club requires people to come together physically to play the game at a given location and usually within a discrete time frame. Other recreational activities, particularly those that focus on the exchange of goods or information, can have a virtual existence, and indeed may flourish more readily within this environment because they can access many more people than those found in any given physical location.

Smith et al. (2000) specifically omitted the word community from their Internet research, and instead used the concept of 'social cyberspace' to evoke a better sense of interactivity and its importance in social groups. These authors discovered a social structure within virtual communities that emulated that of a physical community and suggested close social and personal connections between the on-line individual and their off-line life. The continuum between virtual and physical communities has been furthered explored by Fox (2004: 49) who suggested that, 'Long before the imagined landscape of cyberspace became a haven for developing communities of Internet and niche, critical and cultural theorists developed an understanding of communities as imagined. Within each community was a notion of solidarity or collectivity that was the glue of the community and dependent on leaders and followers'. Such a flexible 'imagined' environment provided opportunities for identity shifting and even deception because 'the identity cues that define one's identity in the physical world – such as gender, age, class, ethnicity, sexuality, and so on – are enacted in much more complex ways on-line . . .' (p 52).

Online interaction and the emergence of groups

Kollock and Smith (1999) identified at least five forms of on-line interaction that can mediate the emergence of virtual groups. All of these have relevance to the collection of abuse images, but some (especially those involving synchronous communication) might be thought to be more powerful in terms of the development of a strong sense of group identity. The following reviews the forms of on-line interaction to indicate the broad framework within which communication on the Internet can take place:

- **Email and discussion lists.** Email allows a user to send a message directly to someone, rather in the form of a traditional letter. Discussion lists extend this concept, however, by automatically sending the message to a group of people on an email list, rather than an individual. The direction of a series of messages, and their responses, to the list generates a form of group discussion, which can extend across hundreds, and even thousands of individuals. Typically, the list is 'owned' by one individual because the messages must pass through a single point. The 'owner', therefore, has the capacity to monitor and exclude or edit material flowing through the discussion list. On a large list, this may take a considerable amount of time and energy, so a more manageable format is to keep the list 'open' and without detailed editing. Even so, disruptive, inappropriate or malicious material can still be included without detailed monitoring.
- **Usenet newsgroups and BBSs.** Bulletin board systems (BBSs) are a form of asynchronous communication that allows participants to create topical groups in which a series of messages can be listed, one after another. Well known systems of this type include the Usenet newsgroups, the WELL, ECHO and BBSs run on commercial services, such as AOL and Microsoft Network. For each there is a wide collection of discussion topics and communication between participants. Usenet is the largest of these conferencing systems and carries thousands of newsgroups. A new site joins the Usenet simply by finding any existing server that is willing to pass along to other servers it is networked with a copy of the collection of messages it receives. No one owns most Usenet newsgroups, and there is no central authority controlling content. Almost anyone can read the contents of a Usenet newsgroup, create new newsgroups or contribute to an existing one. Furthermore, this can be done in circumstances of almost complete anonymity. This in turn makes the Usenet a different social space than is possible in the off-line world. In the sense in which we are interested here, Egroups are similar proprietary structures, although access may be limited to 'members'.
- **Chat rooms.** This differs from email and BBSs in that it allows for synchronous communication. People can chat in real time by sending text messages to one another. Such chat on the Internet is organised around 'channels', which are also referred to as rooms. The majority of chat systems support a great number of these channels dedicated to a wide array of topics. Text chat uses a centralised server that gives the server owner control over access to the system and to particular channels. Commercial systems are often 'policed' by staff or appointed volunteers. Non-commercial systems, such as Internet Relay Chat (IRC) may have channel owners (termed operators) who can eject people from the channel, control who enters it and restrict membership, and there may be some central monitoring of activity. However, chat networks also allow for private one-to-one communication outside of any given chat room, which is both unmonitored and uncontrollable by external agents. Such direct communication need not necessarily pass through network servers. Chat rooms may also include moving visual imagery through video conferencing protocols, such as CuSeeMe or ICUII. A real time moving image from a camera on one computer is transmitted via a server to other computers on the same network. As in IRC channels, video communication can also be private. Using these protocols, visual communication may be supplemented by either voice or text transmissions. In effect, video conferencing protocols such as CuSeeMe and networks such as ICUII are effectively visual versions of text chat protocols, with similar capacities, although bandwidth constraints limit the numbers on any one server channel, and also visual quality. Commercial systems (such as ICUII) tend to route communications through central servers to enhance video streaming, and to give added commercial value.
- **MUDS.** Multi-User Domains or Dungeons (MUDS) attempted to combine a sense of physical place with face-to-face interaction. This is achieved through 'rooms', which are

textually constructed but which are detailed enough to provide a real sense of physical space. Everything about the MUD is invented, although it is rule-governed by the administering programme. They typically have more than one user connected at any given time, and all communication is synchronous, in real time.

- **World Wide Web.** Often abbreviated to WWW or 'the Web', this is increasingly becoming an access point (or portal) for other forms of computer-mediated communication. People can access their emails, look up newsgroup messages or enter a chat room through the World Wide Web. Access is through a browser, which is a programme that downloads instructions taken from the Internet and displays them on the desktop computer as text, images, animation and sounds. Typical examples of such browsers are Netscape Navigator and Microsoft explorer. Different audiences can be targeted in different ways, and because it can integrate images and sounds, it can be a more intuitive and a potentially richer context for communication on the Internet. BBSs and various forms of chat facility (including video conferencing) can all be accessed through web browsers.

Not withstanding the involvement of video conferencing, at the moment social groups tend to be mediated through text-based media, but for the future there is a growing potential for richer forms of sound and visual communication through the various forms of video conferencing, and other visual and auditory media formats.

Online and off-line communities

While there is clear evidence that people do come together to form groups on the Internet, as we have already noted there is continuing debate as to whether these aggregations of people can be called communities. In part, the debate is influenced by traditional definitions of community, which are based on the sense of relatedness and shared experiences among people living in the same locality. Such definitions require shared proximity as well as a degree of common experience and interests. However, spatial or temporal proximity of communicants is almost never part of computer-mediated communication over the Internet. 'More often than not, the human beings involved are geographically dispersed, and their

common place on the Internet is accessible only as textual fragments on the computer screens' Gotved (2002). Watson (1998) has suggested that instead of emphasising geographical proximity, we should look to preserve the connection between communication and community, as without ongoing communication amongst its participants, a community dissolves. Neighbourhood and kinship ties are only a portion of people's overall community networks, because cars, planes and 'phones can maintain relationships over long distances. The emphasis is on a move from defining community in terms of space to defining it in terms of social networks. In a similar way, Nip (2004) saw the interconnectivity and interactivity of the Internet as fostering an 'empty space', a cyberspace that is not defined by geographical place but a social space for the development of interpersonal relationships and a public space for the formation of communities.

Within a more traditional definition of community, relationships among people carry with them a sense of stake or obligation to that community (Postman, 1993). A criticism of the term 'virtual community' is that on-line collectives seem not to contain that stake or obligation that exists in off-line or real communities, and lack the consequences of not meeting or participating in the common obligation of that community. Internet groups are mainly formed out of common interest, not obligation. Wood and Smith (2001: 110) therefore argued that 'Virtual communities thus allow people to transcend geographic boundaries and unite with others who share their common interests, whether that's watching a particular television series or buying plastic figures of Charlie Brown and Bugs Bunny'.

However, not all such communities function in the same way, and this has been explored by Norris (2002) in his analysis of the bridging and bonding functions that they might have. Bridging refers to social networks that bring people together of different sorts, whereas bonding brings people together of a similar sort. We can think of many communities whose focus is building social capital, generating interpersonal trust and reinforcing community ties. In contrast, homogeneous bonding communities can also serve positive functions, but the danger is that they can exacerbate and widen social cleavages. Norris (2002) gave examples of what he called 'dysfunctional types of bonding networks' in the

Ku Klux Klan in Mississippi, La Cosa Nostra in Sicily, and the IRA in Belfast. We could add to this on-line paedophile communities, participation in which reinforces like-minded beliefs, similar interests and therefore ideological homogeneity amongst its members. Norris (2002) has suggested that with the wide availability of groups, organisations and associations on-line, it is exceptionally easy to find the niche website or specific discussion group that reflects one's particular beliefs and interests. One consequence of this is an avoidance of exposure to alternative points of view. In addition, the lack of barriers to entry means that once social groups are on-line, most virtual communities are fairly permeable to its members.

Online paedophile communities

Durkin and Bryant (1995: 187) have discussed how such ideological homogeneity within on-line paedophile communities can be used to sanction and justify beliefs, attitudes and behaviours amongst its members that might otherwise be challenged or seen as deviant. They suggested that the Internet 'can provide an enormous, and extremely rapid, contact network for people of related interests, including those related to sexual deviancy. Individuals can seek, identify and communicate with fellow deviants of a similar carnal persuasion across the country, and even around the world. Information from deviant subcultures can be broadly disseminated, and interested new persons can be recruited'. Other research, in the context of the Internet and adult sexual interest in children, has supported this notion of community. Jenkins (2001) talked of those who use Internet abuse images as being members of a subculture, as they possess a huge corpus of specialised knowledge, but in this context without direct face-to-face contact. Jenkins suggested that such communities are made up of highly deviant individuals who in most cases operate as loners, never having personal contact with another deviant.

A further study by Durkin and Bryant (1999) attempted to gather data from a Usenet discussion group, which reflected a community of adults with a sexual interest in children outside of an incarcerated group. The discussion group was alt.support.boy-lovers and at the time the data was accessed there were 41 people participating in this forum. The research question for the study was, 'How do paedophiles who use

the Internet account for their deviance?' The authors performed a content analysis on all of the postings to the Usenet newsgroup for a period of one month (93 postings) and the data was examined to look for the presence or absence of themes. The following categories were used as part of the analysis:

- *Account offered* – the posting contained some type of explanation offered in defence of paedophilia or adults having sexual contact with children.
- *Condemnation of condemners* –the poster attempts to shift the focus from paedophiles and their behaviour to the actions of those who condemn them. Targets of condemnation may include law enforcement officers, social workers, psychologists or psychiatrists, and others.
- *Denial of injury* – the poster claims that adults engaging in sexual contact with children do not cause harm to children. It may involve a claim of benefit assertion.
- *Claim of benefit* – this particular account is an extension of the denial of injury account. The poster goes a step beyond simply asserting that adult-child sex does not harm the child and claims that such behaviour is actually beneficial to the child involved.
- *Appeal to loyalties* – the poster attempts to justify paedophilia and adult-child sex by claims of an allegiance to 'children's liberation' or 'children's rights'.
- *BIRGing* – the poster makes the assertion that 'great men' have also been paedophiles.
- *Polythematic accounts* – the posting contains an appeal to more than one defensibility. It includes any combination of the previous accounts.

The study concluded that paedophiles made extensive use of accounts, with denial of injury and condemnation of condemners being particularly prevalent, with the Internet providing a highly effective mechanism for the aggregation and dissemination of accounts. The Internet allowed such adults to advertise and propagandise their ideological position. Durkin and Bryant (1999: 122) also suggested that, 'The fact that a substantial number of these paedophiles are offering accounts may lead to the generation of a consolidated body of accounts. In turn this may help the scores of paedophiles who read this newsgroup to justify or legitimate their deviant orientation and behaviour'.

Such a consolidated body of accounts might function to normalise or legitimise sexual engagement with children by adults, and many authors have suggested that the Internet provides the perfect medium for such behaviour. Medaris and Girouard (2002) have gone so far as to suggest that, 'Cloaked in the anonymity of cyberspace, sex offenders can capitalise on the natural curiosity of children, seeking victims with little risk of interdiction. These offenders no longer need to lurk in parks and malls. Instead, they roam from chatroom to chatroom looking for vulnerable, susceptible children'. Other authors have also taken up such a position, suggesting that 'child predators are forming an on-line community and bond that is unparalleled in history. They are openly uniting against legal authorities, discussing ways to influence public thinking and legislation on child exploitation' (Mahoney and Faulkner, 1997).

Functions of communities

Hagel and Armstrong (1997) talked of on-line communities in terms of their function and how they meet consumer needs. Within this context, they identified four such needs:

1. Communities of interest are formed by individuals with a shared interest, expertise and passion for a wide variety of subjects.
2. Individuals who express a need to meet or engage with others who have shared similar experiences form communities of relationships. This is clearly seen in the growth of 'mutual help' groups for people who have chronic illnesses, or who have undergone traumatic experiences.
3. Communities of transaction which have as their focus the exchange of information to facilitate an economic process.
4. Communities of fantasy, which provide people with the opportunity to explore new identities through enacting fantasy games and exchanges.

In the context of abuse images, it could be argued that the Internet and the communities that emerge on it meet all four needs. In particular, the Internet facilitates the development of a community of consumers, whose very activities may help promote social relationships. This is also evidenced in off-line as well as on-line activities such as collecting, '. . . demonstrates

that consumption creates social relationships – both real and imagined. Consumption is a shared as well as an individual activity forging links between self-object and others, that is between consumers as well as between producers and consumers' (Houlton and Short, 1995). The significance of collecting as an element of community will be examined in more detail in the next chapter.

According to Jones (1997) virtual communities distinguish themselves from a simple on-line gathering when they feature:

1. *A minimum level of interactivity* – in order for a virtual community to exist, there must be a flow of messages among the participants. If one person were to post a newsgroup and no one were to comment on it, there would be no basis for a virtual community. The community comes from interactivity amongst participants.
2. *A variety of communicators* – more than two contributors need to join the conversation for a community to arise. Virtual communities are enhanced by the variety of people who participate and the contribution they make.
3. *Common public space* – virtual communities still need to identify with a cyber place. Jones (1997) suggested that these are the forums in which the community participants most regularly engage in communication. In the early days of computer-mediated communication, BBS were the place where individuals went to post and read messages. Today, chat rooms serve the same purpose, but allow people to interact in real time rather than in delayed messages.
4. *A minimum level of sustained membership* – one visit or a simple exchange does not constitute membership in a virtual community. Rather, those who form the community have relationships to one another that are perpetuated through time.

For a community to exist, therefore, there have to be sufficient people who engage with each other, who occupy a common space and who are prepared to expend energy to sustain relationships. Hauben (1997) talked of such people as 'netizens', and suggested that true netizens distinguish themselves through active contributions to the development of a sustained community. 'Netizens are the people who actively contribute on-line towards the development of the Net. These people understand the value of collective work and the public aspects of public communications. These are the people who actively discuss and debate topics in a constructive manner, who e-mail answers to people and provide help to new-comers, who maintain FAQ files and other public information repositories, who maintain mailing lists and so on. These are the people who discuss the nature and role of this new communications medium . . . Netizens are people who decide to make the Net a regenerative and vibrant community and resource'. Clearly, not everyone who visits a virtual community is a netizen at least in this activist sense. Wood and Smith (2001) cited some specific terminology to designate non-participants, who clearly do not fulfill the requirements for netizen status. These include the surfer (an infrequent and detached visitor); lurkers (who are present but offer no comment or contribution); and privateers (people who use the net for profit). They do not qualify because of their selfish, rather than selfless, use of technology. However, on-line communities are not static but dynamic and the roles of respective members changes over time or in accordance with the purpose of the community. This has been described also in the context of 'fan' communities, 'Those who do penetrate a fandom's core community may earn a status, particularly among newer recruits to the fandom, as more authentic and authoritative fans . . . those on the periphery are more likely to be spurned should they boast about exhaustive video libraries, whether because they disturb that chain of privilege, disregard shared codes of courtesy and displays of community mindedness or, as if often is the case, confirm their outsiderness by misapprehending the etiquette for solitary trades' (Bjarkman, 2004).

Trust

Central to the notion of community and its management, is trust, an issue of particular significance in communities that engage in illegal activity such as trading or exchanging abuse images. Ba (2001) defined trust in exchange in terms of three central characteristics: reliability, predictability and fairness.

- The exchange partner is expected to be credible in such a way that their word or promise can be relied on.
- The exchange partner will behave in ways that equitably protect the welfare of both parties.

- The exchange partners are dedicated to reciprocating the obligations and commitments between them under an environment of uncertainty and vulnerability.

While Ba's (2001) theoretical analysis is in the context of commercial exchange, it remains valuable when considering the importance of trust in paedophile communities. While such communities are not driven by commercial considerations, the nature of the products that are exchanged (both text and pictures) requires a high level of trust between parties. There is also a sense in which abuse images can be thought of as a form of currency in the trading process, thus making it more relevant to notions of commercial exchange.

However, we know that in the off-line world, trust is not automatically given to people that we do not know. The same could be said of the Internet, where the problems of establishing an identity in which to trust have to be negotiated. Slater (1998: 93) talked about his research participants operating 'within a dialectic of cynicism and belief: they experienced their on-line world with a mixture of cynical detachment on the one hand (a refusal to believe anything on-line and therefore a refusal to treat events or relationships there as serious), and on the other hand a desire to trust and invest in on-line relationships which depended on pursuing strategies of authentication (and a constant concern about being deceived, ripped off and otherwise hurt by others' inauthenticity'). There are many examples of breaches of trust on-line, whether through others pretending to be children when they were in fact adults (e.g., Quayle and Taylor, 2001) or where people claim to be something other than who they are. For example, Feldman (2000) reported four cases of 'Munchausen by Internet' where people in on-line support groups claimed illnesses that they did not have. In a similar way, adults may retain sexual images for trade that are used as evidence to others in a social network or community that they actually are who they say they are with regard to their sexual proclivities.

Very often we trust people with whom we have long-standing relationships or who occupy a position within our social hierarchy. Such hierarchies also exist on-line, and reference is made to positions on that hierarchy, such as 'newbie', 'wise one' and 'operator'. However, hierarchies emerge out of interactions that take place over time (the very term newbie implies some sort of temporal context). On the Internet people's identities are, in the main, inextricably tied up with nicknames (nicks) which can be changed at any time. It would be hard to imagine living in the off-line world where the names of people in your communities could be changed at any moment, or worse, taken over by somebody else – to arrive into work to find that somebody is using your name and that you either have to battle it out with them or find another! With protocols such as Internet Relay Chat (IRC) it is possible to go on-line only to find that someone is already there using your nickname. The converse is also true, that someone presents themselves with a familiar 'nick' but who turns out not to be the same person you were talking to last time.

Slater (1998: 96) talks about this in relation to trading 'sexpics', 'Recognizing someone as the same or as different over time and tracking down unique others (in order to make them ethically responsible for emotional commitments or trading obligations) is a central practical issue which obsesses participants and centres on the obvious matter of tracing multiple presences to unique identities and bodily locations . . .'. In the context of Internet abuse images, an individual's social position may relate to longevity, level of knowledge (for example, about issues to do with security) having a 'good' collection or having new material to trade. Along with position comes power and influence, both of which appear to be very potent factors within this community.

Communities arise spontaneously on the Internet when a group of likeminded people share a commitment to set standards about their communication which is maintained over time. However, communities can also be artificially created around the particular focus of abuse images and adult sexual interest in children. It would appear that for those with a sexual interest in children, the Internet provides a sense of community that can be related to on multiple levels. For some people, the Internet is a resource, a means of obtaining desired objects (pictures, fantasy stories, videos) from other like-minded people. The illicit nature of such material means that the person has to take one step inside of that community to find the right language and skills to gain access, but need not communicate in any other way.

Such passive community membership clearly does not qualify the person to be a 'netizen'. While there is passion about the products, and

possibly about the process of engagement with the Internet, it does not carry with it 'sufficient human feeling, to form webs of personal relationships in cyberspace' (Rheingold, 1993). In fact, for many people the fears about safety and the feelings of social discomfort about meeting others on the Internet appear to be sufficient reasons to stop further communication.

What then moves people from being passive participants to being active communicators within these communities? One significant factor may be the ability to trade material, as opposed to simply downloading from BBSs or Web pages. Trading means that the person has more control over the material available to them, and ultimately this is reflected in the quality of their collection. However, trading images for some participants is not the sole function of the community but also becomes a vehicle for new friendships. Bjarkman (2004) talked about video trading communities where exclusive trading circles admit only highly experienced collectors by invitation or recommendation (a comparative situation is discussed later on in this chapter in relation to wØnderland, an IRC based trading and social network). Erecting internal social hierarchies within such communities yields psychological rewards by 'shoring up a sense of privilege, authority and insider identity'.

The importance of such friendships must be emphasised, for in a tightly knit community there is a need to be able to trust the other individuals. Members of such communities may not expose themselves through face-to-face introductions, but they reveal a lot about themselves through their collections, asking and giving advice, sharing personal information, sharing fantasies and 'real-life' accounts and through the very medium by which they communicate – text. Furthermore, communities clearly exist within communities, with ever more secret and complex layers of security to protect the respective members. As previously discussed, such communities have many of the qualities seen in the off-line world.

wØnderland

One example of a secret community within a broader illegal context is that of wØnderland, which at the time received such extensive coverage in the press. It is worth exploring this at some length, for whilst it is an extreme example, it contains within it many of the qualities of less extreme more usual virtual communities related to abuse images. wØnderland was composed of a group of people, many of whom called themselves paedophiles, who were interested in trading pornographic images of children. They came from a wide range of countries and were equally diverse in terms of age and socio-economic background. They communicated with each other through IRC and Jenkins (2001) suggested that there were approximately two hundred members in over forty countries, many of whom were not apprehended by the police. The community had a clear set of rules (not always adhered to or enforced) about the purpose of the channel, its 'moral boundaries', and who was allowed to join. While trading pictures of children was seen as the core activity of the group, the relationships formed on-line were also important, both because they allowed for the acquisition of other desirable goods (new computer software), and also because they fostered a sense of fellowship.

They had already identified the people who sought to be members of the inner circle that was wØnderland as being sexually interested in children. Moving from the periphery only took place when the person had proved themselves to be trustworthy. Central to this community was the ability to protect its members from law enforcement agencies, and it achieved this by moving from a channel identified with paedophile material to one that allowed them to effectively remain hidden.

Protecting the community meant that it became increasingly closed to new members, as access was through a complex layer of passwords. The rules that protected this closed community also became more complex, starting with general rules about not physically meeting other people and rules about behaviours that related to the content of the pictures. These rules were also positioned within a moral framework – downloading, trading and looking at abuse images was seen as a lesser crime than physically abusing children, and was even presented as a way of preventing child abuse. Indeed, should these rules be infringed by, for example, somebody trying to trade pictures of babies or sado-masochistic pictures, then they might be banned from the channel.

As the wØnderland community became more secretive and more exclusive, the rules for the channel became increasingly complex and ultimately resulted in a fracturing of the community. Frequent arguments were common and emphasised the tension between freedom and control within the group. The result of one argument resulted in the oldest member being excluded. This, however, was not the end of wØnderland, but the beginning of two new but related communities. In part the original community broke up because not all members agreed with the ground rules, and also because there was a jockeying for power within the group. Examples of rule breaking included members of the community meeting each other off-line. A further example of rule breaking included the production of photographs, as this clearly involved the actual and current abuse of a child. More than one member of wØnderland became involved in production and made his photographs available to selected members of the community (and eventually to other Internet users).

Within this community, trading abuse images reduced as members reached saturation point within their collections. However, the desire for new material remained and gave power and status to people who were able to make and distribute videos that were of good quality and highly pornographic. Power obtained in this way was a destabilising factor on the group as a whole, challenging other sources of status such as technical experience.

Shirky (1995: 92) has suggested that synchronous communication on the Internet promotes a greater sense of community than asynchronicity can, 'When people use real time chat, they are usually less interested in what's being discussed than in who is doing the discussing, less interested in text than in the community'. This is clearly demonstrated in wØnderland, where as trading reduced, communication and intensity of relationship increased. This was the case whether or not members went on to meet each other off-line. Jenkins (2001: 152) suggested that wØnderland came to an end because 'police found some illegal activity largely through chance and put pressure on accused individuals to act as informants until a wider and much more serious network was identified and wound up'. As with other cases, the discovery partly emerged through the identification of a child who was being abused who disclosed the abuse. However, it is also the case that the end of the wØnderland community may simply have marked a transition point for the emergence of another version of the same. By the time that arrests had been made and the channel had been closed, wØnderland had already been through several cycles of creation. It is unlikely that all the members have been apprehended and there is little evidence to suggest that those who have 'gone underground' are not still actively engaged in similar communities. The nicknames of those who were caught have also entered into the folklore of Internet child pornographers, and such names are now emerging in the Newsgroups, presumably borrowed by new traders. wØnderland expressed a complex structure, which whether intentional or otherwise enhanced mutual dependence. Similar more contemporary organisational structures can be found in egroups.

Significant issues in wØnderland as in any group, virtual or real, are notions of power and status. As in real life communities, members of virtual communities differ in terms of status. As already noted, the capacity to give advice, to have access to a large collection of photographs, but above all to be able to make available new photographs greatly enhances an individual's status within on-line paedophile communities. The effects of this can be seen in the selective release of pictures, for example, relating picture availability to receipt of other material.

One final factor relates to temporal issues, and time spent on the Internet as a consequence of active membership of a virtual community. Given that the time available to people is finite, extensive involvement in the Internet which characterises membership of a virtual group necessarily impacts on off-line social relationships. Internet communication in real-time tends to be slow, and we have already noted the length of time people can spend on-line. This can be a factor in causing relationship problems with partners or others, and/or can clearly exacerbate existing social or relationship tensions and weaknesses. In extreme circumstances, a viscous circle of increased Internet involvement fuelling diminishing social contact fuelling in turn further increased Internet engagement can emerge. The consequences of this can be experienced not only in terms of diminished social contact but also diminished influence of social mores and constraints, an issue of particular significance for adults with a sexual interest in children.

Points of concern

- There are different levels of engagement with Internet communities, from passive downloading of images through web sites to active engagement within, for example, a private egroup.
- Increasing engagement may increase the likelihood of trading images, either as evidence of group membership or as part of a collecting community.
- Social engagement with homogeneous on-line communities can lead to the exclusion of others within the person's off-line social network, and a reduction in any challenges or barriers to their activity.
- Exclusive on-line socialisation may result in a negative mood state, which paradoxically increases the likelihood of going on-line.
- Engagement with homogeneous on-line communities may expose people to, or reinforce existing, ways of thinking of children as legitimate sexual targets.
- Communities may not only provide access to illegal images of children but encourage participation in information sharing about children or about the means of avoiding detection.
- Status is important in Internet communities and, in the context of abuse images, may be achieved through size of collection, longevity within the group, or ability to produce images.

Working with the client

This chapter is of particular importance to those who have engaged with Internet protocols such as IRC, ICQ or egroups, where there has been a willingness to establish relationships with others on-line. As noted above, such relationships may have functioned to the exclusion of other social contacts and limited the availability of 'reality checks' to their Internet behaviour. Points to note are the ways in which Internet involvement may have exacerbated existing social relationship difficulties or social tensions, and/or the extent to which Internet social contact begins to substitute for more normal off-line social engagement, either socially or more specifically with a partner. With particular respect to partner relationships, the sexual nature of on-line activity is of course a further aggravating factor. In some cases a further factor might be the extent to which the financial cost of maintaining Internet social contact impacts on the client's capacity to engage in off-line social behaviour.

Important issues in relation to assessment include:

- An examination of the levels of engagement your client has had with Internet communities, and the different types of social relationships that were formed with each.
- What was happening to your client's off-line social relationships while engaged with the Internet.
- What was the function of these on-line relationships and what needs did they meet for the client.

Changing behaviour

For many offenders, the Internet offers opportunities to meet others who share similar ways of thinking. Meeting in this sense does not necessarily imply actual or even virtual contact, but rather a sense that there may be others 'out there' who are thinking or doing the same things. For others, access to communities brings with it friendships that are very 'real' and which fulfil many emotional needs. The Internet also brings safety, because on-line a person can choose to exit from contact with individuals or the community whenever they choose to.

It is hard to imagine a better social environment for people who may feel insecure about themselves, who have difficulty forming friendships, or whose interests limit the opportunity to engage socially with others. On-line, people are not given access to the community because of how they look, or their educational or social status. Entry is relatively easy and movement within that community can be rapid. It is also the case that on-line relationships may be preferred to off-line ones because there is a reduction in the capacity of others to be hostile or critical (or an increase in the person's ability to avoid or exit when necessary).

In asking clients to describe their engagement with Internet communities, we hope that they will arrive at an understanding that on-line relationships may have reinforced offence related cognitions and damaged off-line social relationships with partners, families and friends. Whilst we may hope that this will promote change, it is important to realise that we are asking clients to give up relationships that may

have assumed great importance, and which they will be reluctant to abandon. But we are also asking them to give up a *way of relating* to others, which left them feeling confident, important or even 'their real self'. This is not to say that all people who use the Internet in this way lack social competence, but that social engagement on-line has met a need that was maybe unfulfilled in the off-line world. Asking someone not to do the very things that made them feel wanted, accepted or special is a hard thing to do and needs to be negotiated in terms of what is needed to move towards a 'better life'. In the context of social relationships this is not easy. We have all given (or been given) advice about making friendships and improving our social life, but in reality this is difficult.

In helping the client make sense of what was important about their social world on-line, it is possible to target areas of problematic social relationships. For example, the person who likes to download pictures to masturbate to because his relationship with his partner is not sufficiently sexually fulfilling; the person who felt unsure of themselves with others because of the way that they looked; the person who feels more confident with children than with adults. For each of these examples, any intervention will be different, and may range from couple therapy to weight management to social skills training. It is outside the remit of this book to try and provide an intervention model that is exhaustive. Perhaps what is important is to stress that a given behaviour (social activity on-line) may look similar across all offenders, but may in fact be meeting a variety of needs. Our task is to try with the client to understand the function of these activities and in doing so generate specific goals that are congruent with our client's values and which enable him to set small but achievable goals in areas that can be changed.

Exercises

1. Levels of engagement. Use the circles exercise (at the end of this chapter) to help the client locate the different types of social relationships and engagement they had with the Internet.
2. Look at these social relationships within a temporal framework (use a time line if necessary), and get your client to create a parallel chart to look at what was happening to off-line relationships as on-line ones developed.

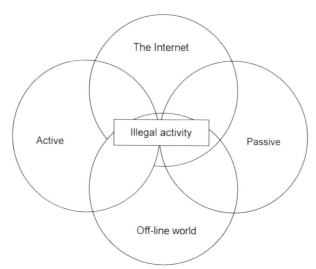

Figure 7.1 Circles of community involvement

3. Explore similarities and differences. In what ways were these relationships similar to those off-line and in what ways were they different?
4. What was the function of these relationships, and what gaps were they filling in the client's life? How can these gaps be filled in the off-line world?
5. Describe any of these relationships which were sexual. What were the benefits of such relationships over off-line ones. What were the drawbacks?
6. What does the client value about real life relationships, and what ACTION might be taken to achieve what is valued?

Completion criteria

By the end of this chapter the client should have:

1. Used the circles exercise to identify their level of engagement with the Internet community.
2. Created a time line to look at on-line social relationships and their development, and what was happening in parallel in their off-line world.
3. Written down a list of similarities and differences between on-line and off-line relationships.
4. Identified what on-line relationships might have meant and how this might be met in their off-line social world.
5. Generated a set of **actions** which might help bring about changes in they way they relate to others off-line.

Materials

Circles exercise of community involvement.

Each of the circles represents a different type of involvement with the Internet, the off-line world and illegal images. Highlight the areas on the diagram which describe your past involvement with the Internet and illegal images or activities. The circles are labelled 'The Internet', 'Passive', 'Active' and 'Off-line world'. There are also areas that indicate illegal activity. Activities such as trading on egroups or IRC would be considered 'Active', while downloading images from websites or newsgroups would be 'Passive'. Mark each area that applies to you. How many of these areas fall within 'Illegal activity'?

Example 1

'I have used the Internet in both a passive and active manner but I have never engaged in any illegal activity'. In this case, you would shade the areas that are in the 'Active' and 'Passive' circles, but you would not include any shading within the 'Illegal activity' area.

Example 2

'I have used the Internet in both an active and passive manner and I have in the past downloaded images from newsgroups or websites'. In this case you would shade the same areas as in Example 1 but you would also shade the area contained by 'Passive', 'Illegal activity' and 'Internet' circles.

Example 3

'I have never passively downloaded illegal material from the Internet but I have actively traded pictures on egroups and engaged in illegal activities with children in real life'. In this case, you would shade the areas contained by 'Active', 'Illegal activities' and 'Off-line world'.

Chapter Eight

Collecting Images

The aims of this chapter are to provide:

- A review of the literature concerning the psychology of collecting and the importance of the Internet.
- A summary of why this might be relevant for some people with a sexual interest in children who commit offences through the Internet.
- Ways of assessing the extent of the problem.
- Strategies for changing offending behaviour.

Background

Many people collect things, from stamps and comics to paintings and diamonds. Bookshops (both on-line and off-line) are full of books that relate to the collection of specific items and whose goal is to help you become a *good* collector. There are even magazines whose selling point is the inclusion of a collectable – a miniature teapot, toy soldier, teddy bear and so on. Many famous people have been collectors. Freud, for example, has been described as '. . . a proper collector, not just an accumulator, being concerned with differentiated objects which often [had] exchange value . . .' (Ucko, 2001). This quote already introduces some important ideas into our understanding of collecting. It contrasts collecting with accumulating, suggests that the objects collected had to have some 'shared' value, and that the objects should not all be the same. More critically, it argues that not all collectors are equal. Most of us would probably agree with this, although we might think in terms of how 'serious' someone was about their collection: how much time and money were they prepared to spend on it, for example. Ucko (2001: 282) says of Freud, '. . . [his] apparent reticence concerning his passion to collect . . . hid a collecting activity which he likened to smoking in its addicting habit . . . and which might even have enabled him to give up smoking if only he had been able to afford to buy sufficient antiquities . . .'

Many offenders convicted of downloading illegal images of children from the Internet will differentiate themselves from 'paedophiles' by calling themselves 'collectors'. While we might conclude that this is one way of rationalising and normalising their interests and distancing themselves from a problematic and stigmatising identity, it clearly is, for some, an important aspect of their offending behaviour. If the function of the images was solely sexual, it would be difficult to make sense of why many seized collections are so large. Indeed, the importance of the process of collecting abuse images for the adult with a sexual interest in children can both distract from and distort the central sexual significance of the material collected. On the other hand, we cannot ignore the fact that collecting does embody certain features that can drive and enhance engagement with Internet related abuse images. This chapter will briefly examine the sparse literature on the psychology of collecting (as opposed to the huge literature on being a collector) in order to try and understand some of the important functions of collecting.

Defining collecting

Police, probation and child protection services all use the terms collecting and collector when talking about an individual who has actively acquired and retained illegal images of children. The term has slipped into common usage, and this may be due to the desire to make sense of what offenders are actually doing. The product of this activity, the collection, may vary from an aggregation of items, to something more focused and organised, that has an identifiable structure.

Of course, as we have already noted, collections can be of any objects, not only abuse images. At a very general level, we can define collecting as the selecting, gathering and keeping of objects of subjective value (Muensterberger, 1994). The emphasis on the subjective value placed on the objects is important, because the intensity of the feelings expressed about a given object, or about the aggregation of objects, does not always relate to its financial, aesthetic or commercial value. An example of this can be seen in people who collect Sylvanian family toys. These are small, soft-toy animals (cats, rabbits etc.) dressed to resemble humans living in an idealised rural, western community and produced by a Japanese company to conform to three-generation families, with all the artifacts that human families require. These are avidly collected by both children and adults (Houlton and Short, 1995).

Belk (1995) places emphasis on the emotional intensity attached to collecting behaviour for those who collect, '. . . the process of actively, selectively, and passionately acquiring and possessing things removed from ordinary use and perceived as part of a set of non-identical objects and experiences'. This definition is a useful one in relation to abuse images and it draws our attention to a number of important features of collecting:

1. Collecting is a process, whose development depends upon what has gone before, and the availability of items to be collected in the future.
2. The process is an active and selective one, in that generally a collection involves some definite and identifiable objects.
3. Collections are organised around sets of related but different items (although for purposes of trading and exchange duplicates may be retained).
4. The objects collected share common qualities but are non-identical.
5. There is an emotional intensity to collecting, which has been described as passionate.
6. Collecting often occurs within a social context, as collectors interact with each other to acquire desired objects.
7. The subjective value of the collection may have a competitive element to it, expressed in relation to collections held by others (bigger, rarer etc.).

An important feature of collecting is that the objects collected also have some personal relevance for the collector, as well as having a public or social context. As suggested by Muensterberger (1994), while two collectors may crave the same object (seen, for example, in intense and competitive bidding in a salesroom) their causal reason for desiring it, and their way of going about obtaining it, may be very different. The collected objects are seen therefore, to have a use or a function for the collector. Belk and Wallendorf (1997) have argued that collections are a reflection of an individual's identity, in that they offer the opportunity to express personal qualities and reflect individual experiences. Clifford (1995: 238) suggested that possessions serve to shape our identities, separating self from others, 'A boy's accumulation of miniature cars, a

girl's dolls . . . in these small rituals we observe the channelling of obsession, an exercise in how to make the world one's own . . . An excessive, sometimes even rapacious need to *have* is transformed into a rule-governed, meaningful desire. Thus the self which must *possess,* but cannot have it all, learns to select, order, classify in hierarchies – to make 'good' collections'. Muensterberger (1994) goes beyond this to suggest that collectors assign power and value to objects because their presence and possession seems to have a modifying function in the owner's mental state, such as keeping anxiety and uncertainty under control. Collecting then becomes more than the experience of pleasure from having obtained yet another object. Collectors are never satisfied with the acquisition of one object, but make repeated acquisitions. Within a psychodynamic framework, such acquisitiveness is seen as a vehicle to cope with inner anxiety and to distance oneself from the future anxieties, with all the confusing problems of need and longing. This analysis may have great relevance when applied to collections of abuse images.

Accumulation, hoarding, dealing and collecting

However, whilst we all accumulate objects in the course of our lifetime, it is important to distinguish between accumulation and collecting. Accumulation does not have the specificity of collecting, nor does it have the same selectivity. It is more like a refusal to get rid of objects (they might have some use in the future!) and has some of the characteristics of hoarding. Although scholars have debated the distinctions between terms such as 'normal collecting', 'obsessive collecting' and 'pathological hoarding' (Wu and Watson, in press), hoarding is typically defined as the collecting of, and inability to discard, excessive quantities of useless or valueless items (Frost and Gross, 1993). Hoarding may have some reference to future need (even though this may have little basis in reality), and at times may become problematic because of volume. There is also relative agreement that for hoarding to be seen as pathological, the items must occupy excessive amounts of space and also interfere with daily functioning (Frost et al., 2000). For example, while hoarding rubber bands is unlikely to present difficulties, large cardboard boxes may intrude on everyday social space. But the sense of specificity and selectivity that characterises the collection is missing in the hoard. It is also the case that the word hoarding carries with it very different attributions to that of collecting. The latter tends to be associated with objects that have, or will acquire, some extrinsic value. When we talk about hoarding, we rarely make reference to the aesthetic value of the items collected. We also know that compulsive hoarding occurs in 20–30 per cent of people diagnosed as having Obsessive Compulsive Disorder (Frost et al., 1996). The distinction between hoarded abuse images and collected abuse images has yet to be explored; but quite clearly it might have an important bearing on our understanding of offenders in possession of illegal images of children.

In the context of collecting, we also need to distinguish between the collector and the dealer. The latter may also be a collector, but monetary considerations motivate the acquisition of at least some of the objects. However, the dealer may also engage in this process in order to support their own collecting behaviour, and reap the rewards of both dealing and collecting. This has relevance in the context of abuse images, where dealing in images may play an important role in the acquisition of other pornography for the person's collection. Collections therefore are not simple aggregations of items; they may have utility and value and reflect structured and deliberate choices. Such choices may be very specific, as when the person searches for a particular item, or more general, as when someone looks for a class of items. Collections can be quite personal and private, but they generally are given meaning by being held in relation to other people's collections. Bjarkman (2004) described this in relation to two research participants who collected video-tapes, 'Dave and John are both networked into tightly knit trading loops of archivists who grant each other 'free run'. . . of their collections, instead of orchestrating trade on a one-for-one basis, BUT . . . much tape collecting activity is fuelled by the spirit of competition, even among long-time friends . . .'

Qualities of items collected

A necessary element of a collector's approach to collecting is recognition of the 'whole' to which their collection relates as a 'part'. The collector has a sense (however unapproachable and ill defined) of the extent and nature of the possible items within the category collected, of which their collection is a fraction. Acquisitiveness may well be a factor in collecting behaviour, but the selectivity shown by the collector suggests that choices are strategically made in relation to a sense of the overall category of items collected. Recognition of this may help in understanding the driven qualities of collectors, in that completeness provides a powerful motivator to focus and drive collecting. Bjarkman (2004: 222) suggested that, 'For the self who wants but cannot possess it all, the mere fact of desired objects that cannot be held within the corpus of the collection can cause considerable distress'. For Benjamin (1969), ownership was seen as the most intimate relationship that one can have to objects – a will to own and not just enjoy, that admits items into the growing collection. Muensterberger (1994) argued that one central aspect of collecting behaviour is that there has to be a more or less continuous flow of objects to collect and that it is this flow that captivates the collector. There is therefore a point at which interest in a collection may change when supply diminishes beyond a certain point. Part of the thrill of collecting relates to surmounting the obstacles that get in the way of securing the desired object, but there has to be some real possibility of obtaining it. This is clearly of great significance in relation to collecting abuse images.

Cataloguing

A related feature of collecting is cataloguing. Such cataloguing occurs at different levels, but appears to be an important part of the collecting process, giving a structure to the collection and some notion of order. It is what the collector does after he has acquired the objects (although some types of collections may already have a pre-existing structure to them). The collection needs to be accessible and the objects need to be stored in some way that protects their physical integrity. Collections of dried flowers, for example, are stored and displayed in a particular way so as to protect them. Keeping them loose in a cardboard box would be likely to cause damage, but would also render the collection largely inaccessible. Accessibility may have a public or a private quality, such that the collection may be openly displayed or kept only for viewing by the collector. Any collection will also display some level of organisation, and this organisation may change over time as the number of variety of objects within the collection increases. A collection of paintings for example may focus on artists from a particular era. As the numbers of paintings accumulate, the collector may further organise the works according to particular themes across paintings or within the category of each artist. What is important about such organising behaviour is that it increases the engagement that the collector has with the objects collected. Such cataloguing may change over time in relation to the unwieldiness of the collection. For example, Dinsmore (1998: 218) in the context of videotapes, reported on the collectors 'gradual and reluctant 'imposition' of rule-governed organisational systems as their collections grow unwieldy'.

Problematic collecting

Most of us think of collecting as a harmless and even useful past time. Indeed, we may actively encourage collecting as a way of passing time, meeting other people and generating a sense of satisfaction or pleasure in our lives. Many historical collections provide an important educational function, while others may have led to the retention of social artefacts that would have otherwise been lost. But there are ways in which collecting can be problematic. Problems may arise in relation to:

1. *Level of engagement and rate of behaviour associated with collecting* – here the process of collecting becomes all engrossing and takes place to the exclusion of other activities, such as caring for children, engagement with work, relating to family or friends. This also of course makes reference to the driven quality of collecting.
2. *Social and financial exclusion* – here collecting takes place in the context of an intensive focusing on a narrowly defined collection, to the exclusion of other interests, at perhaps financially unsustainable or damaging levels, and may diminish social opportunity. The psychological and temporal space for family contacts and parenting are necessarily reduced in such circumstances.
3. *Content* – an issue of obvious relevance to the concerns about abuse images. Where the content of collections is illegal, then openness is not possible, and the social context to the collection is necessarily different. This seems to suggest that some forms of collecting can be much more solitary than others, where the

intrinsic value to the individual of the item collected itself is the principle, if not the only, factor driving collecting. Associated with this may be the thrill of the risk that comes with the collection of illegal materials.

Collecting abuse images

Abuse images on the Internet are an obvious example where level of engagement and rate, social exclusion and content may all be problematic. However, there is remarkably little empirical data about collecting abuse images. Lanning (1992) from the perspective of law enforcement, suggested that one feature of paedophile behaviour is that they almost always collect abuse images or child erotica. The emphasis is on collection as it relates to saving material, rather than simply viewing it. He lists the kinds of items collected and includes: books, magazines, articles, newspapers, photographs, negatives, slides, movies, albums, drawings, audiotapes, videotapes and equipment, personal letters, diaries, clothing, sexual aids, souvenirs, toys, games, lists, paintings, ledgers, photographic equipment and so on. The defining feature of such collections is that in some way, they all relate to children.

Until the advent of the Internet, accessing actual pornography (as opposed to erotica) was difficult, risky and expensive. The size of collections was therefore related to the ability to source and buy pornography, as well as having a secure space in which to keep it. The fact that abuse images was so difficult to obtain in the past also increased the likelihood that it would have to be obtained over a long period of time, and may have had consequences in terms of the age of the collector. Lanning (1992) has also asserted that there are differences between types of 'child molesters' in the variety of material collected. The COPINE data would suggest that where there is not an exclusive sexual interest in children, but an interest in a variety of illegal or unorthodox material, then abuse images becomes one aspect of the collection, rather than the totality. This is seen very clearly in relation to the acquisition of Internet pornography, where collectors have categories based on some characteristic of the material saved. Prior to the advent of the Internet, collections were likely to be limited to whatever was readily available, and certainly animal and rape pornography, for example, would not have been easily obtained.

Collectors of pornography

In the context of abuse images, Hartman et al. (1984) identified four types of collectors that they called closet, isolated, cottage and commercial:

1. *The closet collector* was one who acquired material from commercial sources, kept the collection a secret and was thought not to be actively engaged in the molestation of children.
2. *The isolated collector* was described as actively molesting children as well as collecting abuse images or erotica. The fear of discovery ensured that this collector used pornography either for solitary sexual behaviour or in the context of the victim. The materials collected might also include those of the victim produced by the collector, as well as those from other sources.
3. *The cottage collector* was said to share his collection and sexual activity with other individuals, primarily as a means of validating their own behaviour and without any monetary consideration.
4. *The commercial collector* sees his collection as a commercial proposition and will sell duplicates of his collection to others. Hartman et al. (1984) suggest that although primarily motivated by profit, such collectors are also likely to be actively engaged in the abuse of children.

This early work clearly makes no reference to the Internet, and the contemporary ease of access to abuse images. But in essence, the same analysis seems as relevant today as it did 20 years ago.

Why do paedophiles collect abuse images?

There is little research that has explored why paedophiles collect abuse images and erotica. Lanning (1992) argued that collecting this material may help paedophiles satisfy, deal with or reinforce their compulsive, persistent sexual fantasies about children, and fulfil a need for validation. As we have already considered in earlier chapters, many people with a sexual interest in children need to justify their own interest, and the availability of material to collect is one way of achieving this. Collections can also act as trophies, memorabilia of previous relationships with children. They fix the victim at the very age they were at when most attractive to

the paedophile and this may be one of the reasons why many paedophiles carefully date and label their collections. In another context Nora (1989) had talked about collecting as a way 'to stop time, to block the work of forgetting . . . to materialise the immaterial' so that our experiences can be transformed into tangible records to be re-accessed at will, in journals, scrapbooks and photo-albums.

Lanning (1992) discussed five ways in which those with a sexual interest in children may use their collections of abuse images:

1. *For sexual arousal and gratification*. In this context, its function is similar to adult pornography in that it enables fantasy and masturbation.
2. *Lowering of children's inhibitions* by exposing them to pictures of other children apparently enjoying sexual activity. This form of vicarious learning can also serve to normalise the activities for the child, and increase the possibility of elevating both curiosity and arousal.
3. *Blackmail*. While there have been very few studies of those who are the victims of abuse images, it is agreed that such victimisation is a source of extreme shame (Svedin and Back, 1996). Children are likely to assume some of the responsibility for what has taken place, and photographs are a permanent record of what has happened. Threat of disclosure of such material may be used as blackmail to ensure the child's silence, although detailed and reliable evidence of this is not easily come by.
4. *Exchange* – Lanning talked about this exchange in the context of information. The paedophile may exchange part of their collection for information about a given child, the value of the exchange lying in the extreme qualities of the pictures.
5. *Profit* – in that historically, where material was difficult to find, there was a commercial value attached to it. Even non-pornographic pictures that can function as erotica may have commercial value if used in the context of a magazine.

Collecting and the Internet

If we consider the role of the Internet in collecting behaviour, we can see that this new technology facilitates collecting in many ways. Primarily, it increases ease of access to material that is clearly pornographic, as opposed to erotic, across a wide number of categories, including abuse images. Access can be secret without all the risks associated with attempting to purchase commercially produced items. Pictures can be downloaded without the need to identify oneself or to communicate with another person. Equally, such activity can take place within the context of an identifiable community. Bjarkman (2004) likened the notion of a collecting community to a series of concentric social circles, with a core that can seem, for many, impenetrable. While such complex communities are united in their allegiances, they are often internally divided by 'factions, fractions, fiction and flaming'. The innermost circles of such communities divide up what power they have, but do so without having to throw open the doors to every newcomer (newbie) who expresses an interest in their hard-won collection.

Along with ease of access through the Internet comes volume. As there is relatively little commercial exchange in relation to abuse images, most images can be obtained without any financial cost. Rapid acquisition is facilitated by trading images with others, or by accessing somebody else's collection. Paedophiles who use IRC (Internet Relay Chat) can make available the contents of their hard drive to other users using, for example File Transmission Protocols (FTPs). Slater (1998: 94) has provided a good description of how this works, 'If you can transmit lines of text over IRC, you can transmit anything that is digitised, thus any kind of representation: photos, drawings, video clips, sound files, streamed sound or video, software program files. Hence the sexpics trade: 'sexpics' usually refers to any kind of sexually explicit material circulated within this scene. People meet up or advertise their wares in and around designated channels, chatting either publicly in the channel or privately. Alongside the chat, they can send files to each other (technically, this is done by a facility called DCC, direct computer to computer communication). They can also use a facility called 'fserve' (file server): someone offering an fserve allows others (usually by way of a 'trigger' word that can be typed in a channel window) to access and peruse directly the hard disk of their local computer, looking through subdirectories and lists of files, and then to select and download the files they want, usually up to a limit (a specified number of kilobytes) . . . people can also

set up ratios (you can download x bytes for every y bytes you upload): these are like exchange rates or prices'.

Along with ease of access is also ease of storage. Unlike hard copies of photographs, images stored electronically, either on a hard disk, diskettes, CD-ROMs or data sticks, take up very little physical space. Images can even be stored electronically at a location both anonymous and distant from the location of the collector's PC. Storage also implies some level of organisation. Whether this is simply placing all images within one file or folder, or sorting them according to some complicated system of categories, depends on the collector and the importance placed on rapid access to material. Organising material electronically means that photographs can be moved easily, so that there is a dynamic to the collection. As the quantity increases, or the focus changes, there is a potential parallel change in the way that a collection is catalogued. Cataloguing is an important feature of collecting and is probably one factor that differentiates the collection from an accumulation. Bjarkman (2004) suggested that for her research participants, cataloguing was not only a practical necessity but one of its central pleasures. Retrieval systems acted as data bases that facilitated cross-referencing and allowed for multiple field searches. The author concluded that, 'It affords a comforting sense of coherence, achievement, control and authority (even authorship) as John and Dave pour proudly over the content of their collections'. As the person's collection grows, so does their catalogue, which may start out as a by-product of the collection but increasingly becomes a project in its own right, that '. . . presents its own managerial challenges and material pay-offs as missing episodes are obtained and slotted into the data base like pieces in a jigsaw puzzle, cut from 'want' lists and pasted into 'have' lists.'

In the context of sexually explicit material on the Internet, it is of interest that cataloguing systems tend to be very traditional, and the images traded and their organisation into categories is virtually indistinguishable from the way that magazines and videos are organised on the shelves of adult stores or sex shops. 'These routinely organise body imagery into a conventional repertoire of sex acts (couples in action, group sex, lesbian, oral, cum shots, anal); into conventional body types (blondes, brunettes, redheads); into degrees of 'hardness' (celebrities, poses, lingerie, hard, weird, xtreme); into conventional fetishes and kinks (bondage, voyeur/exhibition, mature, latex, etc.)' (Slater, 1998: 100). This conventionality can also be seen in the types of fantasies portrayed in on-line sexual imagery of children.

Abuse images, as they appear on the Internet, often emerge as a series of photographs. Series of pictures often 'tell stories' (for example, a sequence of pictures showing a child undressing) or they illustrate a theme (e.g., oral sex). The series are identified by a name and each picture by the series name and usually a number, although the person producing or distributing the series does not necessarily release them in the production sequence, nor necessarily name them in the way a collector might. Collecting on the Internet often means looking for material that is new to the collector, or completes part of a series. The advantage to the collector of collecting series of photographs of a child, as opposed to single shots from a series, is that it adds value to the collection, both subjectively and with regard to the community. For the individual, there is satisfaction in completing a series, but there is also potential for increasing the capacity to create sexual arousal.

The seeking out of new material is an important aspect of collecting per se, but in the context of abuse images it has a more sinister aspect. Many of the images available on the Internet are relatively old and in order to supply the demand by collectors for new material, more photographs have to be taken that depict the ongoing sexualisation or abuse of children. Within the complex social network of the Internet, accessing new or private collections requires the exchange of material that is of interest to other collectors. For some collectors, this has directly led to the production of new material through the abuse of children in the collector's immediate social network, to enable access to other material. Notions of status and power are intimately associated with this, both with respect to the producer and the collector who can distribute pictures to others.

When we discussed collecting, we noted that a distinction needs to be made between collectors and dealers, although they are not mutually exclusive. Whilst there is an increase in the amount of commercially available abuse images on the Internet, the vast majority of images are not commercially produced. In relation to video collecting, it has been suggested that although there is evidence of quasi-economic discourses of scarcity, supply and demand and 'trade-value', the symbolic or social value of rare recordings converts into actual monetary value less readily than might be expected (Bjarkman, 2004).

The advent of the digital camera has meant that individual collectors can easily become producers of abuse images if they have access to children (usually in the context of domestic or institutional proximity to a child or children). As the move from collector to producer and distributor of such images is not commercially driven, we might assume that what motivates the individual is power. Given access to a child or a group of children with whom they have influence, the producer can choose what photographs to take, when to take them and when, where and to whom to distribute them; likewise the distributor or trader. The release of new material is followed by a flurry of Internet communications demanding more images of the same child or children, release of parts of a missing series, and even requests for specific types of abuse within the images. Some new images may be privately distributed to a chosen group of people on the Internet. Such private images are invariably not for general release, although the control that the individual who produced them has over these images is illusory once traded or exchanged, as invariably they will eventually become part of a larger distribution network. The selective release of material to enhance the status of the poster (and perhaps producer if they are the same person) can frequently be seen in the Internet abuse images environment, and is undoubtedly an important factor in sustaining trading behaviours.

Points of concern

- In the context of the Internet and the enormous amount of material available, the qualities of an individual's collection relates largely to preference, rather than to availability.
- However, where pictures have a currency in terms of trade, then there may be items within a given collection that have no direct appeal for the collector, but are retained as potential tradable items attractive to others. This may be difficult to assess without access to a forensic report of trading activity, but it is important for practitioners not to assume that because given types of images form part of the collection that they relate directly to an offending fantasy held by the offender. It would therefore seem that

although there is a paucity of research in this area, we can at least discriminate between:

1. Accumulating, hoarding and collecting.
2. The presence or absence of cataloguing systems.
3. The presence of multiple or single pornographies.
4. Where the focus is exclusively illegal images of children, the dominant gender of the children portrayed.

In a way, it might have been supposed that the advent of new technologies should have made collecting activities less likely, rather than more. Once in active circulation, digitised images are permanently accessible, and degradation and storage constraints become things of the past. At present, this does not seem to be the case, and as technology advances, so does the size of individual collections of illegal images. In making sense of such offending activity, we need to be mindful of the individual's collection, their level of engagement with it and the way that it functioned in meeting both sexual and non-sexual needs.

Working with clients

As previously discussed, many clients convicted of downloading abuse images will deny that the primary function of the material was for their sexual use, but will instead focus on themselves as collectors. Indeed, distinctions are often made by offenders between paedophiles and collectors (serving to distance collectors from paedophiles). Clearly, for some offenders the function of collecting will have assumed an enormous importance and may have moved them further along the offending process. However, the function of the material remains sexual, and offenders need to acknowledge this.

Another aspect of collecting behaviour is its compulsive qualities. Again, clients will often describe this in terms of 'addiction' and loss of control. Many such offenders will have thought of their early engagement with the Internet as being a means of controlling many of the unsatisfactory things within their lives, only to find that as engagement escalates, feelings of control are often replaced by those of compulsion and chaos.

The aims for the practitioner are to:

• Examine the client's collecting behaviour and the role that it played in the commission of the offence.

• Help clients recognise relationships between collecting and unsatisfactory qualities of their lives.
• Help clients identify and control the compulsive qualities of their own inappropriate collecting behaviour.
• Help generate new ways of meeting needs outside the context of collecting.
• Identify what their 'new me' would be like, in the context of stopping collecting behaviour, being mindful of where this fits with identified values (Chapter 6).

This is of particular importance for those who traded images and whose collections were highly organised (put into directories and folders and catalogued), and who spent a lot of time off-line sorting through the pornography they had downloaded. It is also of particular relevance to those whose offence includes the production of images to trade whether through the photography of a child, or through the construction of pseudo images.

Changing behaviour

For at least some offenders, the intense, compulsive quality of the collecting behaviour associated with Internet images of children is seen as being problematic. This is not necessarily in relation to the content of the images, but the negative impact that it has on their social and emotional lives. In addition, the very act of collecting can be used by offenders to distance themselves from the content of their collection. Again, it is important for practitioners not to underestimate the compulsive qualities to some of this collecting behaviour and what we are asking offenders to both forego and endure on 'giving it up'. It may also be the case that some offenders collect, accumulate and possibly hoard across many artefacts.

The first step in working on this with offenders is for them to be part of the process of assessing in what ways their collecting behaviour might have been problematic for them. This is important because while it is easy to see that it was a problem because it was a breach of the law, for some the devastating effect that other aspects of the behaviour has had on their lives may not be so transparent. Practitioners also need to differentiate between accumulating and hoarding activity from collecting per se. The former may have many of the qualities of Obsessive

Compulsive Disorder, may be part of a spectrum of obsessional behaviour, and may require specialist treatment in and of itself. Driven and passionate collecting is likely to have been accompanied by cataloguing and trading behaviour, and it may be that these are both specific targets for change. Helping the client look at how their collection was structured and the function of some of the images retained is important in understanding the meaning of the collection for the individual. In a similar way, engaging the client in an analysis of the amount of time dedicated to the collection may be useful. If we think of this in terms of the client's values, it is possible then to look at where it fits with what the client aspires to in their lives, and how collecting might have been used as a means of avoiding other important life issues.

Giving up collecting Internet images is likely only to be seen as relevant to the individual if it is seen as a way of 'doing things differently' to improve their lives. In working with the client to understand what needs might have been met through collecting and how these might be achieved in a way that is more life enhancing is an important part of changing behaviour. This is not about imposing our values on someone else, but trying to help the individual look at what they value and how this might be lived.

Exercises

1. Ask the client to describe their collection and what factors made it problematic (content; amount of time spent engaged with the collection; exclusion of other valued activities etc).
2. How was the collection of pornographic pictures organised? Ask the client to identify the organising principal behind the collection and to name the directories and folders that were used. What would these have meant to someone who did not collect child abuse images?
3. Was there anything in the collection that the client did not find sexually arousing? Name any such categories (such as 'baby sex' or 'boy-animal') or series. Why might such material be kept?

4. How much time was spent on or off-line sorting the photographs or video clips? Using a pie chart, ask the client to specify how much time they had available each day, and what portion of this was spent on such activities, distinguishing between 'on-line' and 'off-line' time periods. Compare with a 'new me' chart.
5. What function did collecting have for the client? What role did it occupy or what did it substitute for? What was missed out on (that the client valued) because of the time spent collecting?
6. What did the client tell him or herself to justify collecting abuse images? What personal significance did the photographs have for the client?
7. What strategies might the offender use to:
   (a) Cope with the withdrawal from the emotional intensity of offending and any 'cravings' that might follow (the exercises in Chapter 6 may be very significant here).
   (b) Put in place strategies to avoid the social context of collecting.
   (c) Accept the loss of the collection and make a commitment not to further collect abuse images.

Completion criteria

By the end of this section the client should have:

1. Given a written description of their collection and identified the factors that made it problematic.
2. Given a detailed account of how their collection was organised, and looked at whether material was collected which was not sexually arousing.
3. Created a pie chart of the proportions of time spent on-line and off-line engaged in collecting activities.
4. Described the function that collecting had in their life.
5. Listed the self-statements used to justify collecting abusive images.
6. Generated ACTIONS that would reduce the likelihood of future collecting.

Materials

What made collecting problematic for me?

1. Describe any problems which resulted from collecting the child abuse images. What changes (if any) did it make to your usual lifestyle at the time? How important was your collection to you? What other activities did it replace? What other activities did you not do as a result?

2. Describe your personal and social relationships at the time of your Internet use. What effect did your use of the Internet have (if any) on your personal and social relationships?

Materials *continued*

3. Describe your financial situation, before and during your Internet use. Were there any changes as a result of your Internet use? If so what were these?

4. Describe the content of your collection. (Size of your collection, type of images, sexual activities portrayed, age race and gender of the children in the images.)

5. How did you organise the images in your collection? What categories did you use? What names did you use for your directories and folders?

Chapter Nine

Maintaining Change

Aims of the chapter

This is the final chapter in this book, and in some ways is the most difficult. While there is an emerging literature about offending related to Internet abuse images, there are as yet no evidence-based programmes that inform practitioners about the effectiveness of intervention over the long term. As already noted, there is still confusion over basic issues as to what we hope to achieve through intervention. Is it reducing the likelihood of a person accessing or trading abuse images on the Internet, or is it to do with reducing the risk of a future contact offence? If it is the former, would something as simple as an abstinence model in relation to accessing the Internet be the most effective approach? If it is the latter, we need to have more evidence about the relationship between viewing images and the commission of contact offences, or at least be able to distinguish between people and contexts that increase the likelihood of one influencing the other.

Throughout the book we have tried to integrate the disparate research in this area and to provide guidelines for practitioners about the nature of offending on the Internet and some of the issues that need to be addressed when working with offenders. It has been important to note the heterogeneity of such offenders, and to distinguish between different kinds of offending activities. In doing so our emphasis has been on the importance of taking a dynamic, rather than static, perspective about offending behaviour and noting that individuals both approach and react to offending contexts in different ways. We have also emphasised the importance of a functional analytic approach to offending activity.

The following review of the literature attempts to consider three therapeutic approaches, which it is hoped will not confuse but help clarify some of the complexities covered by earlier chapters. These are:

- Relapse Prevention Models
- Good Lives Models
- Acceptance and Commitment Therapy

All three of these have emerged from very different theoretical contexts, and there is always the risk of loosing all coherence and integrity by trying to look at how, in practice, they may compliment each other. You, the reader, will have to decide whether that is a risk that was worth taking.

The aims of this chapter therefore are:

- To reconsider the explicit values identified by the offender and whether these have changed over the course of treatment.
- To set goals for the future that will help the person continue to act in a way that they value.
- To identify factors that may inhibit movement, such as contexts, behaviours, emotions and thoughts.
- To identify the resources, both internal and external that can be drawn upon to optimise the likelihood of acting in a way that is congruent with the participant's values.

Background

Relapse prevention model

To date, research indicates that manual-based cognitive-behavioural treatment (CBT) programmes that are structured and implemented in a systematic and therapeutically responsive manner, by qualified and well-trained staff, in a supportive environment, are more likely to produce the desired effect of lower re-offending rates (Andrews and Bonta, 1998). Therapy, within a cognitive behavioural framework, aims to work towards a negotiated goal (or set of goals) within a collaborative relationship, with the expectation that therapeutic gains should be maintained after the therapy ends. In the context of CBT with sex offenders, the beneficiaries of intervention are thought to go beyond the individual in therapy to include adults and children who are possibly at risk should the offender go on to commit further offences. Therefore one goal of therapy is the reduction of risk to others through change in the offender's behaviour. Within this framework, one model has tended to dominate treatment programmes – a relapse prevention model, which was developed by Martlatt and Gordon (1985) to aid the treatment of a variety of addictive behaviours, such as substance abuse and over-eating. Treatment programmes that include a relapse prevention element tend to focus on helping the individual to identify high-risk situations, avoid usual, problematic coping styles, and increase their perceived self-efficacy in how to deal with such situations. This approach has been used extensively with sex offenders as a maintenance strategy to build on treatment gains (Laws, 1999; Ward and Hudson, 1996; Pithers et al., 1983) and increasingly has become the underlying framework for service delivery.

The original work by Marlatt and Gordon (1985) demonstrated that three high-risk situations constituted almost 75 per cent of relapse episodes for people exhibiting many forms of 'addictive' behaviour. These high-risk situations were:

- negative emotional states
- interpersonal conflict
- social pressure

The therapeutic goal in relation to relapse prevention is one of self-management, and involves teaching the individual alternative responses to high-risk situations (Andrews and Bonta, 1998). Laws (1999: 291) has been critical of the way that relapse prevention has been loosely defined within therapy saying that, '. . . virtually any kind of post treatment intervention has been called relapse prevention'. He went on to identify the following nine core components to a relapse prevention model:

1. The use of an offence chain or cognitive behavioural chain, which teaches the offender to recognise their offence cycle or the cues which may act as a warning of the likelihood of committing a criminal act.
2. Relapse rehearsal, where the offender identifies potential relapse situations, and focuses on the development of skills to address these through a form of corrective feedback, using rehearsal opportunities for low-risk responses.
3. Advanced relapse rehearsal by practicing in hypothetical relapse situations involving increasingly more difficult scenes.
4. Identification of high-risk situations, which are likely to promote criminal activity, and the

development of alternative ways of dealing with such situations.
5. Dealing with failure (relapse) constructively, rather than with discouragement.
6. Reinforcing self-efficacy, and promoting the idea that the offender will be successful as a result of participating in the treatment.
7. The enhancement of coping skills.
8. External support systems involving training family, friends, colleagues and peers to actively reinforce the pro-social behaviours learned in treatment.
9. Booster sessions or aftercare, which focus on supplementing the original treatment programme.

Dowden et al. (2004) have noted that there is very little controlled outcome research to formally evaluate the effectiveness of this treatment approach and that this is surprising given the current emphasis in establishing 'what works' and an emphasis on empirically validated strategies for the treatment of offender populations. An earlier meta-analytic review by these authors (Andrews et al., 2003) had highlighted the lack of controlled outcome studies in this area but suggested that for studies which did use a relapse prevention component, the preliminary findings were positive. Dowden et al. (2004) further analysed 24 studies as part of this meta-analysis, which revealed that relapse prevention programmes were associated with a moderate mean reduction in recidivism. However, they identified that certain elements of relapse prevention are associated with more positive treatment effects than others. These included:

1. Training of significant others.
2. The identification of the offence chain and high risk situations, along with role play of these situations.
3. Increasing the number of relapse prevention components targeted within the programme.
4. A detailed specification of relapse prevention elements.

Of interest, teaching an offender how to deal with failure situations and the provision of booster sessions were not as effective. In addition, programmes that did not predominantly target criminogenic needs along with relapse prevention elements, or failed to use cognitive-behavioural/social learning strategies were not associated with reductions in offender recidivism. Surprisingly, a further finding from this analysis was that setting was not a factor. Programmes that were run inside institutional settings, such as prison, were as effective as those in the community.

However, the uncritical adoption of a generic relapse prevention model in the treatment of sex offenders has not gone unchallenged. Ward et al. (2004: 143) has suggested, '. . . unless we understand the processes involved for an individual offender, how can we credibly identify areas for clinical intervention . . . This is even more profound when we consider that treatment might affect how relapse may occur at some time in the future, that is, the offending process might change'. These authors suggested that even if we see relapse prevention only as a method to help maintain treatment induced change, rather than as a way to structure the intervention, problems still need to be addressed in that relapse prevention plans need to reflect the reality of what might happen and not be arbitrarily constrained by an inadequate model.

Good lives model

Ward and Brown (2004: 244) have also argued that the management of risk of re-offending should be seen as a necessary, but not sufficient condition, for the rehabilitation of offenders. They proposed that the best way to lower recidivism rates is to also equip individuals to live more fulfilling lives, rather than to simply develop increasingly sophisticated risk management measures and strategies, 'At the end of the day, most offenders have more in common with us than not, and like the rest of humanity have needs to be loved, valued, to function competently, and to be part of a community'. The focus is on building on the strengths of the individual rather than repairing weaknesses. As discussed in Chapters 1 and 6, these authors proposed a Good Lives Model as having the conceptual resources to resolve issues in a constructive manner, 'From the perspective of this model, humans are by nature active, goal-seeking beings who are consistently engaged in the process of constructing a sense of purpose and meaning in their lives. This is hypothesized to emerge from the pursuit and achievement of primary human goods (valued aspects of human functioning and living) which collectively allow individuals to flourish; that is, to achieve high

levels of well-being' (p 246). They identify nine classes of primary goods:

1. Life (which may include healthy living and optimal physical functioning, as well as sexual satisfaction).
2. Knowledge.
3. Excellence in play and work (including mastery experiences).
4. Excellence in agency (i.e., autonomy and self-directedness).
5. Inner peace (i.e., freedom from emotional turmoil and stress).
6. Relatedness (which would include intimate, romantic and family relationships).
7. Spirituality (in the broader sense of finding meaning and purpose in life).
8. Happiness.
9. Creativity.

It is argued that such a conception of good lives is always context dependent and that there is no such thing as the right kind of life for an individual that cuts across every conceivable setting. They have also hypothesised that in the case of criminal behaviour, there are four major difficulties:

1. Problems with the means used to secure goods.
2. A lack of scope within a good lives plan.
3. The presence of conflict among goals.
4. A lack of the necessary capacities to form and adjust a good lives model to changing circumstances.

The offender is hypothesised to commit criminal offences because they lack the capabilities to realise valued outcomes, in their environment, in a personally fulfilling and socially acceptable way.

Acceptance and commitment therapy

We have earlier agued that one central way of making explicit the values of the offender is through the assessment and continued exploration of what the person values in their life, for themselves and not in the service of pleasing or agreeing with others. This is not the same as assuming that both therapist and offender will necessarily value the same things, but as indicated by Ward and Brown (2004) there are commonalities across what most of us aspire for in our lives. Equally, there are also inconsistencies in how we live according to these values (which are not the same as 'moral' or 'political' beliefs). For example, we may say that what we value most is a healthy life where we optimise our physical functioning. However, if we look at how we live that value it may be that we face a stark reality of 'not having the time' to exercise, eating fast food and drinking too much alcohol to cope with the immediate stressors of life. Examining the consistencies and inconsistencies between explicit values and the way that we behave can also help us understand the things that 'trip us up' in trying to work towards a valued way of life. In the context of abuse images, it helps the client to consider how far accessing images moves the person forward in terms of their personal values, or whether it blocks that movement by focusing on meeting more immediate needs. Wilson and Byrd (2004: 165) have suggested that from an ACT perspective, '. . . values are not *things* so much as dynamic ongoing patterns of engagement in different life domains. Most critically, values function to organise behaviour and provide a certain sense of direction'. However, these authors have suggested that we must differentiate values from life goals, which are achievable outcomes that might be the embodiment of values, 'A value provides a life course that never ends'. While many clients may have abandoned valued domains over time, we must assume that the underlying sense of direction has not been abandoned.

In contrast to Ward and Brown's (2004) list of primary goods, the work of Hayes et al. (2004), in the context of Acceptance and Commitment Therapy, would argue that emotions such as happiness should not be confused with a value. Many people with 'addictive disorders' attempt to regulate thoughts, feelings or other private experiences even when attempts to do so cause significant behavioural harm. Happiness is something that may or may not be experienced when living life according to one's values, but essentially, unlike overt behaviours, it is not under the direct control of the individual. According to Wilson and Byrd (2004) many clients have got into difficulties by living their lives according to how they feel and what they think. One problem with using thoughts and feelings to runs one's life is that they can be very transient. Wilson and Roberts (2002) have suggested that popular culture embraces the idea that positive emotions, thoughts and bodily states cause good ways of behaving and that the opposite is true – negative feelings, thoughts and

bodily states cause bad behaviour. One consequence of this is that we expend enormous amounts of effort trying to be more confident, have higher self-esteem and be more optimistic. However, attempts to avoid negative private events may work to reduce those states over the short term, but may make things worse in the long term. Hayes and Pankey (2002: 243) argued that the value of any action is its workability measured against the client's true values (those they would have if it were a free choice), 'The bottom line is living well, not having small sets of 'good' feelings'.

One difficulty in relation to the Internet is the way it can be used to either change or enhance existing feelings. This is even more the case with abusive images where access might culminate in masturbation and ejaculation. As yet it is unclear as to what might act as discriminative stimuli (or cues) for future offending. This may include feeling states (anxiety, anticipatory excitement), thoughts about going on-line, sensory cues such as seeing a computer or touching the mouse, or behavioural contexts such as being alone with access to the Internet. We might also note in this context there may also be distinctive criminogenic qualities associated with both the physical qualities of the Internet and how we engage with those qualities (Taylor and Quayle, in press). Much of the literature relating to relapse prevention has as its focus relapse as part of a chain, mediated by 'seemingly unimportant (or irrelevant) decisions (SUDs)' which increase the possibility of placing the individual in a situation where they may offend (Steen, 2002). In identifying the parts of the chain, it is anticipated that the client will be able to engage in an alternative response. In many ways this is similar to much of the work on self-control theory, '. . . because crime and deviance are inherently gratifying, all people are motivated to do them. But because low self-control renders people less able to anticipate and respond to potential long range costs of misbehaviour, they tend to succumb to temptation. Therefore, criminal behaviour is an outgrowth of low self-control, in combination with opportunity', (Tittle and Botchkovar, 2005). However, these authors suggested that criminal opportunity, and in most instances deviant peer association, was found to predict the indicators of misbehaviour as well as or better than, and independently of, self-control.

Making values explicit may be important in that they indicate what the person may aspire to and also act as reminders of how operating in relation to short-term goals may ultimately move us further away from what we value. Tittle and Botchkovar's (2005) analysis also reminds us that opportunities and peer associations are also important influences on criminal activity in general, and we can assume, abusive behaviour in relation to Internet images. Unfortunately the Internet and the availability of illegal images of children increases the opportunity for offending, and ease of association with a deviant peer group can be established quickly and with apparent privacy and reduced fear of being caught. Both therapist and client need to be aware of this when looking at a future where the possibility of re-offending is reduced.

Points of concern

While as yet we have no evidenced based model to help us distinguish between what factors might reduce the likelihood of re-offending in relation to Internet abuse images, we know that the activities involved served a function for that individual and that it is important to address how these basic needs may be met in a more pro-social way.

A process model of offending would suggest that such functions may change over time. For many offenders, accessing images on the Internet has been a high rate behaviour which is often described as compulsive or addictive. This may be part of an avoidant pathway to the presence of negative emotions or it may be an approach pathway to meet existing emotional needs. Such differences are important in determining what issues increase the likelihood of re-offending.

It is important that you are aware of your values in relation to this therapy as well as the values of your client. Therapy is never values-free.

Working with the client

In working with the client, the goals of this section are to:

- Help prevent the client from returning to previous problematic behaviours involving the Internet.
- Move the person forward and on with a life whose goals are underpinned by values.

This final section incorporates relapse prevention with values work, and it builds on the material of

the previous chapters. At this stage, the offender should now have a greater understanding of how and perhaps why, they used illegal images of children, and realise that it is a process that is destructive, not only for the children used in the images but for the offender and those around them. What is important is that the people we are working with are left with a sense of optimism about their future (Beech and Scott Fordham, 1997) and a sense of autonomy in their ability to manage future problems.

Changing behaviour

The focus of this chapter is on consolidating change that has occurred and an examination of how the client might build on these changes to maintain change into the future. Essentially it is about meetings one's social and sexual needs without bringing harm to others or engaging in behaviour that is not socially sanctioned. It is about helping the client to identify the resources (both internal and external) that may help support them to lead a rewarding life, but which is also about living well and in accordance with what is valued. Common problems that emerge in values work include compliance with actual or perceived social convention, confusion about values, switching values in the service of emotional avoidance and the absence of values in key areas (Wilson and Byrd, 2004: 169). These authors have suggested that, 'If it is the case that the client literally values nothing but getting high and not getting caught, there is nothing to work on in therapy. By contrast, it is entirely *possible* that the person does value something, but is so frightened, demoralized, resigned, that values have been pushed out of awareness'. In this context, they have suggested that strategies to reveal avoided values could include asking whether in the past there was a time when the person wanted something, to be something or to do something. 'We are asking what they want – in a world in which what they really want is possible' (p 169).

Exercises

1. Review the original homework on the process and history of offending and get the participant to comment on how much progress they have made and where they may still be experiencing difficulties.
2. Repeat the Values Assessment (Chapter 6) and ask the participant to comment on whether

there is less of a gap between what they value and how they live those values. Be clear whether any of those values have changed. Select important values domains and help the participant to generate further goals in relation to these. Break each goal down into smaller, realisable steps. Be clear about what might be stumbling blocks in working towards these goals.

3. Develop a relapse prevention plan with the participant. This should be detailed and may involve role-playing situations which the participant anticipates that they will have particular problems with.
4. Emphasise positive life changes, rather than simply managing risk. Generate a list of pros and cons to these changes, and what long-term benefits they may bring to the person.

Completion criteria

By the end of this chapter the client should have:

1. Reviewed their personal model of their offence activities and identified what has changed and what may still remain potentially vulnerable areas.
2. Repeated the values assessment and compared the results with their original ones.
3. Set some target goals for the future in relation to their values and have broken these down into further small steps.
4. Identified and written down factors that may 'trip them up'.
5. Developed a relapse prevention plan and have role played any areas that are particularly problematic.
6. Created a table of 'consequences' in relation to leading an offence-free-life.

Materials

Relapse prevention

1. Understanding what a relapse is

A relapse can happen very easily and very quickly. A relapse has a number of stages, as shown in the 'How might a relapse happen?' section below, and although these stages occur in quick succession (very often without someone realising that they are about to have a relapse) being aware of them can help you to understand the process of relapse and how to prevent it. With self-control and determination you can prevent a relapse at any of these stages, up to and including

the 'giving up' stage. Should you go through this stage and on to the next only then will you have had a relapse because you will have done something illegal. Obviously this is not the desired goal, but rather than giving up altogether you should view this as a setback – a relapse – that ultimately you can overcome. The saying 'If at first you don't succeed, try, try and try again' is very relevant here.

How might a relapse happen?

Look at the steps below, understand them, because if you are serious about changing your behaviour you face the possibility of a relapse. Should a relapse be about to happen, by identifying the stage you are at, if possible, you might be in a better position to prevent it from happening.

The Road to Relapse

Abstinence – Non-offending. At this stage you are not engaged in any illegal activities involving children and the Internet. For example, you are not accessing illegal images of children on the Internet. With self-control and determination you can decide to stay at this stage. You know it will not be easy, but you also know that it is the right thing to do.

Seemingly Irrelevant Decisions. Going down this road is the start of a slippery slope. The decisions you make at this stage may seem innocent enough – for example, deciding to look for holiday destinations on the Internet. BUT such decisions can be risky because they place you in a position that increases the possibility of you doing something illegal.

Dangerous Situations. At this stage you are placed in a situation where you have the opportunity to offend. For example, although you may be using the Internet to gather information on holiday destinations, you will be very much aware that just a few clicks away are illegal images of children. Knowing this makes it more likely that you will decide to access illegal images. However, with self-control and determination you can stop yourself from doing so.

Lapse. A lapse can be a behaviour that brings you very close to offending. For example, you may put key words into a search engine that you know will bring up illegal sites, which you can then choose to access. A lapse can also take the form of fantasy. Perhaps you fantasise about accessing illegal images of children. Lapses such as these put you very close to offending and make it much more difficult to turn away.

Giving up. At this stage **you believe** that you have passed the point of no return, that you have failed. Your attitude is likely to be 'What the heck. I might as well do it'. After a lapse, as described above, it is very, very easy to give up.

Offending. If you decide to follow through the other stages you will eventually reach this stage. You will have made the decision to engage in illegal activities involving children and the Internet.

(Steen, 1993)

Generating alternatives

Admittedly the Internet can be useful for many things such as seeking holiday destinations, house hunting, banking, finding information and so on, but the Internet is a fairly recent phenomenon and almost anything that the Internet is used for can be obtained by other means. For example, estate agents, banks and libraries still exist because there is a need for them, as people still use them. Rather than use the Internet, and putting yourself at risk, think of alternative ways of seeking what you want.

For example:

1. You could have asked a travel agent for advice or guidance about suitable holiday destinations.
2. You could have got brochures and other literature from the travel agents.
3. You could have looked in the papers or on Teletext for holiday information.
4. You could have tuned into the holiday shows on the television.
5. You could have asked friends or family to recommend holiday destinations.

When is a relapse most likely to occur?

You are more likely to have a relapse if you are feeling bad. You may remember that earlier we looked at ways of 'Dealing with bad feelings' and you might want to read over this material again. Feeling bored, anxious, depressed or lonely makes us feel bad and leaves us vulnerable. When we are feeling bad we tend to do things that we believe will make us feel better, for example, going on-line to access illegal images of children. The thing to remember is that while choosing to do this may make you feel better at the time, in the long term you will feel worse for it. For example, afterwards you may feel guilty about what you've done, you may feel annoyed with yourself for having given in and you may

feel depressed about having had a relapse. What is more, these feelings are likely to stay with you for longer. The point is that while not giving in to our urges can make us feel bad, urges do pass and we do feel better (more so for not having given in) but doing something that we know we shouldn't be doing or having been trying not to do, will also make us feel bad and these feelings will last much longer.

2. Placing value on your values

Relevant to this, and also covered in our earlier work, is values. You may recall that we all have values and very often what we value is at odds with what makes us feel good. The problem with trying to feel good, rather than trying to tolerate feeling bad, is that it can take us away from what we really value because all our energies go into making sure that all our feelings are good ones. If you look again at your values assessment you will be able to see what it is that you really value about yourself and your life. Being clear about what you value will help to give you direction and move you forward in life. Think about setting yourself **realistic** goals that **you believe** you can achieve and which will guide you in the direction you want to go.

But remember, life is such that at some time or other we all feel bad. Learning to tolerate these feelings can help.

3. Contexts

A relapse is also more likely to happen if we associate with people who support or encourage our problematic behaviour and very often these are the very people that are prone to the same destructive behaviours. Making friends on-line is relatively easy and often these friendships are based on common interests. Friendships can be difficult for us to distance ourselves from but when the friendship is based on common interests (such as illegal images of children on the Internet) which are destructive and illegal, it is best to try to distance ourselves and perhaps try to form new friendships. Admittedly, making friends in the 'real world' is more difficult than making friends on-line but by forming new interests, perhaps by joining a club or starting a night class, it is possible. Think about making more of an effort with family and existing friends and consider getting in touch with friends that you may have ignored in favour of your computer! If you work, perhaps you could arrange a social evening. Think of new ways of meeting people and making new friends and try to follow these through.

The point is if you can avoid the people, places and situations that you know are likely to provide temptation, you are much less likely to have a relapse.

To make your life a little easier . . .

1. If you need the use of a computer, consider moving your computer to a more public place, if possible, so that people can see what you are doing. The mere thought of people being able to see what you are doing should help you to resist the temptation to view illegal images of children on the Internet.
2. If you have access to the Internet at home, consider if you really need the use of it.

Perhaps you could cancel your on-line subscription and save yourself some money! Remember, if you really need to use the Internet you could always go to an Internet Café.

3. If you feel you could confide in a friend or family member about your problem, consider doing so and ask them if they would act as a support person – someone you can call upon to talk to when you think you are going to have a relapse.
4. Consider writing a list of what you value and attaching it to the computer. Looking at this list should help you to resist the temptation to access illegal images of children on the Internet.

My Good Life Plan

This is how I would like to see me living my life over the next five years:

1. Work
These are the goals that I need to set in relation to work:

They are important to me because:

2. Leisure
This is how I will use my leisure time:

I want to do these things because:

My Good Life Plan *continued*

3. Personal needs
These were the needs met by going on-line and accessing abuse images:

I can now meet these needs by:

4. Ways of living
My old ways of living used to be:
My thoughts . . .

My feelings . . .

My Good Life Plan *continued*

My behaviours . . .

I will know that I'm going back to these if:
I feel . . .

I think . . .

I act this way . . .

My Good Life Plan *continued*

If I notice that any of these are happening I will:

Others may notice that things are slipping . . .
How I will look . . .

What I might say . . .

What I may do . . .

My Good Life Plan *continued*

If I am told about this I will:

I have developed strengths in the following areas:

This is how I would like to be thought of by others:

These are areas that I need to keep working on:

This is how I will work on these issues:

Consequences

If I re-offend, the effects will be:

For me	For others

Consequences *continued*

If I live an offence-free life, the effects will be:

For me	For others

References

Abel, G. et al. (1994) Screening Tests for Pedophilia. *Criminal Justice and Behaviour.* 21: 1, 115–31.

Abracen, J. and Looman, J. (2001) Issues in the Treatment of Sexual Offenders: Recent Developments and Directions for Future Research. *Aggression and Violent Behavior.* 1, 1–19.

Adler, A. (2001) The Perverse Law of Child Pornography. *Columbia Law Review.* 101 Mar. 209–73.

Akdeniz, Y. (2001) Controlling Illegal and Harmful Content on the Internet. in Wall, D.S. (Ed.) *Crime and The Internet.* London: Routledge.

American Psychiatric Association (1999) *Diagnostic and Statistical Manual of Mental Disorders: DSM-IV-TR.* Washington, DC: American Psychiatric Association.

Andrews, D.A. and Bonta, J. (1998) *The Psychology of Criminal Conduct.* 2nd edn. Cincinnati, OH: Anderson Publishing.

Andrews, D.A., Dowden, C. and Gendreau, P. (2003) *Clinically Relevant and Psychologically Informed Approaches to Reduce Reoffending: A Meta-Analytic Study of Human Service, Risk, Need, Responsivity and Other Concerns in Justice Contexts.* Carleton University, Ottawa, Canada.

Ashcroft, V. Free Speech Coalition (2002) Available online from Straylight.Law.Cornell.Edu/Supct/Html/00-795.ZS.Html.

Ba, S. (2001) Establishing Online Trust Through a Community Responsibility System. *Decision Support Systems.* 31, 323–36.

Baer, R., Smith, G. and Allen, K. (2004) Assessment of Mindfulness by Self-Report: The Kentucky Inventory of Mindfulness Skills. *Assessment.* 11: 3, 191–206.

Bandura, A. (1977) *Social Learning Theory.* Englewood Cliffs, N.J.: Prentice-Hall.

Barron, M. and Kimmel, M. (2000) Sexual Violence in Three Pornographic Media: Toward a Sociological Explanation. *The Journal of Sex Research.* 37: 161–8.

Beard, K.W. and Wolf, E.M. (2001) Modification of the Proposed Diagnostic Criteria for Internet Addiction. *Cyberpsychology and Behavior.* 4, 377–83.

Beauregard, E., Proulx, J. and Rossmo, D.K. (In Press) Spatial Patterns of Sex Offenders: Theoretical, Empirical and Practical Issues. *Aggression and Violent Behaviour.*

Bechar-Israeli, H. (1995) *From 'Bonehead' to 'Clonehead'; Nicknames, Play and Identity on Internet Relay Chat. Play and Computer-Mediated Communication.* 1: 2 Available Online at Ascusc.Org/Jcmc/Vol1/Issue2/Bechar.Html

Becker, J.R. (1994) Offenders: Characteristics and Treatment. *The Future of Children: Sexual Abuse of Children.* 4, 176–97.

Beech, A.R. and Scott-Fordham, A. (1997) Therapeutic Climate of Sexual Offender Treatment Programs. *Sexual Abuse: A Journal of Research and Treatment.* 9: 3, 219–37.

Beech, A.R. and Ward, T. (2004) The Integration of Etiology and Risk in Sex Offenders: A Theoretical Framework. *Aggression and Violent Behavior.* 10, 31–63.

Beech, A.R., Fisher, D.D. and Thornton, D. (2003) Risk Assessment of Sex Offenders. *Professional Psychology, Research and Practice.* 34, 339–52.

Belk, R.W. (1995) *Collecting in a Consumer Society.* London: Routledge.

Belk, R.W. and Wallendorf, M. (1997) Of Mice and Men: Gender Identity and Colleting. in Ames, K. and Martinez, K. (Eds.) *The Material Culture of Gender: The Gender of Material Culture.* Ann Arbour, MI: University of Michigan Press.

Benjamin, W. (1969) Unpacking My Library. A Talk About Book Collecting. in Arendt, H. (Ed.) *Illuminations.* New York: Schocken Books, (Originally Published as ''Unpacking My Library'': Literarische Welt, 1931).

Berlin, F.S. (1983) Sex Offenders: A Biomedical Perspective and a Status Report on Biomedical Treatment. in Greer, J.G. (Ed.) *The Sexual Aggressor: Current Perspectives on Treatment.* New York: Van Nostrand Reinhold.

Bickley, J. and Beech, A.R. (2001) Classifying Child Abusers: Its Relevance to Theory and Clinical Practice. *Journal of Offender Therapy and Comparative Criminology.* 45, 51–69.

Bjarkman, K. (2004) To Have and to Hold .The Video Collector's Relationship With an Ethereal Medium. *Television and New Media.* 5: 3, 217–46.

Bogaert, A.F. (2001) Handedness, Criminality and Sexual Offending. *Neuropsychologia.* 39: 5, 465–9.

Briggs, D. (2003) Personal Communication.

Brookes, D.G. (2003) *Paedophile Activity on the Internet: Concept Analysis and Risk Assessment Management of Internet Paedophiles.* Bramshill: National Police Library.

Browne, K.D., Foreman, L. and Middleton, D. (1998) Predicting Treatment Dropout in Sex Offenders. *Child Abuse Review,* 7: 402–19.

Brownmiller, S. (1975) *Against Our Will.* NY: Simon and Schuster.

Burdon, W.M. and Gallagher, C.A. (2002) Coercion and Sex Offenders: Controlling Sex-Offending Behavior Through Incapacitation and Treatment. *Criminal Justice and Behavior.* 29, 87–109.

Burgess, A.W. et al. (1984) Response Patterns in Children and Adolescents Exploited Through Sex Rings and Pornography. *American Journal of Psychiatry.* 141: 5, 656–62.

Burk, L.R. and Burkhart, B.R. (2003) Disorganized Attachment as a Diathesis for Sexual Deviance: Developmental Experience and the Motivation for Sexual Offending. *Aggression and Violent Behavior.* 8, 487–511.

Byers, E.S. (1998) Sexual Intrusive Thoughts of College Students. *Journal of Sex Research.* 35, 359–69.

Calder, M.C. (2004) The Internet: Potential, Problems and Pathways to Hands-On Sexual Offending. in Calder, M.C. (Ed.) (2004) *Sexual Abuse and the Internet: Tackling the New Frontier.* Lyme Regis: Russell House Publishing.

Caplan, S.E. (2002) Problematic Internet Use and Psychosocial Well-Being: Development of a Theory-Based Cognitive-Behavioral Measurement Instrument. *Computers in Human Behavior.* 18, 553–75.

Carter, D. et al. (1987) Use of Pornography in the Criminal and Developmental Histories of Sexual Offenders. *Journal of Interpersonal Violence.* 2: 2, 196–211.

Cautela, J.R. (1993) Insight in Behavior Therapy. Annual Meeting of the Association for the Advancement of Behavior Therapy (1992, Boston, Massachusetts) *Journal of Behavior Therapy and Experimental Psychiatry.* 24: 2, 155–9.

Clifford, J. (1995) Paradise. *Journal of the Society for Visual Anthropology: Visual Anthropology Review.* 11: 1, 92–117.

Collins, M. (2003) *Victimisation.* Paper Given at The Fourth COPINE Conference, Cork, Ireland.

Condron, M.K. and Nutter, D.E. (1988) A Preliminary Examination of the Pornography Experience of Sex Offenders, Paraphiliacs, Sexual Dysfunction Patients and Controls Based on Meese Commission Recommendations. *Journal of Sex and Marital Therapy.* 14, 285–98.

Conte, J.R. (1991) The Nature of Sexual Offenses Against Children. in Hollin, C.R. and Howells, K. (Eds.) *Clinical Approaches to Sex Offenders and Their Victims.* Oxford: John Wiley and Sons.

Cooper, A. (Ed.) (1998) *Sex and the Internet. A Guidebook for Clinicians.* New York: Brunner Routledge.

Cooper, A. et al. (1999) Sexuality on the Internet: From Sexual Exploration to Pathological Expression. *Professional Psychology: Research and Practice.* 30, 154–64.

Cooper, A., McLoughlin, I.P. and Campbell, K.M. (2000) Sexuality in Cyberspace: Update for the 21st Century. *Cyberpsychology and Behavior.* 3: 4, 521–36.

Court of Criminal Appeal Division (2002) *Regina -V- Mark David Oliver, Michael Patrick Hartney, Leslie Baldwin.* Neutral Citation Number: [2002] EWCA Crim 2766.

Covell, C.N. and Scalora, M.J. (2002) Empathic Deficits in Sexual Offenders: an Integration of Affective, Social, and Cognitive Constructs. *Aggression and Violent Behavior.* 7, 251–70.

Cowburn, M. and Pringle, K. (2000) The Effects of Pornography on Men. *The Journal of Sexual Aggression.* 6, 52–66.

Craig, L.A., Browne, K.D. and Stringer, I. (2003) Treatment and Sexual Offence Recidivism. *Trauma, Violence and Abuse.* 4, 70–89.

Davis, R.A. (1999) Internet Addiction: is It Real? *Catalyst.* Available at MACROBUTTON HtmlResAnchor Http://Www.Victoriapoint.Com/Internetaddiction.Htm.

Davis, R.A. (2001) A Cognitive-Behavioral Model of Pathological Internet Use. *Computers in Human Behavior.* 17, 187–95.

De Silva, P., Menzies, R.G. and Shafran, R. (2003) Spontaneous Decay of Compulsive Urges: The Case of Covert Compulsions. *Behaviour Research and Therapy.* 41: 2, 129–37.

Detriou, C. and Silke, A. (2003) A Criminological Internet Sting. *British Journal of Criminology.* 43, 213–22.

Dinsmore, U. (1998) Chaos, Order and Plastic Boxes: The Significance of Videotapes for the People who Collect Them. in Geraghty, C. and

Lusted, D. (Eds.) *The Television Studies Book.* London: Arnold.

Dowden, C., Antonowicz, D. and Andrews, D.A. (2003) The Effectiveness of Relapse Prevention With Offenders: A Meta-Analysis. *International Journal of Offender Therapy and Comparative Criminology.* 47: 5, 516–28.

Durkin, K. (1997) Misuse of the Internet by Paedophiles: Implications for Law Enforcement and Probation Practice. *Federal Probation.* 61: 2, 14–8.

Durkin, K.F. and Bryant, C.D. (1995) Log on to Sex: Some Notes on the Carnal Computer and Erotic Cyberspace as an Emerging Research Frontier. *Deviant Behaviour.* 16, 179–200.

Durkin, K.F. and Bryant, C.D. (1999) Propagandizing Pederasty. A Thematic Analysis on the Online Exculpatory Accounts of Unrepentant Pedophiles. *Deviant Behaviour.* 20, 103–27.

Eccles, A. and Marshall, W.L. (1999) Relapse Prevention. in Marshall, W.L., Anderson, D. and Fernandez, Y. (Eds.) *Cognitive-Behavioral Treatment of Sex Offenders.* Chichester: Wiley.

Eldridge, H. (1998) *Therapists Guide for Maintaining Change: Relapse Prevention Manual for Adult Perpetrators of Child Sexual Abuse.* Thousand Oaks, CA: Sage.

Elliott, M., Browne, K. and Kilcoyne, J. (1995) Child Sexual Abuse Prevention: What Offenders Tell Us. *Child Abuse and Neglect.* 19, 579–94.

Feldman, M.D. (2000) Munchausen by Internet: Detecting Factitious Illness and Crisis on the Internet. *Southern Journal of Medicine.* 93, 669–72.

Fennell, M. (2004) Depression, Low Self-Esteem and Mindfulness. *Behaviour Research and Therapy.* 42, 1053–67.

Ferster, C. (1972a) An Experimental Analysis of Clinical Phenomena. *The Psychological Record.* 22, 1–16.

Ferster, C. (1972b) Psychotherapy From the Standpoint of a Behaviorist. in Keehn, J.D. (Ed.) *Psychopathology in Animals: Research and Clinical Implications.* New York: Academic Press.

Finkelhor, D. (1994) The International Epidemiology of Child Abuse, *Child Abuse and Neglect: The International Journal.* 18, 409–17.

Finkelhor, D. (Ed.) (1984) *Child Sexual Abuse: New Theory and Research.* New York: Free Press.

Finkelhor, D. and Jones, L.M. (2004) *Explanations for the Decline in Child Sexual Abuse Cases.* Washington, DC: Office of Justice Programs, US Dept. of Justice.

Finkelhor, D. and Lewis, I.A. (1988) An Epidemiologic Approach to the Study of Child Molestation. in Prentky, R.A. and Quinsey, V.L. (Eds.) *Human Sexual Aggression: Current Perspectives.* New York: New York Academy of Science.

Finkelhor, D. and Ormrod, R. (2000) *Characteristics of Crimes Against Juveniles.* Washington, DC: US Dept. of Justice, Office of Justice Programs.

Finkelhor, D., Hotaling, G., Lewis, I.A. and Smith, C. (1990) Sexual Abuse in a National Survey of Adult Men and Women: Prevalence, Characteristics and Risk Factors. *Child Abuse and Neglect: The International Journal.* 14, 19–28.

Fisher, D., and Beech, A.R. (1999) Current Practice in Britain with Sexual Offenders. *Journal of Interpersonal Violence.* 14, 240–56.

Fisher, D., Beech, A. and Browne, K. (1999) Comparison of Sex Offenders to Non-offenders on Selected Psychological Measures. *International Journal of Offender Therapy and Comparative Criminology.* 43: 4, 473–91.

Flor-Henry, P. (1987) Cerebral Aspects of Sexual Deviation. in Wilson, G.D. (Ed.) *Variant Sexuality: Research and Theory.* Baltimore, Maryland: The Johns Hopkins University Press.

Forsyth, J.P., Parker, J.D. and Finlay, C.G. (2002) Anxiety Sensitivity, Controllability, and Experiential Avoidance and Their Relation to Drug of Choice and Addiction Severity in a Residential Sample of Substance-Using Veterans. *Addictive Behaviors.* 27, 1–20.

Fox, S. (2004) The New Imagined Community: Identifying and Exploring a Bidirectional Continuum Integrating Virtual and Physical Communities Through the Community Embodiment Model. *Journal of Communication Inquiry.* 28: 1, 47–62.

Frost, R.O. and Gross, R.C. (1993) The Hoarding of Possessions. *Behavior Research and Therapy.* 31: 4, 367–81.

Frost, R.O., Krause, M.S. and Steketee, G. (1996) Hoarding and Obsessive-Compulsive Symptoms. *Behavior Modification.* 20: 1, 116–32.

Frost. R.O., Steketee. G., Williams. L.F. and Warren. R. (2000) Mood, Personality Disorder Symptoms and Disability in Obsessive-Compulsive Hoarders: A Comparison With Clinical and Nonclinical Controls. *Behavior Research and Therapy.* 38: 1071–81.

Galbreath, N.W., Berlin, F.S. and Sawyer, D. (2002) Paraphilias and The Internet. in Cooper,

A. (Ed.) *Sex and The Internet. A Guidebook for Clinicians.* New York: Brunner Routledge.

Gebhard, P.H. et al. (1965) MACROBUTTON HtmlResAnchor Sex Offenders: an Analysis of Types. New York: Harper and Row.

Gee, D.V., Devilly, D.J. and Ward, T. (2004) The Content of Sexual Fantasies for Sexual Offenders. *Sexual Abuse: A Journal of Research and Treatment.* 16: 4, 315–31.

Geer, J., Estupinan, L. and Manguno-Mire, J. (2000) Empathy, Social Skills and Other Relevant Cognitive Processes in Rapists and Child Molesters. *Aggression and Violent Behaviour.* 5, 99–126.

Gifford, A. (2002) Emotion and Self-Control. *Journal of Economic Behavior and Organisation.* 49, 113–30.

Gillespie, A.A. (2003) Sentences for Offences Involving Child Pornography. *Criminal Law Review.* Feb., 81–93.

Goldiamond, I. (1974) Toward a Constructional Approach to Social Problems: Ethical and Constitutional Issues Raised by Applied Behavior Analysis. *Behaviorism.* 2, 1–84.

Goldstein, S.L. (1999) *The Sexual Exploitation of Children. A Practical Guide to Assessment, Investigation, and Intervention.* Boca Raton: CRC Press.

Gotved, S. (2002) Spatial Dimensions in Online Communities. *Space and Culture.* 5, 405–14.

Griffiths, M. (1998) Internet Addiction: Does it Really Exist. in Gackenbach, J. (Ed.) *Psychology and The Internet: Intrapersonal, Interpersonal, and Transpersonal Implications.* New York: Academic Press.

Griffiths, M. (2000) Sex on the Internet. in Von Feilitzen, C. and Carlsson, U. (Eds.) *Children in the New Media Landscape.* Kungälv: UNESCO.

Grossman, P. et al. (2004) Mindfulness-Based Stress Reduction and Health Benefits: A Meta-Analysis. *Journal of Psychosomatic Research.* 57: 1, 35–43.

Groth, A.N. (1979) *Men Who Rape.* New York: Plenum Press.

Groth, A.N., Hobson, W.F. and Gary, T.S. (1982) The Child Molester: Clinical Observations. in Conte, J. and Shore, D.A. (Eds.) *Social Work and Child Sexual Abuse.* New York: Haworth.

Grubin, D. (1997) Inferring Predictors of Risk: Sex Offenders. *International Review of Psychiatry.* 9, 225–31.

Grubin, D. (1999) Actuarial and Clinical Assessment of Risk in Sex Offenders. *Journal of Interpersonal Violence.* 14, 331–43.

Hagel, J. and Armstrong, A.G. (1997) *Net Gain: Expanding Markets Through Virtual Communities.* Boston, MA: Harvard Business School Press.

Hall, G.C. (1995) Sexual Offender Recidivism Revisited: A Meta-Analysis of Recent Treatment Studies. *Journal of Consulting and Clinical Psychology.* 63, 802–9.

Hall, G.C. and Hirschman, R. (1992) Sexual Aggression Against Children: A Conceptual Perspective of Etiology. *Criminal Justice and Behavior.* 19, 8–23.

Hammond, S. (2004) The Challenge of Sex Offender Assessment: The Case of Internet Offenders. in Calder, M.C. (Ed.) *Sexual Abuse and The Internet: Tackling the New Frontier.* Lyme Regis: Russell House Publishing.

Hanson, R.K. (2002) *Evaluation of Manitoba's Secondary Risk Assessment.* Unpublished manuscript. Ottawa: Department of the Solicitor General of Canada.

Hanson, R. and Harris, A.J. (2000) *The Sex Offender Need Assessment Rating (SONAR): A Method for Measuring Change in Risk Levels.* Ottawa: Department of The Solicitor-General.

Hanson, R.K. and Bussière, M.T. (1998) Predicting Relapse: A Meta-Analysis of Sexual Offender Recidivism Studies. *Journal of Consulting and Clinical Psychology.* 66, 348–62.

Hanson, R.K. and Harris, A.J. (2001) A Structures Approach to Evaluating Change Among Sexual Offenders. *Sexual Abuse: A Journal of Research and Treatment.* 13, 105–22.

Hanson, R.K. and Thornton, D. (1999) *Static 99: Improving Actuarial Risk Assessment for Sex Offenders.* Canada: Public Works and Government Services.

Hanson, R.K., Scott, H. and Steffy, R.A. (1995) A Comparison of Child Molesters and Nonsexual Criminals: Risk Predictors and Long-Term Recidivism. *Journal of Research in Crime and Delinquency.* 32, 325–37.

Hartman, C.R., Burgess, A.W. and Lanning, K.V. (1984) Typology of Collections. in Burgess, A.W. (Ed.) *Child Pornography and Sex Rings.* Lexington, MA: D.C. Health.

Hauben, M.F. (1997) The Netizens and Community Networks. *CMC Magazine.* Available Online From: Http://Www.December.Com/Cmc/Mag/1997/Feb/Hauben.Html

Hawkins, R.P. (1986) Selection of Target Behaviors. in Nelson, R.O. and Hayes, S.C. (Eds.) *Conceptual Foundations of Behavioral Assessment.* New York: Guilford.

Hayes, S.C. (1994) Content, Context, and the Types of Psychological Acceptance. in Hayes, S.C. et al. (Eds.) *Acceptance and Change: Content and Context in Psychotherapy*. Reno: Context Press.

Hayes, S.C. and Pankey, J. (2002) Experiential Avoidance, Cognitive Fusion, and an ACT Approach to Anorexia Nervosa. *Cognitive and Behavioral Practice*. 9, 243–7.

Hayes, S.C. and Wilson, K.G. (1994) MACROBUTTON HtmlResAnchor Acceptance and Commitment Therapy: Altering the Verbal Support for Experiential Avoidance. *The Behavior Analyst*. 17, 289–303.

Hayes, S.C. and Wilson, K.G. (2003) Mindfulness: Method and Process. *Clinical Psychology*, 10: 161–5.

Hayes, S.C., Strosahl, K.D. and Wilson, K.G. (1999) *Acceptance and Commitment Therapy. An Experiential Approach to Behavior Change*. New York: Guilford.

Hayes, S.C. et al. (2004) Measuring Experiential Avoidance: A Preliminary Test of a Working Model. *The Psychological Record*. 54, 533–78.

Haywood, T.W., Grossman, L.S. and Kravitz, H.M. (1994) Profiling Psychological Distortions in Alleged Child Molesters. *Psychological Reports*. 75, 915–27.

Healy, M. (1997) *Child Pornography: an International Perspective*. World Congress Against Commercial Sexual Exploitation of Children. Available at MACROBUTTON HtmlResAnchor Http://Www.Usis.Usemb.Se/ Children/Csec/215e.Htm.

Hills, P. and Argyle, M. (2003) Uses of the Internet and Their Relationship With Individual Differences in Personality. *Computers in Human Behavior*. 19, 59–70.

Holmes, S.T. and Holmes, R.M. (2002) *Sex Crimes: Pattern and Behavior*. California: Sage Publications.

Horley, J. (2000) Cognitions Supportive of Child Molestation. *Aggression and Violent Behavior*. 5: 6, 551–64.

Houlton, D. and Short, J. (1995) Sylvanian Families: The Production and Consumption of a Rural Community. *Journal of Rural Studies*. 11, 367–87.

Howells, K., Day, A. and Wright, S. (2004) Affect, Emotions and Sex Offending. *Psychology, Crime and Law*. 10: 2, 179–95.

Howitt, D. (1995) Pornography and the Paedophile: is it Criminogenic? *British Journal of Medical Psychiatry*. 68, 15–27.

Hudson, S.M., Ward, T. and McCormack, J.C. (1999) Offense Pathways in Sexual Offenders. *Journal of Interpersonal Violence*. 14, 779–98.

Innocent Images, Operation Candyman Phase 1 (2002) Available at MACROBUTTON HtmlResAnchor Http://Www.Fbi.Gov/ Pressrel/Candyman/Candymanhome.Htm.

Isen, A.M. (1999) On the Relationship Between Affect and Creative Problem Solving. in Russ, S. (Ed.) *Affect, Creative Experience and Psychological Adjustment*. Philadelphia: Taylor and Francis.

Itzin, C. (1997) Pornography and the Organization of Intrafamilial and Extrafamilial Child Sexual Abuse: Developing a Conceptual Model. *Child Abuse Review*. 6: 94–106.

Jacobson, N.S. et al. (2000) Integrative Behavioral Couple Therapy: an Acceptance-Based, Promising New Treatment for Couple Discord . *Journal of Consulting and Clinical Psychology*. 68: 2, 351–5.

Jenkins, P. (2001) *Beyond Tolerance: Child Pornography on The Internet*. New York University Press.

Joinson, A. and Dietz-Uhler, B. (2002) Explanations for Perpetrations of and Reactions to Deception in a Virtual Community. *Social Science Computer Review*. 20: 3, 275–89.

Jolliffe, D. and Farrington, D.P. (2004) Empathy and Offending: A Systematic Review and Meta-Analysis. *Aggression and Violent Behavior*. 9: 5, 441–76.

Jones, L.M. and Finkelhor, D. (2003) Putting Together Evidence on Declining Trends in Sexual Abuse: A Complex Puzzle. *Child Abuse and Neglect*. 27, 133–5.

Jones, S. (1997) *Virtual Culture: Identity and Communication in Cybersociety*. London: Sage.

Kandell, J.J. (1998) Internet Addiction on Campus: The Vulnerability of College Students. *Cyberpsychology and Behavior*. 1, 11–7.

Kavanagh, D., Andrade, J. and May, J. (2004) Beating the Urge: Implications of Research into Substance Related Desires. *Addictive Behaviors*. 29, 1359–72.

Kennedy-Souza, B.L. (1998) Internet Addiction Disorder. *Interpersonal Computing & Technology*. 6, 1–2.

Kincaid, J.R. (1998) *Erotic Innocence: The Culture of Child Molesting*. London: Duke University Press.

Kleinhans, C. (2004) Virtual Child Porn: The Law and the Semiotics of the Image. *Journal of Visual Culture*. 3: 1, 17–34.

Knight, R.A., and Prentky, R.A. (1990) Classifying Sexual Offenders: The Development and Corroboration of Taxonomic Models. in Marshall, W.L. (Ed.) *Handbook of Sexual Assault: Issues, Theories, and Treatment of The Offender.* New York: Plenum Press.

Knopp, F.H., Freeman-Longo, R. and Stevenson, W.F. (1993) *1992 Nationwide Survey of Juvenile and Adult Sex Offender Treatment Programs and Models.* Brandon, VT: Safer Society Press.

Kohlenberg, R.J. and Tsai, M. (1991) *Functional Analytic Psychotherapy: Creating Intense and Curative Therapeutic Relationships.* New York: Plenum Press.

Kohlenberg, R.J., Hayes, S.C. and Tsai, M. (1993) Radical Behavioural Psychotherapy: Two Contemporary Examples. *Clinical Psychology Review.* 13, 579–92.

Kollock, P. and Smith, M.A. (1999) Communities in Cyberspace. in Smith, M.A. and Kollock, P. (Eds.) *Communities in Cyberspace.* London: Routledge.

Kudadjie-Gyamfi, E. and Rachlin, H. (2002) Rule-Governed Versus Contingency-Governed Behavior in a Self-Control Task: Effects of Changes in Contingencies. *Behavioral Processes.* 57, 29–35.

Langevin, R. and Curnoe, S. (2004) The Use of Pornography During the Commission of Sexual Offenses. *International Journal of Offender Therapy and Comparative Criminology.* 48, 572–86.

Lanning, K. (1992) *Child Molesters: A Behavioural Analysis.* Washington, DC: National Centre for Missing and Exploited Children.

Lanning, K. (2004) Compliant Victims. The Fifth COPINE Conference *Psychological and Legal Issues of Internet Abuse Images.* Cork: Ireland.

Lanyon, R.L. (1991) Theories of Sex Offending. in Hollin, C.R. and Howells, K. (Eds.) *Clinical Approaches to Sex Offenders and Their Victims.* Chichester: John Wiley and Sons.

Laws, D.R. (1999) Relapse Prevention: The State of the Art. *Journal of Interpersonal Violence.* 14, 285–302.

Laws, D.R. and Marshall, W.L. (1990) A Conditioning Theory of the Etiology and Maintenance of Deviant Sexual Preference and Behaviour. in Marshall, W.L. Laws, D.R. and Barbaree, H.E. (Eds.) *Handbook of Sexual Assault: Issues, Theories and Treatment of the Offender.* New York: Plenum.

Laws, D.R. and Marshall, W.L. (2003) A Brief History of Behavioral and Cognitive Behavioral Approaches to Sexual Offenders: Part 1. Early

Developments. *Sexual Abuse: A Journal of Research and Treatment.* 15: 2, 75–92.

Leitenberg, H. and Henning, K.(1995) Sexual Fantasy. *Psychological Bulletin.* 117: 3 469–96.

Lenihan, M.M. (1993) Cognitive Behavioral Treatment of Borderline Personality Disorder. New York: Guilford.

Lenihan, M.M. (1994) Acceptance and Change: The Central Dialectic in Psychotherapy. in Hayes, S.C., Jacobson, N.S., Follete, V.M. and Dougher, M.J. (Eds.) *Acceptance and Change: Content and Context in Psychotherapy.* Reno, N.V.: Context Press.

Lévy, P. (1998) *Becoming Virtual: Reality in the Digital Age.* Trans Bononno, R. New York: Plennum Press.

Looman, J. (1995) Sexual Fantasies of Child Molesters. *Canadian Journal of Behavioral Science.* 37, 321–32.

Looman, J., Abracen, J. and Nicholaichuk, T.P. (2000) Recidivism Among Treated Sexual Offenders and Matched Controls: Data From The Regional Treatment Centre (Ontario). *Journal of Interpersonal Violence.* 15, 279–90.

Looman, J., Gauthier, C. and Boer, D. (2001) Replication of The Massachusetts Treatment Center Child Molester Typology in a Canadian Sample. *Journal of Interpersonal Violence.* 16, 753–67.

LoPiccolo, J. (1994) Acceptance and Broad Spectrum Treatment of Paraphilias. in Hayes, S.C. et al. (Eds.) *Acceptance and Change: Content and Context in Psychotherapy.* Reno, NV: Context Press.

Luciano, C. and Wilson, K.G. (2002) *Acceptance and Commitment Therapy: A Behavioral Treatment Focused on Values.* Madrid: Pirámide.

Mahoney, D. and Faulkner, N. (1997) *Brief Overview of Pedophiles on the Web.* Available from: MACROBUTTON HtmlResAnchor Http://Www.Healthyplace.Com/ Communities/Abuse/Socum/Articles/ Pedophiles.Ht m

Malamuth, N.M. and Check, J.V.P. (1985).The Effects of Aggressive Pornography on Beliefs in Rape Myths: Individual Differences. *Journal of Research in Personality.* 19, 299–320.

Maletsky, B.M. and Field, G. (2003) The Biological Treatment of Dangerous Sex Offenders: A Review and Preliminary Report of the Oregon Pilot Depo-Provera Programme. *Aggression and Violent Behaviour.* 8: 4, 342–91.

Marcks, B.A. and Woods, D.W. (2005) A Comparison of Thought Suppression to an

Acceptance-Based Technique in the Management of Personal Intrusive Thoughts: A Controlled Evaluation. *Behavior Research and Therapy.*

Margalit, A. (1996) *The Decent Society.* Cambridge, MA: Harvard University Press.

Marlatt, G.A. and Gorden, J.R. (1985) *Relapse Prevention: Maintenance Strategies in the Treatment of Addictive Behaviors.* New York: Gilford.

Marques, J.K. et al. (2000) Prevention Relapse in Sex Offenders: What We Learned from SOTED's Experimental Treatment Program. in Laws, D.R. (Ed.) *Remaking Relapse Prevention with Sex Offenders.* 321–40. California: Sage.

Marshall, W.L. (1989) Pornography and Sex Offenders. in Zillman, D. and Bryant, J. (Eds.) *Pornography: Research Advances and Policy Considerations.* Hillsdale, NJ: Lawrence Erlbaum Associates.

Marshall, W.L. (1996) Assessment, Treatment and Theorizing About Sex Offenders: Developments During the Past Twenty Years and Future Directions. *Criminal Justice and Behavior.* 23, 162–99.

Marshall, W.L. (2000) Revisiting the Use of Pornography by Sexual Offenders: Implications for Theory and Practice. *The Journal of Sexual Aggression.* 6: 1, 67–77.

Marshall, W.L. and Anderson, D. (2000) Do Relapse Prevention Components Enhance Treatment Effectiveness? in Laws, D.R. (Ed.) *Remaking Relapse Prevention With Sex Offenders.* California: Sage.

Marshall, W.L. and Laws, D.R. (2003) A Brief History of Behavioral and Cognitive Behavioral Approaches to Sexual Offender Treatment: Part 2. The Modern Era. *Sexual Abuse: A Journal of Research and Treatment.* 15: 2, 93–120.

Marshall, W.L. and Marshall, L.E. (2000) The Origins of Sexual Offending. *Trauma, Violence and Abuse.* 1, 250–63.

Marshall, W.L. et al. (1995) Empathy in Sex Offenders. *Clinical Psychology Review.* 15: 2, 99–113.

Marshall, W.L. et al. (1998) Conclusions and Future Directions. in Marshall, W.L. et al. (Eds.) *Sourcebook of Treatment Programs for Sexual Offenders.* New York: Plenum.

Marshall, W.L. et al. (Eds.), (1998) *Sourcebook of Treatment Programs for Sexual Offenders.* New York: Plenum.

Marshall, W.L. and Barbaree, H.E. (1990) Outcome of Comprehensive Cognitive-Behavioural Treatment Programmes. in Marshall, W.L., Laws, D.R., Barbaree, H.E. (Eds.) *Handbook of Sexual Assault.* 363–85. New York: Plenham Press.

Marshall, W.L. and Pithers, W.D. (1994) A Reconsideration of Treatment Outcome With Sex Offenders. *Criminal Justice and Behavior.* 21, 10–27.

Maruna, S. (2001) *Making Good: How Ex-Convicts Reform and Rebuild Their Lives.* Washington, DC: American Psychological Association.

Marx, B.P., Miranda, R. and Meyerson, L.A. (1999) Cognitive-Behavioural Treatment for Rapists: Can We Do Better? *Clinical Psychology Review.* 19: 9, 875–94.

McCracken, L.M., Vowles, K.E. and Eccleston, C. (2004) Acceptance of Chronic Pain: Component Analysis and a Revised Assessment Method. *Pain.* 107, 159–66.

McGrath, R.J. et al. (2003) Outcome of a Treatment Program for Adult Sex Offenders: From Prison to Community. *Journal of Interpersonal Violence.* 18, 3–17.

McLaughlin, M.L., Osborne, K.K. and Smith, C.B. (1995) Standards of Conduct on Usenet. in Jones, S.G. (Ed.) *Cybersociety: Computer-Mediated Communication and Community.* Thousand Oaks, CA: Sage.

Medaris, M. and Girouard, C. (2002) *Protecting Children in Cyberspace: The ICAC Task Force Program.* Juvenile Justice Bulletin, US Dept. of Justice. Available MACROBUTTON HtmlResAnchor Http://Www.Ncjrs.Org/Pdfiles1/Ojjdp/191213.Pdf

Middleton, D. (2004) Current Treatment Approaches. in Calder, M.C. (Ed.) *Child Sexual Abuse and The Internet: Tackling the New Frontier.* Lyme Regis: Russell House Publishing.

Middleton, D., Beech, A. and Mandeville-Norden, R. (2005) What Sort of a Person Could Do That?–Psychological Profiles of Internet Pornography Users. in Quayle, E. and Taylor, M. (Eds.) *Viewing Child Pornography on The Internet: Understanding the Offence, Managing the Offender, Helping the Victim.* Lyme Regis: Russell House Publishing.

Mitra, A. (2001) Diasporic Voices in Cyberspace. *New Media and Society.* 3: 1, 29–48.

Money, J. (1970) Use of an Androgen-Depleting Hormone in the Treatment of Male Sex Offenders. *Journal of Sex Research.* 6, 165–72.

Morahan-Martin, J. and Schumacher, P. (2000) Incidence and Correlates of Pathological Internet Use Among College Students. *Computers in Human Behavior.* 16, 13–29.

Muensterberger, W. (1994) *Collecting: an Unruly Passion.* Princeton, NJ: Princeton University Press.

Mulloy, R. and Marshall, W.L. (1999) Social Functioning. in Marshall, W.L., Anderson, D. and Fernandez, Y. (Eds.) *Cognitive Behavioral Treatment of Sexual Offenders.* England: John Wiley.

Murphy, W.D. (1990) Assessment and Modification of Cognitive Distortions in Sex Offenders. in Marshall, W.L. Laws, D.R. and Barbaree, H.E. (Eds.) *Handbook of Sexual Assault: Issues, Theories, and Treatment of the Offender.* New York: Plenum.

Nicholaichuk, T. and Yates, P. (2002) Treatment Efficacy: Outcomes of the Clearwater Sex Offender Program. in Schwartz, B. (Ed.) *The Sex Offender: Current Treatment Modalities and Systems Issues.* New Jersey: Civic Research Institute, Inc.

Nicholaichuk, T., Gordon, A., Gu, D., Wong, S. (2002) Outcome of an Institutional Sexual Offender Treatment Program: A Comparison Between Treated and Matched Untreated Offenders. *Sexual Abuse: A Journal of Research and Treatment.* 12, 139–53.

Nip, J. (2004) The Relationship Between Online and Offline Communities: The Case of the Queer Sisters. *Media Culture and Society.* 26: 3, 409–28.

Nora, P. (1989) Between Memory and History. *Realms of Memory.*1, 1–20.

Norris, P. (2002) *The Bridging and Bonding Role of Online Communities.* Available at MACROBUTTON HtmlResAnchor Http:// Ksgnotes1.Harvard.Edu/Degreeprog/ Courses.Nsf/Wzbydirectoryname/Pippanorris

Paul, R.H., Marx, B.P. and Orsillo, S.M. (1999) Acceptance Based Psychotherapy in the Treatment of an Adjudicated Exhibitionist: A Case Example. *Behavior Therapy.* 30, 149–62.

Pirke, K.M., Kockott, G. and Dittmar, F. (1974) Psychosexual Stimulation and Plasma Testosterone in Man. *Archives of Sexual Behavior.* 3, 577–84.

Pithers, W.D. (1999) Empathy: Definition, Enhancement, and Relevance to the Treatment of Sexual Abusers. *Journal of Interpersonal Violence.* 14: 3, 257–84.

Pithers, W.D. et al. (1983) Relapse Prevention With Sexual Aggressives: A Self-Control Model of Treatment and Maintenance Change. in Greer, J.G. (Ed.) *The Sexual Aggressor: Current Perspectives on Treatment.* New York: Van Nostrand Reinhold.

Polaschek, D.L., Ward, T. and Hudson, S.M. (1997) Rape and Rapists: Theory and Treatment. *Clinical Psychology Review.* 17, 117–44.

Postman, N. (1993) *Technology: The Surrender of Culture to Technology.* New York: Vintage Books.

Pratarelli, M.E. and Browne, B.L. (2002) Confirmatory Factor Analysis of Internet Use and Addiction. *Cyberpsychology and Behavior.* 5: 1, 53–64.

Proulx, J., Perreult, C. and Ouimet, M. (1999) Pathways in the Offending Process of Extrafamilial Sexual Child Molesters. *Journal of Research and Treatment.* 11: 2, 117–29.

Quayle, E. (2004) The Impact of Viewing on Offending Behaviour. in Calder. M.C. (Ed.) *Sexual Abuse and The Internet: Tackling the New Frontier.* Lyme Regis: Russell House Publishing.

Quayle, E. and Taylor, M. (2001) Child Seduction and Self-Representation on the Internet. *Cyberpsychology and Behavior.* 4: 5, 597–608.

Quayle, E. and Taylor, M. (2002) Child Pornography and The Internet: Perpetuating a Cycle of Abuse. *Deviant Behavior: an Interdisciplinary Journal.* 23, 331–61.

Quayle, E. and Taylor, M. (2003) A Model of Problematic Internet Use in People With a Sexual Interest in Children. *Cyberpsychology and Behavior.* 6, 93–106.

Quale, E., Holland, G., Linehan, C. and Taylor, M. (2000) The Internet and Offending Behaviour: A Case Study. *Journal of Sexual Aggression.* 6: 1–2, 78–96.

Quayle, E., Vaughan, M. and Taylor, M. (In Press) Sex Offenders, Internet Child Abuse Images and Emotional Avoidance: The Importance of Values. *Aggression and Violent Behavior.*

Rada, R. et al. (1983) Plasma Androgens in Violent and Nonviolent Sex Offenders. *Bulletin of The American Academy of Psychiatric Law.* 11, 149–58.

Rada, R.T., Laws, D.R. and Kellner, R. (1976) Plasma Testosterone Levels in the Rapist. *Psychosomatic Medicine.* 38, 257–68.

Regehr, C. and Glancy, G. (2001) Empathy and Its Impact on Sexual Misconduct. *Trauma, Abuse and Violence.* 2: 2, 142–54.

Rheingold, H. (1993) *The Virtual Community: Homesteading on the Electronic Frontier.* Reading, MA: Addison Wesley.

Rosler, A. and Witztum, E. (2000) Pharmacotherapy of Paraphilias in the Next Millennium. *Behavioral Sciences and The Law.* 18, 43–56.

Schwartz, B.K. (1995) Characteristics and Typologies of Sex Offenders. in Schwartz, B. (Ed.) *The Sex Offender: Corrections, Treatment and Legal Practice (Vol. 2).* New Jersey: Civic Research Institute.

Scott, S. (2001) *The Politics and Experience of Ritual Abuse: Beyond Disbelief.* Philadelphia: Open University Press.

Scully, D. and Marolla, J. (1984) Convicted Rapists' Vocabulary of Motive: Excuses and Justifications. *Social Problems.* 31: 5, 530–44.

Scully, D., and Marolla, J. (1990) Convicted Rapists' Vocabulary of Motive: Excuses and Justifications. in Brissett, D. and Edgley, C. (Eds.) *Life as Theater: A Dramaturgical Sourcebook.* 2nd edn. Hawthorne, NY: Aldine De Gruyter.

Seidman, B.T. et al. (1994) An Examination of Intimacy and Loneliness in Sex Offenders. *Journal of Interpersonal Violence.* 9, 518–34.

Sentencing Advisory Panel (2002) *Sentencing Advisory Panel's Advice to the Court of Appeal on Sentences Involving Child Pornography.* MACROBUTTON HtmlResAnchor Http:// Www.Sentencing-Advisory-Panel.Gov.Uk/C_ And_A/Advice/Child_Offences/ Advice_Child_Porn.Pdf

Seto, M.C., Maric, A. and Barbaree, H.E. (2001) The Role of Pornography in the Etiology of Sexual Aggression. *Aggression and Violent Behavior.* 6, 35–53.

Shingler, J. and Strong, L. (2003) Putting the B Back into CBT: The Use of Behavioural Contingencies in Sex Offender Treatment. *NOTA News.* July 9–12.

Shirky, C. (1995) *Voices From The Net.* Emeryville, CA: Ziff-Davis Press.

Silbert, M.H. (1989) The Effects on Juveniles of Being Used for Pornography and Prostitution. in Zillman, D. and Bryant, C. (Eds.) *Pornography: Research Advances and Policy Considerations.* Hillside, NJ: Lawrence Erlbaum.

Simon, L.M. et al. (1992) Characteristics of Child Molesters: Implications for the Fixated-Regressed Dichotomy. *Journal of Interpersonal Violence.* 7, 211–25.

Simons, D., Wurtele, S.K. and Heil, P. (2002) Childhood Victimization and Lack of Empathy as Predictors of Sexual Offending Against Women and Children. *Journal of Interpersonal Violence.* 17, 1291–307.

Singh, N.N. et al. (2004) A Mindfulness-Based Treatment of Obsessive-Compulsive Disorder. *Clinical Case Studies.* 3: 4, 275–87.

Skinner, B.F. (1953) *Science and Human Behavior.* New York: The Macmillan Company.

Skinner, B.F. (1957) *Verbal Behavior.* New York: Appleton-Century-Crofts.

Skinner, B.F. (1974) *About Behaviorism.* New York: Alfred Knopf.

Slater, D. (1998) Trading Sexpics on IRC. Embodiment and Authenticity on The Internet. *Body and Society.* 4: 4, 91–117.

Smith, D.W., Letourneau, E.J. and Saunders, B.E. (2000) Delay in Disclosure of Childhood Rape: Results From a National Survey. *Child Abuse and Neglect.* 24, 273–87.

Song, I. et al. (2004) Internet Gratifications and Internet Addiction: on the Uses and Misuses of the New Media. *Cyberpsychology and Behavior.* 3: 4, 384–94.

Steen, C. (1993) *The Relapse Prevention Workbook for Youth in Treatment.* Vermont: Safer Society Press.

Stein, D.J. et al. (2001) Hypersexual Disorder and Preoccupation With Internet Pornography. *American Journal of Psychiatry.* 158, 1590–4.

Sturmey, P. (1996) *Functional Analysis in Clinical Psychology.* Chichester: John Wiley and Sons.

Sullivan, J. (2002) *The Spiral of Sexual Abuse: A Conceptual Framework for Understanding Child Sexual Abuse.* NOTA News, April.

Sullivan, J. and Beech, A. (2004) Assessing Internet Sex Offenders. in Calder, M.C. (Ed.) *Child Sexual Abuse and The Internet: Tackling the New Frontier.* Lyme Regis: Russell House Publishing.

Svedin, C.G. and Back, K. (1996) *Children Who Don't Speak Out.* Stockholm, Sweden: Swedish Save The Children.

Sykes, G.M. and Matza, D. (1957) Techniques of Neutralization: A Theory of Delinquency. *Sociological Review.* 22, 664–70.

Taylor, M. and Quayle, E. (2003) *Child Pornography. an Internet Crime.* London: Bruner Routledge,

Taylor, M. and Quayle, E. (2005) Abusive Images of Children. in Cooper, S. et al. (Eds.) *Medical and Legal Aspects of Child Sexual Exploitation.* Saint Louis: GW Medical Publishing.

Taylor, M. and Quayle, E. (In Press) The Internet and Abuse Images of Children: Search, Precriminal Situations and Opportunity. in Wortley, R. (Ed.) *Situational Perspectives of Sexual Offences Against Children.*

Taylor, M., Holland, G. and Quayle, E. (2001) Typology of Paedophile Picture Collections. *The Police Journal.* 74, 97–107.

Terry, K.J. and Tallon, J. (2004) *Child Sexual Abuse: A Review of The Literature.* Available at Http://Www.Usccb.Org/Nrb/Johnjaystudy/Litreview.Pdf.

Tittle, C. and Botchkovar, E. (2005) The Generality of Self-Control in Predicting Criminal Behavior: A Comparison of Russian and US Adults. *Social Science Research.*

Tyler, R.P. and Stone, L.E. (1985) Child Pornography: Perpetuating The Sexual Victimization of Children. *Child Abuse and Neglect.* 9, 313–8.

Ucko, P.J. (2001) Unprovenanced Material Culture and Freud's Collection of Antiquities. *Journal of Material Culture.* 6: 3, 269–322.

US Postal Inspection Service and Operation Avalanche (2003) Available at MACROBUTTON HtmlResAnchor Http://Www.Usps.Com/Postalinspectors/Avalanch.Htm.

Ward, T. (2002) Good Lives and the Rehabilitation of Offenders. Promises and Problems. *Aggression and Violent Behavior.* 7, 513–28.

Ward, T. and Brown, M. (2004) The Good Lives Model and Conceptual Issues in Offender Rehabilitation. *Psychology, Crime and Law.* 10: 3, 243–57.

Ward, T. and Hudson, S.M. (1996) Relapse Prevention: A Critical Analysis. *Sexual Abuse: A Journal of Research and Treatment.* 8, 177–200.

Ward, T. and Hudson, S.M. (1998) The Construction and Development of Theory in the Sexual Offending Area: A Metatheoretical Framework. *Sexual Abuse: A Journal of Research and Treatment.* 10, 47–63.

Ward, T. and Keenan, T. (1999) Child Molesters Implicit Theories. *Journal of Interpersonal Violence.* 14, 821–38.

Ward, T. and Marshall, W.L. (2004) Good Lives, Etiology and the Rehabilitation of Sex Offenders: A Bridging Theory. *Journal of Sexual Aggression.* 10, 153–69.

Ward, T. and Siegert, R. (2002) Toward a Comprehensive Theory of Child Sexual Abuse: A Theory Knitting Perspective. *Psychology, Crime, and Law.* 9, 319–51.

Ward, T. et al. (1995) A Descriptive Model of the Offense Chain for Child Molesters. *Journal of Interpersonal Violence.* 10, 452–72.

Ward, T. et al. (2004) The Multifactorial Offender Readiness Model. *Aggression and Violent Behavior.* 9, 645–73.

Ward, T. et al. (2004) *The Self-Regulation Model of the Offense and Relapse Process.* Victoria, BC: Pacific Psychological Assessment Corporation.

Ward, T., Hudson, S.M. and Siegert, R.J. (1995) A Critical Comment on Pithers' Relapse Prevention Model. *Sexual Abuse: A Journal of Research and Treatment.* 7, 167–75.

Ward, T., Keenan, T. and Hudson, S.M. (2000) Understanding Cognitive, Affective, and Intimacy Deficits in Sexual Offenders: A Developmental Perspective. *Aggression and Violent Behaviour.* 5, 41–62.

Watson, N. (1998) Why Should We Argue About Virtual Community? A Case Study of the Phish.Net Fan Community. in Jones, S.G. (Ed.) *Virtual Culture: Identity and Communication in Cybersociety.* London: Sage.

Whittal, M.L., Rachman, S. and McLean, P.D. (2002) Psychosocial Treatments for OCD: Combining Cognitive and Behavioural Treatments. in Simos, G. (Ed.) *Cognitive Behaviours Therapy: A Guide for Practising Clinicians.* London: Brunner-Routledge.

Wilson, K., Hayes, S. and Byrd, M. (2000) Exploring Compatibilities Between Acceptance and Commitment Therapy and 12-Step Treatment for Substance Abuse. *Journal of Rational-Emotive and Cognitive – Behavioral Therapy.* 18: 4, 209–34.

Wilson, K.G. and Byrd, M.R. (2004) ACT for Substance Abuse and Dependence. in Hayes, S. and Strosahl, K. (Eds.) *A Practical Guide to Acceptance and Commitment Therapy.* New York: Springer-Verlag.

Wilson, K.G. and Luciano, C. (2002) *Terapia De Aceptión Y Compromiso: Un Tratamiento Conductal Centrado En Los Valores.* Madrid: Editorial Pirámide. (Translation Available From The Authors).

Wilson, K.G. and Roberts, M. (2002) Core Principles in Acceptance and Commitment Therapy: an Application to Anorexia. *Cognitive and Behavioral Practice.* 9, 237–43.

Wolf, S.C (1985) A Multi-Factor Model of Deviant Sexuality. *Victimology: an International Journal.* 10, 359–74.

Wood, A.F. and Smith, M.J. (2001) *Online Communication: Linking Technology, Identity and Culture.* Mahwah, NJ: Lawrence Erlbaum Associates.

Wright, R.C. and Schneider, S.L. (1999) Motivated Self-Deception in Child Molesters. *Journal of Child Sexual Abuse.* 8, 89–111.

Wu, K.D. and Watson, K. (2005) Hoarding and Its
    Relation to Obsessive–Compulsive Disorder.
    Behaviour Research and Therapy. 43: 7, 897–921.

Index